Inscribed by the Author
for the Reverend Mother Prioress & Community
of the Carmelite Monastery, Concord. N.H.
With happy memories of your courtesies to
me when I lectured on the
Poetry of St. John of the Cross at
the Carmelite Monastery in Roxbury in 1936.

Gratefully in the Lord,
Maurice Leahy.

Feast of Our Lady of Lourdes
1953.

108 - E 78th St.

This book is presented by
Mrs John Schley Behr,
in memory of John Schley Behr, a
Convert to Holy Church,
(Requiescat in Pace, 1936)

The Flower of Her Kindred

A Biographical Study of

NANO   NAGLE   OF   IRELAND

Foundress, Pioneer of Popular Education and Noted Leader in
Sociology in the Eighteenth Century

By MAURICE LEAHY

With a Preface by His Grace
THE MOST REVEREND JOHN J. GLENNON, D. D.
Archbishop of Saint Louis

MAURICE LEAHY

991 Fifth Avenue   New York. N. Y.

This book is manufactured
under wartime conditions

Printed by The Etheridge Company, Grand Rapids, Michigan

To

His Grace The Most Reverend Francis J. Spellman, D.D.,
Archbishop of New York, Military Vicar for the Armed
Forces of The United States, Distinguished Prelate and
Great American — beloved in Church and State, Wise
Counsellor and Devoted Father-in-God to all

This Biography of Mother Nagle
is gratefully and affectionately dedicated
by the Author

Nihil Obstat:

ARTHUR J. SCANLAN, S.T.D.
Censor Librorum

Imprimatur:

†FRANCIS J. SPELLMAN, D.D.
Archbishop of New York

New York,
Feast of Saint Monica,
May 4th, 1944.

In obedience to the Decree of Pope Urban VIII, I protest that, for the miraculous deeds and gifts ascribed in this book to certain servants of God, I claim no other belief than that which is ordinarily given to history resting on mere human authority; and that, in giving the appellation of Saint or Blessed to any person not canonized or beatified by the Church, I only intend to do it according to the usage and opinion of men.

AUTHOR.

TABLE OF CONTENTS

Foreword

By His Grace The Most Reverend John J. Glennon, D. D., Archbishop of Saint Louis; Assistant at the Pontifical Throne.

E RIN is a fair land, and of its four provinces Munster, which lies to the South, is its fairest. There you find a varied tender beauty — a blending of mountain and valley, of crystal lake and rushing river, of fairy springs and laughing waterfalls, and over all an atmosphere of mystic and misty splendor — suggesting to the traveller that here at last he has discovered the long lost Eden, or as the poet more boldly described it: "A little bit of Heaven that fell from the skies one day."

He who wanders down that way will find at every step some expression of natural beauty and God's benediction. In the valleys as they run towards the sea, he will be greeted by a warm fragrant atmosphere found only in sub-tropical lands; glancing up the mountain-side, he will note its varied garb of lichen, moss and blooming heather, while a mile higher the white clouds veil and caress its topmost peaks. And all this landscape comes to him in reflected beauty from the lake that lies in stillness at his feet.

That Southern Ireland should be so dowered seems strange and inexplicable, for looking at the map we note that Ireland lies in a far northern latitude, as near to the North Pole as is Northern Canada, almost as near as these Aleutian Islands, which our armed forces stationed there tell us are lands of continuous snowstorms carried by northern blasts that sweep over ice-bound islands. Only the polar bear finds comfort there. Fancy one of these monsters swinging with ungainly gait from a Kerry Moun-

tain on his way to the Lakes of Killarney, determined to
get something or somebody for breakfast.

That Ireland is not afflicted as are these lands in similar
latitude is due to the tidal wave of warmth known as the
Gulf Stream, which emerging from the Gulf of Mexico
moves northeastwardly over the Atlantic Ocean bearing its
orange blossoms, its scented woods, its exotic forests — in
a word all the riches of the tropics. The Gulf Stream is
the Creator's gift to Western Europe, and Ireland is the
first to receive it — proof perhaps of the ancient saying:
"God loves the Irish."

The America of today is giving much to Europe; millions of men to help her regain her liberties, her faith in
herself and in Almighty God. America is doing much
through her "Lend-Lease Act" (extended to the United
Nations) to feed and clothe her dense population and
equip her armed forces. But these pale into insignificance
when compared to the blessings that have come to Europe
on this mighty wave of waters, which with America's
greeting, continues to fulfill the mission its Master gave
it in the beginning of the world.

We are told by the ethnologist that where the climate is
pleasant and food-stuffs plentiful, you find an easy-going
people, who having little else to do, incline to day-dream-
ing, romance — "looking at the solemn autumn fields and
thinking of the days that are no more."

And this is in part true of the Southern Irish. At eventide they watch "the splendor that falls on castle walls" and
hear a bugle call echo along the mountain-side, reminding
them of the brave days of old when the pibroch sounded
the chieftain's call to his faithful clansmen, to come to the
hosting, there to gird themselves once more for a fight in
defence of faith and fatherland. Again, I believe, you find
many of the young ready to go a-playing with the "fairies"
as they dance around the lone-tree, or mingling their song
with the winds that "whisper through the groves of
Blarney."

But the Irish, though they retain pleasant memories of

the heroic past, though they rejoice in and gather what
comfort they can from the newer freedom and prosperity
that are theirs, yet can they never forget that now, as in
days gone, there is given a mission — yes, a glorious mission which, if true to themselves, they must fulfill. Lionel
Johnson defines that mission when he writes:

> "Somehow to Ancient Innisfail
> Shall come the majesty and awe
> Of martial truth that must prevail
> To lay on all the eternal law."

To a world that is in revolt against the laws of God —
where tyranny follows revolution and nations seek to destroy their sister nations — the Irish nation, which never
engaged in a war of conquest, and never enslaved another
people, however defenceless it might be, has taken to itself
the noble task of bringing to the world of men the Christian Faith and that unchanging law that is of God.

Now it is Southern Ireland that furnishes a scene
where the fulfillment of that mission is best illustrated.

Every traveller to Europe has seen or heard of the
"Cove of Cork" — the little protected bay that lies South
of Cork and has Cobh (formerly called Queenstown) as a
background. It is the port in Ireland to which all the great
liners call. One of these lies out in the open sea — the
little tender plies in and out from pier to steamer; the
incoming tender has a few passengers, visitors to Ireland;
on the outgoing one you can see huddled together a group
of ten to twenty young men — they are Irish priest-
missionaries. On the same tender a large number of nuns
— the mission of both is to "teach the nations" — "they
go to seek new nations with their living, and mark them
with their dead."

They have said "Ave" in yonder Cathedral before starting on their journey. And now as with tear-filled eyes they
look back on the land of their birth to which many will not
return, they hear the Cathedral bell tolling, not their

requiem, but "God be with you" — "Ave atque Vale" — "Hail and Farewell."

It was in this delightful southland that Nano Nagle was born in the early part of the 18th Century. She descended from one of those ancient Irish Catholic families that survived hundreds of years of bitter opposition and persecution.

The chroniclers tell us her family was an "aristocratic" one. I have no objection to the descriptive word "aristocratic" if taken according to its original Greek signification, but since it grates on modern democratic nerves, I would prefer to title her family as one of those "fine old families" that in face of insults of every kind was able to preserve its dignity, gracious spirit of hospitality and that sterling faith that flourished in Ireland in the days of her glory.

Nano grew up in the refined atmosphere of a Catholic home. Her family lived in peace with their Protestant friends, of whom they had many. Some of these were relatives. The son of the famous poet Edmund Spenser had married into the Nagle family; while the great orator and statesman Edmund Burke was her first cousin. Burke was a friend and admirer of the American Colonies. He noted their just demand for an ordered liberty and self-government, and the most famous of his many speeches was a plea to England for the reconciliation of the Colonies. His pleading fell on deaf ears. It was just as well that it did, since in its stead a victorious army gave America her independence. There are many today waiting for another Burke to help maintain that same independence the fathers sought for. But though her Protestant friends might tolerate Nano's faith and even applaud her in the practice thereof, the invading government deemed it a sacred duty to destroy that faith and, if necessary thereto, they put to death those that refused to conform.

To this end the alien government had closed all Catholic schools, so that Nano must grow up ignorant or attend schools which were brazenly Protestant.

Fortunately the Nagle family had friends at the Court of Louis XV of France. Thither Nano was sent so that she might receive a Catholic education, but being associated with a frivolous court she was expected to take part in all its doings; its receptions, theatre parties, grand-balls and the rest. Nano, young, unsophisticated and beautiful, found the varied programme attractive.

Soon she grew tired — the court lights dimmed, their pleasing palled. Returning from a Court function one wintry Sunday morning she saw a crowd of poor people huddled together before the Church doors, waiting for their opening, so that entering they might enjoy the warm friendship, protection and presence of Him Who is Father of the poor. She thought then of her own country, where the poor and lowly were just then seeking some hidden chapel, there to give to God their heart and receive His benediction.

She returned to Ireland and in its Southern Capital began the great work with which her name is associated. She gathered the poor famished children around her; obtained comfortable quarters where she and her organized helpers fed, comforted and taught them. She established many such centres, and spending in their purchase and equipment her own considerable fortune, as also all she obtained from friends. God blessed her work and it grew so that her long cherished dream of founding an Order of Nuns, whose special mission would be to teach the children of the poor was realized.

The new Community was placed under the protection of the Blessed Mother and under the title of the Presentation. She would ask the Blessed Mother to help her daughters to present to the Lord in His Temple the children of the poor.

Nano Nagle, Foundress of the Nuns of the Presentation, died in the year 1784. The Order prospered from the start. The broader liberties that were coming to the Irish Catholic helped its growth, while their migration to the other countries gave the Nuns of the Presentation the opportunity to follow them in faith and service.

Today the Presentation Order is found in every English speaking country, and in many pagan countries as well, and, wherever they may be, that white virginal flame that was Nano Nagle lights their way.

We pray that sometime — in God's good time — Holy Church may declare the pious, humble, devoted Nano Nagle worthy to be presented to a place in the temple of God as one of those who follow the Lamb whithersoever He goeth.

Meanwhile, I commend to the kind reader Maurice Leahy's story of Nano Nagle which follows. It is written by a pilgrim from her homeland and therefore one fitted by nature and grace to write her "Life."

✙ JOHN J. GLENNON,
Archbishop of Saint Louis.

August 5, 1943.

Author's Preface

"For she hath wrought a good work upon Me. For the poor you have always with you; but Me you have not always.

Amen, I say to you, wheresoever this Gospel shall be preached in the whole world, that also which she hath done shall be told for a memory of her."

— *From the Holy Gospel according to St. Matthew.*

TELL us a story. That is an old cry in life and literature. This is the story of a valiant woman — Nano Nagle of Ireland. She was the Lady Elect of Catholic Education in days when the submerged Irish nation seemed without health, hope, or leadership.

I could kneel all night in prayer to heal your many ills. So sang Mangan to the beautiful being called Dark Rosaleen. Nano Nagle knelt many a night in prayer to heal her people. She worked many a day to lift up her race in body and soul. She is the bright ring of light round the dark day. Lethargic and leaderless lay her people in the Eighteenth Century that became blest by her radiant labours. If ever a woman needed the golden glorious virtue of God's highest Hope it was Nano Nagle in that cheerless dawn that saw the faithful Irish Catholics slowly emerge towards long-prayed-for emancipation.

With heart-aching eloquence the noble Henry Grattan expressed his hope for the nation that no repression could quench. "Yet I do not give up my country. I see her in a swoon but she is not dead; though in her tomb she lies helpless and motionless, still on her lips is the spirit of life and on her cheeks the glow of beauty."

It was Nano Nagle's special task to restore to educational life that hapless nation which was anaesthetized by coercive measures that forbade learning to the Catholic majority. Her cousin Edmund Burke knew how unshakable was the Irish Faith: "You cannot make the people Protestants," he wrote. And again: "The Papists of Ireland have sustained many injuries, they have inflicted none." Mother Nagle in her charity seems to have put into practice that beautiful saying of the renowned Spanish poet and mystic Carmelite, Saint John of the Cross: "Where there is no love put love and you will find love." Her peace, patience, and perseverance won the day — a lesson for us all. And hers was a wild and stormy day.

A resolve is here made to tell her story clearly and simply — amidst all the enthusiasm of the author's pledge to write of a saint of his country. There is much about her that we do not know, much about her that we should like to know. But perhaps it is well not to know all about whom one writes: it keeps modesty in the sketcher and mystery in the sketched. "Always remain a bit of a mystery to the people." That is venerable Irish advice from the old pastor to the new curate.

To quote St. Paul, Mother Nagle seems "as unknown, yet known." But: "It is really astonishing how very little is known of Nano Nagle, even by those who glory in being called her children." Thus wrote one of her biographers, The Venerable Archdeacon Hutch, nearly seventy years ago in Ireland. Fifty years ago in the United States, the great crusading apologist, of California, Father Peter C. Yorke vigorously panegyrized her as a pioneer of popular education — "but whose very name seems to be unknown to the thousands in this country who are the heirs of her achievements."

I have appended, to this book, enthusiastic messages sent to me by members of the Hierarchy. They all plead that Nano Nagle should be better known. When I decided that I would publish this work, do or die, I was met with the objection that nobody knows anything about her. This should be one good reason for writing about her. She wrought her fruitful work in wintry weather and desert places that we might dwell in greener pastures. Time will but make her more dear.

The story of modern Ireland is a happier one. Under an ideal Constitution, the Catholics, Protestants, Jews — all creeds — live in blessed harmony and unity in Eire.

My gratitude goes for ever to the faithful friends listed at the end of this book. As sponsors and advance subscribers they emboldened me in an arduous task. To the esteemed Presentation Sisters themselves I record many thanksgivings for their constantly encouraging kindliness. I realize that it is difficult to do full justice in a few hundred pages to their great Foundress. This chastening thought may prevent me from following the proud proclamation of the writer who said: "My book on Humility, the best book that has ever yet been written on the subject!"

Hundreds of years ago the Irish dedicated a sacred structure to "Saint Mary of Thanks." I always love that title. So, may Our Lady of Thanks reward all who have helped me in the propagation of this book on Nano Nagle. "Wheresoever this Gospel shall be preached in the whole world, that also which she hath done shall be told for a memory of her." In the English-speaking world, and beyond, let us see her works and tell her story. It will serve to lift up our hearts and keep her holy cause green in our souls.

— MAURICE LEAHY

New York, 1943.

CHAPTER I

THE AGE IN WHICH NANO NAGLE WAS BORN

ABOUT one hundred years before Daniel O'Connell won Catholic Emancipation Nano Nagle was born. That name Nano may be rendered as Honora, Honor, Nora. April 9, 1728, is recorded as her date of birth — in the townland of Ballygriffin, in the Parish of Monanimmy, in the Barony of Fermoy, in the County district of Mallow, all by the beautiful River Blackwater, in a fair and fertile region of the richly-endowed County of Cork. About nine months after the birth of Nano Nagle her immortal cousin Edmund Burke was born in Dublin. His mother was Mary Nagle, aunt of Nano. We have much to say of Burke in this book, for in Parliament and on platform he was the loyal champion of those same down-trodden Catholics whom Nano Nagle daringly resolved to educate in chapel and in classroom at a time when the poor proscribed Catholics existed only to be punished, and churches or schools were openly denied them, under pains of fine, imprisonment and even death.

We see that Edmund Burke's mother was a Catholic who practised her religion. His father, Richard Burke, professed himself a Protestant; and the three sons, Garret, Edmund, and Richard were brought up as Protestants, but the daughter, Juliana, followed her mother as a Catholic. To Edmund Burke therefore, the Protestant statesman of world-wide fame in the cause of liberty, we turn momentarily for a description of the age in which Nano Nagle lived and loved and laboured. It will help us in assessing her triumph.

In connection with the history of Ireland you often hear the word "Ascendancy." Nano Nagle's educational work triumphed, despite the opposition of the "Ascendancy."

Edmund Burke boldly explained the allusion as follows: "The Protestant ascendancy is nothing more or less than the resolution of one set of people to consider themselves as the sole citizens of the Commonwealth and to keep a dominion over the rest by reducing them to slavery under a military power."

Mercifully all this is now history long past. It is here introduced to show how Nano Nagle's genial charity abides, and how religious rancours failed. Indeed one may make a meditation herein on deep-rooted Catholic continuity. Nano Nagle's knightly ancestor Jocelyn Nangle, or Nagle, founded a monastery of the Blessed Virgin Mary in the grassy plains of royal Meath in the twelfth century. About four hundred years later when King Henry the Eighth vainly attempted to establish himself as spiritual head of the Irish nation the Mass and Mary's altar and Mary's shrine were soon to be banned with the monasteries. Yonder in England the hallowed shrine of St. Thomas a Becket in the graceful and holy town of Canterbury was sacrilegiously suppressed by Henry. Our friend G. K. Chesterton used to recite for us his own lines on that profane event:

> *The bones of Becket were bundled out*
> *For the fun of a fat white Czar,*
> *And we all became, with the world's acclaim,*
> *The marvellous mugs we are.*

There are always wild people who think that the world will be better by the sacking of shrines. Later generations look back and humanity looks foolish and ashamed. It is the blessed privilege of our generation to see the churches and shrines of the people re-arise, whether it be Our Lady's celebrated shrine, back in Catholic hands at Walsingham in England, or the ancient place of pilgrimage known as Saint Patrick's Purgatory, in Ireland. In Ireland, England, Scotland, Wales, we have seen the Faith of our Fathers re-arise with all the budding profusion of what Cardinal Newman poetically called the Second Spring. Mother Nagle is part of that story.

Protestant settlers from England in the sixteenth century received much of the native land in that smiling region where Nano Nagle was born. Among them was Arthur Hyde. It is noteworthy that one of his Protestant descendants is today the revered head of the Catholic Irish nation—Doctor Douglas Hyde, President of Eire. It is also interesting to note that this good Protestant President has devoted much of his scholarly career to recapturing the religious songs of the Irish people. And amongst them are many songs to Mary the Mother of God. Take the following, translated by Dr. Hyde: it is called "Mary of Graces":—

> O Mary of Graces
>   And Mother of God,
> May I tread in the paths
>   That the righteous have trod.
>
> And mayst thou save me
>   From evil's control,
> And mayst thou save me
>   In body and soul.
>
> And mayst thou save me
>   By land and by sea,
> And mayst thou save me
>   From tortures to be.
>
> May the guard of the Angels
>   Above me abide,
> May God be before me
>   And God at my side.

Jocelyn Nagle in the twelfth century with his monastic shrine to Holy Mary, Nano Nagle in the eighteenth century whose Sisters are dedicated to the name of Mary, Douglas Hyde in the nineteenth century singing anew the olden songs of Mary: here you have an interweaving and a continuity of Catholic traditions in Irish history that must be clearly kept in mind to understand the work which Nano Nagle started and which still goes on at home and abroad, in the name of Mary, whom Pope Pius XI called Queen of Ireland.

.There is a popular and facetious notion that the lives of Foundresses must needs make dull reading, that they are only fit for sentimentally pious people. Here we seek to show that Nano Nagle belongs as vividly and vigorously to the warp and woof of Irish history as does her philosopher kinsman Edmund Burke. She holds an inspiring and romantic place in the essential history of the Catholic Church. Her name flourishes warmly in "the short and simple annals of the poor."

The Penal Laws of her age invidiously insisted that Catholics must remain unlettered. This was galling in heart and mind to the Irish people, who from the earliest dawn to this day, have treasured education beyond all prizes. In their Golden Age, over a thousand years before the epoch of Nano Nagle, they carried the Gospel with their scholarship all over Europe. Their educational footprints may be traced in many lands.

On the Irish love for education let us listen to Lecky, the oft-quoted and weighty Protestant historian, of Trinity College, Dublin. He wrote penetratingly of that eighteenth century in which Nano Nagle's educational work began. Narrow and bigoted souls dismissed the native Irish as being uneducated and uneducable. Looking back, in the light of modern liberty, such souls seem so insignificant and devoid of the wider vision that they might be luxuriously housed in a nutshell. Lecky says: "The passion for knowledge among the Irish poor is extremely strong, and the zeal with which they maintained their hedge schools under the pressure of abject poverty and in the face of the prohibitions of the Penal Code is one of the most honourable features in their history." Plainly, Lecky said their condition was slavery: "The simple profession of the Catholic Faith excluded a man from every form of political and municipal power."

But the subterraneous struggle for education still went on. A century before Nano Nagle's heyday, Father Forde of the Society of Jesus, whose vast history is so inter-allied with the history of education, is described about the year 1654 as founding a school in the midst of incredible desolation in a quaking bog, at a time when priests actually lived in remote caverns. Indeed Bishop Keogh of Clonfert, who ordained many priests in Ireland in the reigns of King Charles II and King James II, lived in a comfortless cabin in a bog to keep clear of what was called the Law. "Papists" could be compelled to answer as to Priests, Mass, Confession.

The poor Friars clung closely to their outlawed people. The spirit of that Charity, which marks Saint Francis of Assisi as the perennial wonder of the wounded world, was a source of consolation to the Irish in those torturing years. A Friar named Burke from Connaught appeared in Kerry, looking like John the Baptist and calling aloud to the people to follow their Faith, forsake their sins and live virtuously so as to bring blessings throughout that Night when no man could work; catechism in hand he drove home those Eternal Truths that men need to know in order to be saved, that mark man off from the ox.

This burning spirit of love for the preservation of the Faith by means of Christian teaching was also to animate Nano Nagle. Young and old among God's poor she will seek in the man-made city streets. She will take care of their spiritual and temporal needs in her carefully organized way; we picture her in that state expressed by Saint James in his first Epistle:—"Religion clean and undefiled before God and the Father is this: to visit the fatherless and widows in their tribulation and to keep one's self unspotted from the world."

CHAPTER 2

THE NAGLE FAMILY

I HAVE called Mother Nagle "FLOWER OF HER KIN-DRED." Her kindred being the Irish Race by blood and the Human Race by charity — the mystic charity of Mary the Mother of us all. We can quote her own words: "If I could be of any service in saving souls in any part of the globe, I would willingly do all in my power." Her charit-able vision went beyond the white-clouded horizon of her native Ireland, and she turned her thoughts to the Negroes of the West Indies long before we talked of race tolerance, and race uplift.

For, in 1770, she had put into operation a plan to teach Religion to the coloured children there and so help to brighten their dim lives. She was ahead of her time in her zeal and charity towards the coloured race. This thought will be amplified by a letter of hers which I must introduce later.

To describe Nano Nagle as a Flower of the Irish Race, I have taken a title from Thomas Moore's lovely lyric, "The Last Rose of Summer," which is known and sung the world over for its feeling sweetness. In the twenties of this cen-tury I used to hear audiences in London demand it as an encore from the lips of Dame Nellie Melba to whom it seemed a sort of Evensong. In studying the age of Nano Nagle it is worth while to reflect briefly upon the poet Moore. With plangent emotion he voiced the cries of the stifled Irish nation and of the penal-plagued Catholics to a world that seemed heedless. He became a literary fashion himself and made the name of Ireland fashionable round the world, so that on St. Patrick's Day, or on any day to this day, North, South, East, or West, whenever the band initiates the stirring measure of "Let Erin Remember" there are hearts that beat high with praise. Attempts have been made to devalue Moore. He is said to be too sentimental, and too sugary. But feeling seems a good thing, especially so when it is controlled. There is tender delicacy in Moore, but there is also an unsurrendering defiance that brings him within the sphere of greatness. There are those popular and patriotic lines:

> Dear Harp of my country in darkness I found thee,
> The cold chain of silence had hung o'er thee long,
> When proudly my own island Harp I unbound thee,
> And gave all thy chords to light, freedom, and song.

Three things which are dear to the Irish mind: Light, Freedom, and Song. To the whole world, as well as to Ireland, Nano Nagle wished to give the Light of the Gospel — which is clearly the Light of the World; her work was to achieve freedom from ignorance and to replace defeatist dirges by songs of Sion. Emerging from darkness and silence she was determined to make her people educationally vocal. She was the true Flower of her Kindred. And what of her lovely companions? They were neither faded nor gone. They were found ready too, high-born Irish ladies like herself, with talents and fortunes and dowries akin to her own, which they generously donated to their community and which were spent in their evangelical efforts to protect the needy, by teaching and feeding and clothing them, all of which was done in the spirit of the Eight Beatitudes.

Our *Oxford* definition warns against that decoying disease, "Lues Boswelliana": the biographer's tendency to magnify his subject; hence see Boswell and his Johnson for some origins of this "Boswellian contagion." In writing of the holy ones of God I firmly believe that we should avoid the saponaceous and the oleaginous and the tendentious. But in the cold light of reason any reader may study the history of Ireland in the Eighteenth Century and realize that no praise is too great for Nano Nagle and her accomplishment. They say that words are given to us to conceal our thoughts. Indeed one feels that words seem frail and helpless to express the spirit of Nano Nagle whose name is

surely writ large in the Book of Life. Lord Byron spoke
of "what I can ne'er express, but cannot all conceal." One
cannot express all of Mother Nagle's story, but it cannot
and should not remain all concealed.

Nano Nagle is accorded some space in the *Dictionary of
National Biography*, side by side with those illustrious
members of her family, Sir Richard Nagle, Admiral Sir
Edmund Nagle, and The Right Hon. Edmund Burke.
Shortly before his lamented death, Father John Fenlon,
Provincial of the Sulpician Fathers, well-beloved ecclesiastical educators in the Old World and in the New,
cheeringly wrote to me: "Edmund Burke had many
cousins but there was only one Nano Nagle, and I know
you will do her the full justice she deserves." One can
only humbly try.

Let us examine her crested and prevailing name. The
name is written Nangle, Nagle, de Nangle, de Nongle,
de Nougle, Nogle, Neagle. Father Woulfe, in his excellent
book on Irish Names, tells us that the name in Middle
English was written "atten Angle," and then again as "atte
Nangle," coming from the Latin form of the name "de
Angulo," meaning at the angle or corner — from residence
thereat. The letter *n* in the article was attracted over and
thus became the initial of the surname proper, so that
instead of Angle we have Nangle. The same change is
credited to the names Ash and Nash: originally there was
"atten Ash," meaning "at the ash." The letter *n* was
attracted over, and it led to "atte Nash," hence the name
Nash. The evolution of names is elusive and tricky and we
pass on to what we can glean of deeds in family history.

King Henry II of England, nearly eight hundred years
ago, gave the smiling land of royal Meath in Ireland to an
invading Norman chieftain — Hugh De Lacy. De Lacy in
turn gave it to his chiefs, among whom was the distinguished Gilbert de Angulo, or Nangle or Nagle. Sir
Bernard Burke in his reference book on the "Landed
Gentry" describes the Nagles as "one of the most ancient
Anglo-Norman families in Ireland." From a precious

fragment of the History of Ireland by Maurice Regan, who was interpreter to King Dermott McMurrough of Leinster, we find that the name Nangle or Nogle is mentioned among the invading families. The Norman commander, Gilbert de Angulo, from whom we now see that the Nagles originated in Ireland, had two sons Jocelyn and Hostilio. The name of Hostilio is also written as Costelo, or Costello. It is said that the name of Costello originated from him — the name being written as Mac Hostilio or Mac Costello, that is, son of Hostilio or Costello. Another explanation is given that the name Costello was taken by the Nagle family from a place called Caosluig, near Ballyshannon, where Hostilio Nangle, the second son of Gilbert de Angulo, is said to have been slain in battle, about 1210, by the native forces of the northern chieftains of the O'Neills and O'Donnells. From these Nagles, who Irished themselves as Mac Costello, it is said that the Barony of Costello in County Mayo is derived. Father Woulfe, in his study of Irish names, says that the name Mac Costello, written in Gaelic as Mac Oisdealb, means son of Oisdealb, and that Oisdealb mean Os-shaped, that is, shaped like the god Os. This patronymic Mac Costello assumed by the Nagle family is said to be the earliest Anglo-Irish Mac surname recorded in the Annals, A.D. 1193.

The Nagle family extended to Westmeath, Kildare, Waterford and Cork.

Jocelyn Nangle became Lord of Navan. He had a son who was surnamed Peter Peppard, and from him originated the family name of Peppard or Pepper. Peter Pepper was Justiciary of Ireland in 1195, and his grandson founded the Abbey at Ardee, in County Louth, to honour the Blessed Virgin Mary. From Jocelyn Nangle's elder son, called Jordan, the Nagles of Leinster and Munster descended. There was also a brother of Gilbert de Angulo who was called Jordan. Thus it is said that from this early family of Nagles there came the family name of Jordan or MacJordan. But there is also another family name, Jordan of Exeter, which has a different history. Merely to show

how the invaders blended with the invaded we mention that
Sir Hugh de Lacy, who gave lands to the Nagles, married
as his second wife the daughter of Roderick O'Connor, the
last High King of Ireland. Many of this de Lacy family
later distinguished themselves in high service in Austria
and Russia.

Even though heraldry has been dubbed the science of
fools with long memories, we recall Emerson's motto that
man is but the sum of his ancestors. Nano Nagle was in
the nobility, and the nobility was in her — which is the
important point for our study. Her great family name runs
in kinship with so many other great Irish families through
the pages of history. We read that Margaret Nagle,
daughter of David Nagle of Monanimmy, in Cork, married
in 1451 John O'Connor, Lord of Kerry, who, in 1470,
founded a Monastery at Lislaghtan where he is buried.
Thus we find Mother Nagle's immediate ancestry linked
with the historic and venerable family of O'Connor Kerry.
We read that the Nagle family was inter-married with the
noted family of Kearney from Tipperary: the Kearneys
were hereditary keepers of St. Patrick's Crozier — a picturesque duty; and members of this family of high place
won fame at the unforgettable Battle of Fontenoy which
was fought when Nano Nagle was seventeen. Sir Richard
Nagle married Jane Kearney, and his brother Pierce Nagle
married Anne Kearney. These will be discussed later.

Another historic family, named Grace, of Norman origin
in Ireland, was allied with the name of Nagle: Oliver
Grace, an Irish Member of Parliament, who died in 1708,
had a daughter Anne who was first married to Richard
Nagle, eldest son of Sir Richard Nagle who was Secretary
of State for Ireland; and secondly she was married to Edmund Butler, the Eighth Lord Dunboyne. She was the
mother of the Ninth, Tenth and Twelfth Lords Dunboyne. It
is the Twelfth Lord Dunboyne that will interest us presently,
for he was John Butler, Catholic Bishop of Cork, who
inexplicably enough was in opposition to Miss Nagle's
edifying projects. He was a family relation of hers, and

he was her Bishop. By all ties she could expect him to co-operate. But from her own letter we are to see that he was her opponent. Her early biographer, The Venerable Archdeacon Hutch, is pretty severe on Bishop Butler, who gave up a Catholic Bishopric on inheriting the title of Lord Dunboyne, and who now openly became a Protestant. His name will recur later. Though his story is a sad one it is also an example of the triumph of God's Grace, for the apostate bishop was received back into the One True Fold of the Catholic Church on his death-bed. Here there is drama for the dramatist. There is Nano Nagle in her youth and beauty and wealth, leaving court and fame and social standing, in order to give herself and her all to God and God's poor. There is her Father in God, Bishop Butler, who at the age of seventy, or more, forsook his flock after being their Bishop for twenty-three years, and who nearly lost his immortal soul through an earthly title and the transient possessions of this unlasting city.

Amongst the list of the Archbishops of Tuam in the sixteenth century we find the name of Richard Nangle, or Nagle, who was a distinguished Augustinian, and who established a house of the Order in Galway. As a Bishop he seems to have come up against the laws of Henry VIII who wished to appoint his own candidates. Richard Nangle was the Pope's choice.

Under the year 1585, Hardiman, in his West Connaught, mentions the name Mac Costello as Nangle. In the early part of King Henry VIII's reign, there is a report made to the monarch, A. D. 1515, on the State of Ireland, wherein the Nagle name occurs. Apparently the area of Ireland in which the King's writ was then observed was small. The English settlers were going native and using the Irish language. Among those listed as "The King's Irish Rebels" there are "30 great Captains of the English noble folk"— and among "the English great rebels in Connaught" is named "The Lord Nangle [Mc Costello] (Mayo)." A list follows of "the countyes that obey not the King's laws." They were "Waterford, Cork, Kilkenny, Limerick, Kerry, all of Connaught, all of Ulster, Carlow, Oriel, Monaghan, ½ of Meath, Dublin, Kildare and Wexford." We are told that "also all of the English folk of the said counties be of Irish habit, of Irish language and of Irish conditions."

From the large list of resisting counties it looks as if neither the Irish nor the English paid much attention to Henry the Eighth's laws at the time, and the Nagles were in the fashion, so it is not too surprising to find a charming young member of the family, a few hundred years later, ignoring the dread Penal Laws, and opening schools in spite of them, for the benefit of these same Irish natives who continuously refused to be deracinated.

A man who had much to say about the Irish natives in the sixteenth century was the English poet Edmund Spenser, whose family was allied with that of the Nagles, and after whom the great Burke was called Edmund. Sylvanus Spenser, eldest son of the poet, married Ellen Nagle, a great-aunt of Burke's mother. Ellen Nagle was the daughter of David Nagle of Ballygriffin, and Ellen Roche — the Roches being a celebrated family in that region, whereby the village of Castletownroche to this day betokens the name. The records refer to "Ballygriffin, a pretty seat of Mr. David Nagle, below which is the ruined church of Monanimy, with a large chancel and in it a modern tomb of the Nagles." The chief antagonist of the newly arrived Edmund Spenser in this locality was Lord Roche who forbade his people to have any trade or conference with the native gentry around Mr. Spenser. It was an early form of boycotting. Yet Spenser's son was to marry the child of a Roche. Indeed the poet himself married an Irishwoman, Elizabeth Boyle — kinswoman to Roger Boyle, Earl of Cork. Hugolin Spenser, one of the poet's grandsons, followed the example of Sir Richard Nagle, the Catholic Attorney-General of King James II, in resisting the Prince of Orange, and was after the Revolution outlawed for treason and rebellion. Such are the strange vicissitudes of

Irish History. The poet Spenser had plans for keeping the Irish down. His grandson was with them as a rebel when they rose up.

The Nagles and Roches are described as Popish families, and both were represented in the Irish Rising of 1641; in this, some of them may have lost their properties. By 1751, there were still descendants of Spenser in County Cork. Spenser wrote of the Knight of the Red Cross, or of Holiness. I have lingered on his period to detail the historical background of Mother Nagle, who may be described as the Lady of the Red Cross of Christ, and whose heroic holiness enabled her to elevate the children of the race that Spenser described as crawling and dying by the wayside from the artificial famine wilfully created by the invaders, Mountjoy and Carew, at that time.

Near to Mother Nagle's birthplace was Kilcolman Castle where lived Spenser who was called "the Prince of Poets in his time." There this Puritan and man of affairs composed his *Faerie Queene*, and there he was visited by Sir Walter Raleigh who introduced the potato and tobacco into Ireland. It was one of the ruined castles of the fallen Earls of Desmond: a pleasant and romantic place, with roses, laurels, apples, oaks. For over three thousand acres of this fruitful native soil the stranger paid an annual rent of about 90 dollars. Here the poet described himself as keeping his flock by the waters of the River Mulla, under cool shades of green alder trees, and tuning his oaten pipe to his fellow shepherds. The river was noted for trout, eels, salmon, carp, perch, tench. These acres were once part of the proud Geraldine possessions — of Gerald Fitzgerald, the last true Earl of Desmond who was one of the great leaders of Europe in his day. He held the rank of a "Prince Palatine" with all the power of a provincial king. He resisted the Reformation and he resisted the English Government. He was finally tracked and slain in a Kerry glen in 1583. His nephew James Fitzgerald joined Hugh

O'Neill but was captured and died a prisoner in the Tower of London. Thus ended the great house of Fitzgerald, Earls of Desmond: their history is spread over many a thrilling page.

Then the Desmond lands were divided among English settlers. Those lands where the mountains were covered with oak forests, where flourished ash, pine, alder, birch, hazel, immense yews, and where wolves and red deer roamed. It cost Queen Elizabeth a couple of million dollars to put down the rebellion of Desmond and his associates. The "Plantation" of Munster in 1586 was the penalty inflicted upon Ireland. Besides Spenser, Sir Walter Raleigh did well with forty thousand acres and a pretty home amid the glories of Youghal. Despite all the "settlements" Lord Mountjoy himself recorded later that, much of the population, even the Old English, had "Papist hearts." Spenser's idyllic peace in Cork was not to last. The Irish Chieftain Hugh O'Neill, Earl of Tyrone, and his forces, swept with promising success from North to South, in the latter part of the sixteenth century, in a final effort to set the Irish nation free: he asked a number of southern chiefs to rise and assist "Christ's Catholic religion." In the blaze of rebellion Spenser's Castle at Kilcolman went up in flames and he and his family were forced to flee. I am reminded of the final ending of his *Faerie Queene:* we seek rest but there is none: our house of rest must be built upon the pillars of Eternity. We are creatures of change and seem to love change, but we are made for the Changeless God in whom alone we can find rest for our souls.

> For all that moveth doth in change delight,
> But thenceforth all shall rest eternally
> With Him that is the God of Sabaoth.

Today Kilcolman Castle is a fragmentary ruin, but the buildings shaped in a stormy age by Nano Nagle abide.

I have dwelt extensively on her family name. Its connections extended far and wide. A Nangle had married into the powerful Loftus family, descended from Adam Loftus who was Protestant Archbishop of Dublin and first Provost of the new Trinity College founded by Queen Elizabeth.

Mother Nagle's ancestors were related to the Plunket family of Meath, to the family of Rochford, to the family of Lord Gormanston and to the Earls of Kildare.

Her family has a historic structure. In keeping with her ancestral name *De Angulo*, which may be interpreted as at the corner, she is in this study the head of the corner. The Family that she set up for us to follow is The Holy Family. We shall see that her work was a corner-stone in the Christian Education of the human family.

CHAPTER 3

THE EDUCATION OF NANO NAGLE

The Penal Laws did not allow Catholic schools to exist, hence Nano Nagle had her primary education from her parents at home. "Both of them less distinguished by their genteel extraction than by the general edification of their good example." So wrote Bishop Coppinger, the patriot Bishop of Cloyne, who would not tolerate any compromise with the Government of the day, which demanded the right to *Veto* priests for the prelacy if unacceptable to the secular powers.

Nano Nagle's mother was of the celebrated family of Matthew, a name made imperishable in Irish history and in social reform by another member of the household, Father Theobald Mathew, whose apostolic toils in the needed cause of temperance led him over the Old World and the New, and won him public statues in Cork and Dublin.

Piety there clearly was in the Nagle home, and Nano benefited by its fruits. Piety, the gift which weans the heart from terrestrial things and centralizes it on God, piety which wards off all killing attachments to the glitter and allure of our enmeshing world, piety which leads the soul to pray and enlivens it with the desire of seeking God in its own interior depths, piety which bids us talk and walk with God in spirit lest we drown in the tempting tangles of things that seduce us downward. Piety, ridiculed by the Rationalist, but beloved by the believer.

True there was a great deal of education and scientific enlightenment going on in the eighteenth century. But materialism became so melancholy that the nature-loving Wordsworth protested against the worldly-minded curiosity of the philosopher who would botanize and peep upon his mother's grave.

In the previous century, not far from Mother Nagle's birthplace, Robert Boyle, "The Father of Chemistry," was born at Lismore Castle, in County Waterford. He improved the Air-pump, and upset the older Alchemists whose ideas on lead, gold, and copper led them to believe that it should be possible to change one into another. Further afield in the eighteenth century Lagrange and Newton treated the world to new marvels in Mathematics; Bradley and Herschell made Astronomy shine anew; Lavoisier discovered oxygen, and Bertholet expounded chemical affinities. A politely perfected and polished Rationalism prevailed. Men talked of themselves as Deists too. In their Liberalism and Deism they declared it ridiculous that people should be punished for particular beliefs, no matter how absurd these beliefs might seem! In a later age Francis Thompson supplied a comment on all this wonderful quest of Science: of a dead priest-astronomer who had naturally sought new stars, Thompson wrote: —"When thou thy starry tube didst let fall, thou didst find the Fairest Star of all." God of course, the poet meant.

But no amount of worldly education could dispense with fear of the Lord, holy fortitude, and the gifts of piety which were made manifest to Nano Nagle in her family circle. There are many details we would wish to know about her early years but unfortunately few facts are preserved. It is good to be told that she was attractively human. In our age writers have set out to humanize the Saints, who were previously pictured as impossibly aloof and remote beings, who never made a mistake, and hardly ever struggled on this our earth. It was my happiness to have known Father Martindale in those days when he was giving a real living picture of the great Saint Aloysius Gonzaga. What a great deal Father Martindale did to make the Saints attractive to the general public. Some *Lives* can be murders. A certain biography was described as an *attempt* on the *Life* of Cardinal Manning.

There were no signs that Nano Nagle would play a tremendous part in the future history of her country. As a child she apparently did not walk about with the precocious airs of a grave young stateswoman or look prematurely wearied from the weight of the cosmos. A certain alarming philosopher of our time tells us that, as a child at the age of five, he was appalled and dismayed at the prospect of a useless, baffling, and disappointing world, with all its coming miseries and gloom. We can imagine what a happy little lad he was at the age of five. As a child Nano Nagle delighted in the things of a child.

We deduce that Nano was wilful and eager and restless and vivacious; evidently and unusually full of those childish human spirits that made her the life of the family, even to the extent of engendering anxiety in her mother who feared that the growing child might become our proverbial problem child. I think of the poet who feared that the first thing the children do when they get into Heaven is to pull all the quills off the Angels' wings. So the mother kept the child in check, well in hand, in the hope of reducing her ardour to a little lower key; even the extras accorded as a reward to the other children, for being so good, were withheld from the mercurial Nano in order to teach her a subduing lesson. But the fond father always intervened for Nano and made pleading apologies for her sprightly childishness. As if in prophetic forecast he used to say that "poor Nano would be a saint yet." It was all the innocent jollity of childhood. The refining influence of her home and surroundings modified and moulded her. Here, her baptismal innocence was assured.

The child looked out on an uplifting countryside. Every prospect pleased. Only the laws of man were vile at the time. The scene was spacious. And space itself makes for culture. When we are cribbed, cabined and confined in crowded cities, perhaps we tend to grate on one another's irritated nervous systems, and lose the finer elegancies. The restful range of *Nagle's Mountains* must have inspired Nano from her windows, and the murmuring waves of the Blackwater must have been as dear a music to her sensitive ears as were, to the poet, the Bells of Shandon "whose sounds so wild would in days of childhood fling round my cradle their magic spells." A young Protestant poet and patriot was cradled by these waves of the Blackwater — Thomas Davis, who is never forgotten. *She is a rich and rare land, she is a fresh and fair land, this native land of mine.* Thus did Davis address the country of his birth. To save her he would dream his lot divine.

Of Poetry and History there were plenty traces round Nano Nagle's home. Here a castle. There the ruins of a church where Knights Templars worshipped in holier days. In a hedge-school at the ruined Castle of Monanimmy Edmund Burke received the elements of his education for about five years. Here in the homeland of the Nagles he spent his early impressionable years; and these scenes he always loved to visit again.

From their estate in life and from their loyal Catholic attachment, which involved many hidden sacrifices, no matter how generous-minded the Protestant neighbours may have been, it is clear that Garret Nagle and his wife gave their daughter a sound and substantial training in the ways of virtue and in the needs of elementary education. The refining grace of the Catholic Faith in which she was grounded was an education in itself, which stood her in good stead when she shortly went to France where the plausibly clever philosophies of Voltaire and Rousseau were, by their reiterated inveighing, to undermine authority and inveigle the common man into disrespect for revealed religion.

It is easy for Catholics to decide upon education for their children in our day. Good boarding-schools and day schools abound on every hand. Education is within the facile reach of rich and poor. In Nano Nagle's day the more privileged Catholic classes, to which she belonged, might stealthily send their children to be educated in Catholic Schools on the continent of Europe. In the eyes of the law this was a grave crime in itself. We almost grow weary of reading enactment after enactment against Papists and *foreign* education. For the poorer Catholics there was no chance of any kind. The richer ones might risk evading the law and receive their education beyond their own shores. France, during her peace with England, had protested against the Penal Code and its crazy injustices against the Catholics.

To the pleasant land of France Nano Nagle was now to go in order to get the education that would fit her for her future station in life among the Catholic gentry of Ireland. Her parents would not place her in a Protestant school at home. To Paris she would go. Paris, where her Franciscan fellow-countryman, Duns Scotus, some centuries previously had set France afire with enthusiasm for the all-pure Mother of God by his warmly Irish defence of Mary's Immaculate Conception. *Ergo, Mater Dei omnino immaculata est.* These words of the learned Irishman were to echo again in the official theology of the Catholic Church in 1854, when the Immaculate Conception of Our Lady was made a matter of Faith. To Mary without stain is the happy land of America dedicated. One could dilate indefinitely on the heavenly and earthly ties that unendingly bind us all within the Ark of Salvation. Sagnificantly, in 1854, Nano Nagle's Sisters of the Presentation of the Blessed Virgin Mary arrived in the United States, to start their good work in the hallowed country that we affectionately know as California, amidst whose treasures and beauties the ancient Order of Duns Scotus had already left the imprint of the Catholic Faith, together with many a name, for many a town, that to this day will remind the traveller of the pervading titles of Holy Mary.

Many of the Irish had gone to France to wear the fleur-de-lis. Balladry bears their name through the winds of time. The most quoted lines reveal a wealth of European history: *On far foreign fields from Dunkirk to Belgrade lie the soldiers and chiefs of the Irish Brigade.* For Nano Nagle it was farewell for the moment to her Munster vale. In her perception of the parting pang who could fail to sympathize with her? For Ireland is such a beautiful country that nobody could willingly wish to part from it.

Emerald meadows, morning dew, buttercups, primroses, fleeting skies, lingering twilights, mountains blue, the song of the lark in the blue serene, the melody of robin or wren from boughs just freshly rainwashed, the call of the wild geese, the curlew, the snipe, the plover, the far-resounding sea that is only sixty miles away from any part, the hawthorn, the fuchsia hedges, the lowing of the kine, the white winding roads, the hush, the silence, the crooning young night winds that seem to rise suddenly from nowhere.

Then as now these were surely sights and sounds that refreshed the soul. One morning as the Irish Spring was awaking with all its fairy train, Nano Nagle set out for France — France, the eldest daughter of the Church, home of chivalry, centre of cultural refinement, the land of many mystics, saints and missionaries. Even if there be other sides to our story we never can fail in our love for France, in its greatness or its fall, in its happiness or unhappiness. With Nano Nagle's story it is engagingly entwined. At home in Ireland she was styled a *Papist*. For almost a century that word marked the official and legal designation of Irish Catholics by the British Government. The Oxford Dictionary tells us that the word Papist means a Roman Catholic — usually in a hostile sense. In France she could be a Catholic and openly belong to the Faith which had so greatly shaped the Culture of Europe, the Faith which twelve thousand converts espouse each year in England in our own time.

CHAPTER 4

NANO NAGLE IN FRANCE

ACCOMPANIED by an uncle Nano Nagle arrived in
Paris. The Nagle family had a deal of contact with
the Continent. When Edmund Burke's only son, Richard,
toured Europe, interviewing rulers and statesmen and
celebrities, the young man was accompanied by one of his
Nagle relatives.

Young Miss Nagle was placed in a convent in Paris for
her further education. Little of her story during that
period is now known to us. Again we turn to Bishop Coppinger who preached a panegyric on her, not so long after
her death. In his Life of her he says that "being gifted
with superior talents, she fulfilled in every particular the
expectations of her friends — uniting with an agreeable
person the most engaging manners, and the most lasting
attractions of a cultivated mind."

Her formal studies were completed and "at the desire
of her friends" she remained on in Paris. It was apparently felt that some contact with Parisian society could,
if needs be, give poise, composure, finish, and a refining
delicatesse to a young lady who wished to move through
life with the proper social graces. And it was easy for
this well-bred Irish girl to be invited to the glittering
parties at the Royal French Court. Let us explain why —
apart from her own rare personal charms. It involves
narrating briefly the historical connections between Ireland
and France. Let me dwell on these.

Numbers of Nano Nagle's relatives had loyally gone
into exile with King James II, who at the age of 68, died
at the Palace of St. Germains, near Paris, on September
16, 1701. King Louis XIV of France had befriended James
and his courtiers, and had actually proclaimed James's
son, "the Pretender," as James III, King of England, and
for that matter, of Scotland and Ireland. Ireland certainly

had done more than its part to defend the Catholic King
of England, James Stuart, who lost the Battle of the Boyne
to William of Orange in 1690, one of the events that completely changed the destiny of the Irish people. By 1695
the Penal Code began against Catholics, and by 1727 it
had reached its complete fury — a year before Nano
Nagle was born. Through this evil Code she found herself
in France. I am reminded of my earliest impressions of
Hilaire Belloc when he declared to us in our youth: "If
you want to have a very adventurous life be a thorough
Catholic." Her Catholicism led to the adventure of exile.

Though it is an unpleasant necessity, we are going to
refer to the leprous degradation of the French Court of
King Louis XV, as depicted for us by the historians. In
that effete and dissipating orbit Nano Nagle was briefly
to move. But of the other Court, not far away, to which
her Nagle relatives had come with King James, we may
say something edifying. There, in his final years, James
lived a life of austere penitence and sublime sanctity —
led to great graces by a Cistercian Abbot. To Belloc,
a fearless English Historian, whom I have esteemed and
admired since the moment I was first associated with him,
I am indebted for facts that portray James's purifying love
of God in the twilight of life.

In his final exile James wrote: — "I abhor and detest
myself for having so often offended so gracious and merciful a God, and having lived so many years in almost a
perpetual course of sin, not only in my youth when I was
carried away with the heat of it, and ill example, but even
after when I was come to years of more discretion, and
that thou hadst been pleased to have called me from the
Pit of Heresy to have opened my eyes, to have known
and entered thy true religion, to have covered my head so
often in the day of Battle, delivered me so many times
from the dangers of the sea and noise of its waves."

I am indebted to Belloc also for the following fragment wherein King James II, in his last days, says: "I am
fixed that the longer I live in this world the more do I

hazard my eternal salvation and that I cannot be in safety till I am freed of this contemptible body, and united with you, O my God. Lord when will that happy day arrive when I shall taste the vision of Beatitude and be one with the Saints who praise and will praise you for ever. It will be at your good time, my God; but Lord delay not long."

To his son, James gave valuable advice as follows: "It is the Grace of God that gives the Faith, and men are to be gained by goodness and example and teaching, not by fear. Do not disturb subjects in their goods or in their religion. Do all to establish freedom of conscience. Keep the Faith against all things and all men."

In that French Court, where his Irish exiles served him, James lay down to die. He made his general Confession. I quote from Belloc on the King's last hours: "The Viaticum had come. The Priest entering the death-chamber held up the Blessed Sacrament asking: *Do you believe Jesus Christ to be really and substantially present in this Host?* To which the King was heard to answer, fervently with ardour gazing on That for which he had given three Crowns and all his House: *I do believe it. I believe it with all my heart.*"

In his stirring book on James II, Belloc has shown us that the Catholic Faith counted for so much in the history of this period. True in Ireland it was a struggle for Faith and Nation. And, if attitudes to the Battle of the Boyne vary according to tastes in gods and men, what really does matter is the demand of General Patrick Sarsfield when the other battle by the Shannon's River, at Limerick, was over: a Catholic School in every parish, a Catholic Church in every parish, and liberty to worship therein. Seemingly simple requests. But Sarsfield's defeated Irish nation was not awarded the rights promised by the Treaty of Limerick. Neither Church, lands, nor Liberty, compensatingly came their way.

In the ship, that bore away the brave General Sarsfield to France, was also Nano Nagle's famous relative, Sir Richard Nagle, who had held high offices in Ireland in the reign of King James II. He was Attorney General for Ireland in 1686, taking the place of a Protestant in that office. We are told that he had a masterly knowledge of the law, that he was employed by many Protestants, and that he had a keen idea of the weak points in their titles. The ancient nobility and gentlemen of Ireland in his time resumed the lands of which they had been deprived by a swarm of seizing Cromwellian adventurers about 40 years previously. He was contemplating a Parliament which might dispossess "Settlers" and at the same time give them compensation. He was made a Knight by Richard Talbot, Earl of Tyrconnel, who had been given command of the Irish Army. Justin McCarthy and Sir Richard Nagle sat as Members of the Irish House of Commons in the Parliament of James II on May 7, 1689.

Nagle was Speaker of the Irish House of Commons and was James II's Chief Secretary. After the Battle of the Boyne he urged James to flee to France while he himself retired to the scene of events in Galway, in what has been called the last stand of Catholic Ireland. He was at the Siege of Limerick with the Earl of Tyrconnel, who trusted him with many secrets during that final battle so gallantly fought by the old Irish nation. When Tyrconnel died, Nagle was one of the three Lords Justices helping to keep the country together. Pathetically, in exile, he still ruled as Secretary of State for Ireland in the shadow Court of King James at the Palace of St. Germains. For the old Catholic nation of Ireland still cherished dreams at home of a Catholic Stuart King coming over the water and rightfully setting Dark Rosaleen on her golden throne. Bards and poets nurtured such visions, but by the time Nano Nagle returned to Ireland the dream was dying, albeit with a touching swansong.

Sir Richard Nagle is supposed to have died abroad. He was an enthusiastic Catholic, a loyal Stuart Royalist, and all this cost him dear. He lost some thousands of acres in his estates in Cork and Waterford. He has been accused by some writers of bigotry towards his separated brethren.

But the general verdict of history is that he was a learned, able, upright, and sincere man. Had he chosen the opposite side, his talents would have been well rewarded and the Nagle estates would have been assured. A member of the Kearney family to which his wife belonged, won fame at the Battle of Fontenoy where the Irish were so victorious in a French cause. They could well wish that their victory was for Ireland instead.

Nagle had a large family. We read of one son marrying a Miss Burke in France. Sir Richard's brother, Pierce Nagle, was notably outstanding in the history of the time. He was High Sheriff of the City of Cork in 1668, and was the last Catholic to fill that office, until O'Connell won a full measure of constitutional Emancipation for Catholics in 1829. He was evidently a man who quietly and fairly did his duty, and was liked by all. The Protestants of the day must have specially esteemed him, and he did not have to go into exile like his brother after the Jacobite collapse. He was so far privileged as to be permitted to carry arms, a thing not allowed to Catholics after King William III came to the throne of England. Pierce had a son named James Nagle, who was Page to James II at the Court of St. Germains, and died at the age of 99.

All these connections and ramifications may help to explain a thing or two. The *Annals* of her own foundation say that she, Nano Nagle, "was a descendant of a family not only highly respectable, but uniformly distinguished for its attachment to the true Faith." It must have been possible to find an excuse or pretext to take young Nano Nagle out of Ireland to be educated in France. Some surmise that she may have been smuggled out. It is possible that kindly Protestants, among the powers that be, helped to clear the road for her uncle and herself. We need documents, letters, and facts which are hard to find among the few precious relics left to us from that obscure period. The *Annals* of the South Presentation Convent in Cork just tersely state that "she was sent to France for her education." Anyway Nano Nagle had plenty of influential friends who might smooth the way a little for her exit and re-entry. And her honoured name was an easy passport into the highest French Society, judging from all that we have now recorded. In France there was a celebrated Irish family named Hennessy, from Cork, among her relatives. Richard Hennessy of Cognac, in France, was an officer in the Regiment of Lord Clare in the French service. Another member, James Hennessy, became a representative in the French Chamber of Deputies, and his son married into the French nobility. Nano's aunt, Margaret Nagle, married James Barrett of another venerable old Cork family, and their daughter was married into the Hennessy family, who held prestige in Cork and in France, where they were related to French Ambassadors and notables.

At this time also, Irishmen served with high-ranking titles not only in the armies of France but of Spain: at the beginning of the eighteenth century there were eight Irish Regiments in Commission in the Spanish service, and among them we find four Don Nagles. Well might the English Statesman, the late Austen Chamberlain, in speaking of Ireland, refer to "the glory of the inheritance which is hers," for the good deeds of her children have given them a claim upon the many lands they serve.

It was a priest belonging to an old family in Ireland who was the Chaplain and loyal friend to the unfortunate King Louis the Sixteenth of France. This was Father Edgeworth who was born at Edgeworthstown, County Longford, Ireland. His father, who was a Protestant Minister, became a convert to the Catholic Church — together with his family. Therefore because of the Penal Laws he moved to France, where his son became a priest. There was also at this time in Paris another prominent Irish priest, Father Moylan, who was a friend to Father Edgeworth, and who is later to play quite a part in the life of Nano Nagle. He became Bishop of Cork. Father Edgeworth grew to be a distinguished figure in France. The Irish Bishops offered him a mitre at home but in his humility he did not accept.

When the Archbishop of Paris was forced to flee, in order to save his life, in 1792, he gave to the courageous Irishman Father Edgeworth the complete care of the great diocese of Paris: as Vicar General therefore the devoted priest carried out his task thoroughly at the very height of the horrors of the French Revolution. He rode in the carriage with the unfortunate Louis to the guillotine: right to the scaffold he helped and comforted the King. How the priest escaped the fanatical mob seems a mystery.

Father Edgeworth was a friend of Edmund Burke. In his correspondence with Burke we find the true note of an apostolic Irishman who was determined to care for the souls of others, no matter what might be the risks to his own body. He was in danger of being torn to pieces by the crazed French Revolutionaries because of his devotion to the hated King, but the holy priest calmly told Burke that he could not leave France as he had to prepare the King of France for death, and perhaps prepare himself for death too. He followed the survivors of the Revolution into exile. Pitt offered him a pension but he declined. He died in 1807 in Russia, while ministering to plague-stricken soldiers. He was a bright light of Irish spirituality at the Court of the hapless descendant of St. Louis, Louis XVI, who partly inherited his fate from his predecessor's profligate Court and its jaded Society — wherein our unstained Nano Nagle must have moved and shone.

Burke said that the "American War brought on ideas of Irish Independence." But the French Revolution affected Ireland also. In France they had corruption and tyranny in high places. In Ireland they had corruption and tyranny in high places too. Both nations revolted against the horror of the thing. In France the Church suffered. In Ireland it was the children of an already suffering Church who rose up against the oppression of their Faith and their Nation, and, odd as it may seem to outsiders, in this they were led by gallant Protestant gentlemen like Wolfe Tone, Robert Emmet and Lord Edward Fitzgerald.

A noble Protestant Englishman, Lord Fitzwilliam, was sent over to Ireland as Viceroy in January 1795. He instantly sacked the corrupt band of officials who obstructed liberal measures; he was intent on overdue reform, and decided that he was going to carry through a full measure of Catholic Emancipation, once and for all. Pitt defeated his plan. Within a month Fitzwilliam was recalled. When he was leaving Dublin on Lady Day, 1795, his coach was drawn by the appreciative people through streets that were draped in mourning. But the young Protestant gentleman, Wolfe Tone, decided that he would try to force Catholic Emancipation, come what may. Even the fires of revolution he would brave in this cause. The poor Catholics were to him the real Irish nation. He said that no change could make their situation worse. To France he too would go, and come back to set his people free. The ideas of Liberty heralded in France echoed in Ireland in mountain and glen. As the poet says, you cannot stir a flower without troubling a star. France and Ireland, Ireland and France. A move here meant a move there.

The eighteenth century was said to be the least Christian and least French Century in French History. Somewhere towards the middle of that century Nano Nagle and her relatives were frequent guests at the sparkling society functions of King Louis XV. The blue-blooded Irish exiles could here find full social recognition. Their families had fought for France. French life they could now enjoy. At home in Ireland the third great Confiscation of native lands had taken place: only one seventh of the whole country was left in the hands of the Catholics. And the Catholics were three times the number of the Protestants. In happier surroundings the Catholic exiles of Ireland were welcomed in Paris to high places in army and senate.

If Courts and their rulers start on a cascade of dissolution, it is said that some of the surrounding society will soon slide down the slippery slope too.

If the only example given by those above be a bad example, one may expect those lower down to take advantage
of the situation, and justify their fleeting fancies by saying
that it is the fashion and everybody is doing it. In this
connection writers have used up enormous stocks of nouns,
adjectives, and verbs, to lash the Court of King Louis the
Fifteenth of France. When Saint Augustine said that, in
his time, dissipation was bubbling round him like fat in a
frying-pan, the description seems almost tame in comparison with the story of the brazen follies of a French Court
in the eighteenth century. They tell us that it would be
difficult to mention the name of any European King whose
private life shows such vulgar vice unredeemed by higher
aims of any kind than that of Louis. The spiritual psy-
chologists in terrifying terms would tell us that he had a
will enervated by lust. The French people paid for it.

Louis the Fifteenth, this great-grandson of the Grand
Monarch, Louis the Fourteenth, was married to a Polish
Princess, a good and just woman. For about fifteen years
he was guided by her virtuous example. Then he irreso-
lutely surrendered himself to a clique of scheming court
intriguers. If he tended to the wilder gaieties they would
make it easier for him. Hence the poor courtesan Madame
du Barry whom the gamblers introduced to him for his
Court; right to the king's death this wretched woman made
and unmade courtiers. Louis built her a mansion. Vengeance to the court, the courtiers, and the courtesan, came
in 1793 when the Revolutionaries cut off her head, and
hell was let loose. There was also the other woman for
whom he bought the estate from which she took her title —
Madame Pompadour. He made it easy for her to be a
Marquise or a Duchess. She made it easy for him to wreck
France. And a little later the canaille would dance the
can-can round royal corpses.

The policy of France since the days of Richelieu had
been to join Germany and thus keep the House of Austria
weak. Madame Pompadour changed this. Why? Because Frederick the Great wrote scandalous verses about

her in Germany. And Maria Theresa of Austria said nice things to her and wrote her a friendly letter. Readers of history may well ask if the King of France had anything to say in all this. One can only quote the Irish proverb which says: There are three kinds of men who do not understand women — young men, old men, and middle-aged men. Madame Pompadour wanted an alliance with Austria. Whatever she wanted, whether it was the suppression of the Jesuits or entanglement with Austria, she did not flinch in insisting. The miserable alliance with Austria brought on the Seven Years' War with all its disasters for France. The previous King of France gave away Newfoundland and Acadia to England, whereby British power was established in North America. Now, Louis XV lost Canada. But Madame Pompadour persisted. There was no office for any courtier except through her choice. She cultivated the writers. Voltaire was her poet in chief. And when finally her unguent charms grew rancid, and Louis tired of her, she merely encouraged his debaucheries. She even tried to hold his fancy by personally staging theatricals for him. When they told her that disease had definitely marked her for death, she gaily dressed herself in full court costume and so departed to meet the final scrutiny of souls, at the early age of 42. How revolting to the French people was her alliance with Austria. Years later this expressed itself when the crowds shouted "Death to the Austrian", and they sent the Austrian Queen Marie Antoinette to the scaffold, and, as Burke said, "the glory of Europe was extinguished for ever."

Madame Pompadour in her soft luxuries at Court had wasted about seven million dollars. Madame du Barry spent so much that the investigators say she inflicted an incubus of about one hundred million dollars on the National Debt of France. The gambling, drinking, and flagitiousness of the Court led to gutters of blood; for Church and State in France the Reign of Terror was coming.

The French people were poor and virtuous. Let us seek a note of consolation from the pages of Edmund

Burke who said: "The Church of France has fallen; but she has attained great glory in her fall; no church, no state is secure from external violence; but the internal part is under the protection of their own virtues and of God's Justice." The Spirit they cannot kill.

Great must have been the internal virtue of Nano Nagle who passed through the whirl of Parisian society without the shadow, suspicion, or whisper of a stain. Great must have been the graces that God gave her to bring her unaffected through the delirious wilderness. The *Annals* of her own Convent may be quoted: she "was introduced into the most brilliant circles of this fashionable metropolis; and so much delighted was she with the gaieties of Paris that she began to think it impossible she could live happy elsewhere. Her unsuspecting innocence seeing nothing in all this which could disturb its calm, she remorselessly yielded to her unhappy inclination for worldly pleasures; but this quiet was soon disturbed." We scarcely need to repeat that she was a romantic Irish beauty, young and vibrant, with all the characteristics of her race that have made them for ever an object of interest and curiosity to the world at large. Said the Public Orator of Oxford University in this generation at the conferring of an honorary degree on a noted Irish Poet: *We have always learnt to expect something new from Ireland; nor are we disappointed.*

Sophie Bryant, in "The Genius of the Gael", tried to explain the dominance of the Irish in the western race-mixture. The Irish social gift is strong. In a community it is apt to be like the little leaven that leavens the whole lump. Expressiveness, responsiveness and interesting individuality mark the Irish character as a social force. Those around it are likely to be transformed to its likeness. "A high-spirited and courageous people" said Lloyd George of the Irish, as he went on to describe "their bright idealism, their inborn genius and their unrivalled gifts."

Neither Society around the French Court nor its dashing and gay cavaliers could hold Nano Nagle from the Eternal

Court for which she was destined. True, France was a change from the routine of quiet days and pastoral peace at her home in Ireland where Catholics might be socially ignored. True, she ardently entered into the Parisian gaieties; her young humanity found joy in the ball, the dance, the salon, the masque, the theatricals. Fine clothes fascinated the instincts of her womanhood. Her life was rounded with pleasure. However, looking back on all this with the sensitivity of her sanctity in later years, she had nothing with which to charge herself except that she had been for the brief hour "a lover of the world, of dress and of vanity."

But the Irish are by nature an other-worldly people. A favourite phrase of theirs is "the Holy Will of God", and He has blest them with the virtue of easy readiness in conforming to it. He wanted Nano Nagle for a work, dear to His Church, Catholic Education. So He led her safely through that aimless and purposeless society whose dance had become the dance of death, whose feet were shuffling upon a floor that was soon to be swept from under them by the pitiless and purging flames of the French Revolution. Such noisy empty pleasure-lovers might be described in his Catholic Epistle by Saint Jude: "Clouds without water which are carried about by winds, trees of the Autumn, unfruitful, twice dead, plucked up by the roots, raging waves of the sea, foaming out their own confusion, wandering stars: to whom the storm of darkness is reserved for ever." Saint Jude finally says: "But others save, pulling them out of the fire."

No streak of Pauline lightning was needed to strike home a lesson to the unseared Nano Nagle. It was a rather familiar daily incident in Catholic life that set her feet on God's royal road for ever. It was the happy sight of people going to morning Mass. This would wean her from the world. And this is the key to our story. The *Annals* of her Convent say that "she was touched by Divine grace, edified and confounded at the sight."

One can almost dramatise the simple symbols of the

scene. It was morning. Nano Nagle was on her way home
from a ball. The idle were going to sleep. The workers
were awake. Some of the poor workers were already
standing on the steps of a church door at that early hour
waiting for the early Mass. It was these poor pious people
that Nano saw as she glanced out of her comfortable carriage. And the salutary sight was not lost on her. It was
the hour of sunrise upon Paris. In another sense it was
the hour of sunrise upon Nano Nagle's soul. Her external
life had been so devoted to pleasure. Her deeper internal
life must have at last revolted against her profitless existence. She had been turning night into day, day into night.
Now, in a spiritual sense God would turn her bleak night
of uselessness into the bright Day that is born of the Sun
of Justice. This was done by a study in contrasts. As
Hamlet says: Look on this picture and on this. She, doing
nothing. The poor, who were toiling, praying, worship-
ping, and making their presence at Mass their morning
offering. The *Annals* of her Convent add that "a circumstance, in itself trivial, made so deep an impression upon
her reflecting and feeling mind that the charms of dissipation by which she had been hitherto so entirely captivated
lost much of their ascendancy on this occasion." Right in
Paris there were two worlds. The world of society where
virtue was mocked. The world of the simple poor people
where God was adored.

One hears a great deal about the sins of Society in all
ages. But, unfortunately, normality and goodness are not
considered *news*. So God gave Nano Nagle His *news* direct, by a glimpse of the virtuous and the normal at the
Church door. She saw that they were seeking the one
thing necessary. What would she do? She would bid
farewell to the coach, the court, and the ball, let the daylight dissolve her earthly dreams, and from the roses that
withered in her boudoir, turn to the Rose that never with-

ers in any wind, the Mystical Rose, as if praying with the
poet to the Mother of Christ:

> To thy breast, to thy rest, to thy glory divine,
> Draw me by charity, Mother of mine.

She was now twenty-two. God's Charity would be her
watchword for the remaining thirty-four years of her life.
She will trudge the streets to find His poor little ones and
teach them. For this He had converted her in the Paris
dawn. The Mass mattered. Christ the King keeps a
Court and He has vacancies *There.*

CHAPTER 5

COME BACK TO ERIN THE LAND OF YOUR BIRTH

NANO Nagle was now going to meditate on *the* question — Why did God make you? One of her kin, the scholarly and distinguished Archbishop Butler, of Cashel, who also belonged to the family of Lord Dunboyne, had in her own generation phrased the answer in the work known as *Butler's Catechism*, a little treasure familiar to all. It is a simple answer, but what a world of importance it contains for the ruling of our lives. God made me to know Him and love Him and serve Him in this life, and be happy with Him for ever in the next. So Nano Nagle decided to serve Him in this life by teaching and caring for His poor. Even if Dives on his throne had left the dogs to do the social welfare on Lazarus and his sores, it must not be ever thus. Saint Paul, in writing to the Galatians, asks us to do something about it: *Therefore while we have time, let us work good to all men, but especially to those who are of the household of the Faith.* Home to help those of the household of the Faith Nano Nagle would soon be going. The energies which she so far mis-directed upon Hedonism were re-directed towards the ancient objectives of her race: *For the Glory of God and the Honour of Ireland.* But it was a winding road.

The *Annals* of the South Presentation Convent, Cork, give news of her next step: —"She was recalled from Paris to Ireland by her friends; and the extraordinary struggle which she felt upon this occasion led to those serious reflections which terminated in a firm resolution to embrace a religious life."

Nano Nagle gave herself up totally to the grace of God. She was resolved to save her own immortal soul as a first duty. Regarding her other particular plans for the future she might ask her Creator the same question that Saint Paul asked at his fiery conversion: *Lord what wilt Thou have me to do.* Back in Ireland she had time to meditate upon the demands of God's Will.

Of course it was a change from the bright bustling city by the Seine to a calm country home by the River Blackwater. To the sound of the lapping waves, and the young winds rustling through olden oaks, or at the sight of the wooded slopes of Nagle's Mountains she could now in peaceful solitude lift up her eyes to the Eternal Hills and even Silence could seem to speak to her. The Irish monks of old were great lovers of Nature. They built their houses by rivers, vales, lakes, and streams. Love of Nature is strong in Irish Literature.

Nano Nagle now had time for devotional contemplation, but there was also room for action. The immortal hero of ancient Irish tradition, Ossian, said he loved the music of the thing that happens. There certainly is always room in this wounded world for the music of a good deed towards the poor. This is so obvious that it sounds like a platitude. But then a platitude may be an epigram with a steady job. There was so much room for human rehabilitation and repair of the social order in Ireland at this time that it was a wise woman who would know where to begin. Even if she were permitted to begin, the task was so wide, so vast, so universal that one might quail in dismay and despair at the prospect of a people and a nation sunk in Night from every point of view — religiously, politically, socially and physically. It is hard to start a job whose circumference seems everywhere and whose centre seems nowhere. The educational regeneration of such a land needed the courage of Saint Michael and of Joan of Arc combined. Could she try it?

A Catholic attempting to teach school, publicly or privately, could, by an Act of King William III, get three months in jail and be fined about one hundred dollars.

It was about the year 1750 when Nano Nagle returned from France to Ireland. A good and genial Protestant, Thomas Davis, who was nurtured amidst the same scenic enchantments in Cork, has left us, in rousing verse, a

picture of the Irish Catholics of that time. Davis says
that a stranger held the land; no Popish lord had lordly
power; the peasant scarce had room to live; a ruined shed
was the poor man's home; there was no tenure but a
tyrant's will; the peasantry were forbid to read, forbid to
plead, disarmed, disfranchised. Only as labourers and
cultivators were the Catholic peasantry considered valuable
to their masters. Turning to the cold prose of history one
learns a story from Sir William Petty who mapped out
the confiscation of Ireland for Cromwell: he says there
were 184,000 houses then in Ireland; only 24,000 had one
chimney or above, and the rest had no chimney. The state
of Ireland was growing steadily worse, before it began to
get better.

George the First was King when Nano Nagle was born.
George the Second was King when she returned to Ireland.
George the Third was King when she founded her Order
and he was still reigning at the time of her death. It was
only in the reign of the Fourth George that Catholic
Emancipation was carried. Had Mother Nagle been born
to do her work then, her troubles would have been less
harassing though her accomplishments would still appear
heroic. But in 1750 the cup of suffering was overflowing.
Ireland was facing Kedron and Calvary, Gethsemani and
Gehenna. Critics may object that things could not have
been possibly as bad as all this, or that the Irish imagination tends to magnify the misery. Very well. Let the
opposite side tell the story. It will equally accentuate the
achievement of Nano Nagle.

A respected Protestant scholar, Dr. Edmund Curtis, Professor of Modern History at Trinity College, Dublin, wrote
an excellent *History of Ireland* in 1936. He says that the
Treaty of Limerick, which was signed by King William in
1692, was broken the same year, when Catholics were
excluded from Parliament. He says that "the iniquitous
Penal code" was begun in 1695 and was not completed
till 1727. Professor Curtis writes: "Another act made it
illegal for Catholics to go for education abroad and for-

bade them to keep a public school at home. The University of Dublin was already closed to them as regards degrees, fellowships and scholarships. This and other *no education* acts were particularly shameful, as well fitted to brutalize a race of aristocratic and learned tradition and reduce it to peasant status and ignorance. The majestic and world-wide system of the Church of Rome could not be treated like some Protestant sect at home seeking a modest toleration; the very greatness of her empire and the completeness of her claims over the souls and minds of believers marked her out for special persecution. The anti-Popery spirit was shown by an act for the banishment of all Roman Catholic bishops and dignitaries, leaving untouched the parish clergy, who, it was hoped, would die out in time for want of due consecration. As an established Church, the Roman Catholic religion now reached its nadir point in Irish history, and those bishops who stood their ground were reduced to less than half a dozen, living the most obscure, and at any moment possibly dangerous, existence. In the next year, 1698, another act excluded members of this Church from the practice of the law except by taking an oath of allegiance and abjuration of the papal authority."

We continue with quotations from Professor Curtis for the reign of Queen Anne. He says: "Unfortunately Anne and the Tories also had the *No Popery* obsession. So the Penal code continued, though Anne was a Stewart. In 1703 another act was passed to banish Roman bishops, regulars, and vicars-general, but a Registration act which accompanied it showed the disposition to allow at least the simple toleration of the Mass. By this any secular priest taking a simple oath of Allegiance could be registered and then perform his priestly functions undisturbed. It was accepted by over 1000 priests, whose numbers showed that it was impossible to suppress the religion of two millions of Irishmen. Unregistered priests remained liable to the penalties of treason under existing statutes. The extinguishing of the Roman faith as a religion was now obviously impossible, and the Church of Ireland (by which name the Protestant Church in Ireland is called) with its great revenues and highly endowed bishops, accepted the fact that as regards the mass of the people itself was a minority religion. The Penal code was finally completed by an act of 1727 by which Catholics were finally debarred from voting for members of Parliament both in counties and boroughs. The Penal laws were to last in their entirety for some seventy years and not to be repealed till 1829."

The foregoing is a summary from our erudite Protestant historian Professor Curtis. He says that "the nation as a whole suffered from all this body of law, which debarred it from all the essential civil rights which even in a despotic State they would have enjoyed, and which allowed a newly arrived minority to hamper them in every natural ambition and self-development." He adds that at this time "the lot of the Catholic peasantry was the worst in Europe," and again that "the religion of the majority, their political and civil liberty and all their racial self-expression were proscribed for almost a century, or worse still, driven underground with disastrous results."

Speaking of the period, 1714 to 1760, Dr. Curtis observes: "The Protestant ascendancy in Church, government, law, parliament, local government, industry, was complete." Indeed I may quote another Protestant, also from Trinity College, who held sway in Nano Nagle's own day. The great champion of human liberty this was — Dean Swift. He described the *papists* as a people completely crushed, "harmless as women and children."

A modest and charming young lady like Nano Nagle, with her delicate physique, might well wonder what she could do to help the unhappy people described so impartially by our two Protestant scholars; her own dear Irish people, with their heavenly patience in enduring social wrongs, were calling to her, but was she not as unhopeful of a solution as they? There were about 24 Catholic Bishops gallantly striving to guide the Catholic Church in Ireland at this time but they were in daily danger, for, by an Act of 1710, anybody betraying a Catholic Bishop to the authorities would be rewarded with a sum equal to about 250 dollars. And the reader may rest assured that there actually were some degraded priest-hunters who were willing to improve their financial position in this shocking way.

A poignant picture of the Irish people at the time is presented to us by the *Annals* of Nano Nagle's Convent in Cork. She was deeply afflicted by seeing the masses of the inhabitants shrouded in "total ignorance." Faith and morals were at stake for want of instruction. With sorrow she beheld "the ruin of their souls." I quote from the *Annals*: "With these feelings she was still more deeply impressed during a visit which she paid to a friend in her father's neighbourhood. Passing some time there, her affable disposition often led her to converse with the poor tenantry of the place; and in these little interviews her heart melted into pity, seeing their complete ignorance of their duty to God, the principal mysteries of religion — the great business of their salvation. Their faith was erroneous; their hope presumptuous; and they had no charity. Their miserable condition was ever present to her imagination: no company or employment, no pleasure or pain, could mitigate her anxiety for those poor people. Not being then able to remedy the misery she beheld, she determined to withdraw at least from the sight of it, and to deplore it for the remainder of her life within the enclosure of a convent. She accordingly took leave of her friends, bidding them, as she thought, a last farewell, and returned to France for the purpose of putting her pious design into execution."

Readers may be shocked at the foregoing description of the poor people from the *Annals*. If only those in power had given them half a chance things might be improved. We even think of the pragmatic human maxim that, if you treat people a little better than they are, they become a little better than they are, and if you treat them worse than they are, they become worse than they are. It is easy to make an apology for the people of the time. History itself makes a perfect apology for them. Of them Thomas Grey might have written that, chill penury repressed their noble rage, and froze the genial current of the soul. But Oliver Goldsmith who was born in Ireland in 1728, the same year as Nano Nagle, will supply us with a native note concerning the desolation of the people:

> No more thy glassy brook reflects the day,
> But choked with sedges, works its weedy way;
> Along thy glades, a solitary guest,
> The hollow-sounding bittern guards its nest;
> Amidst thy desert walks the lapwing flies,
> And tires their echoes with unvarying cries.
> Sunk are thy bowers in shapeless ruin all,
> And the long grass o'ertops the mouldering wall;
> And, trembling, shrinking from the spoiler's hand,
> Far, far away thy children leave the land."

A hundred years ago another Irishman, Sir Robert Kane, made an excuse for the sad state of the people: "We were idle for we had nothing to do; we were reckless, for we had no hope; we were ignorant, for learning was denied us; we were improvident, for we had no future."

All around her Nano Nagle saw the need of work, of charity, and she resolved to do her part. Here again a trifle drove home an unforgettable lesson to her mind. Trifles may of course be tremendous. In the mysteries that rule our lives there seem hosts of tremendous trifles. A group of people at a Church door, waiting for Mass, may seem to some a trifle. To Nano it was a tremendous revelation as we have seen. Saint Patrick used the trifle of a trefoil to teach the ancient Irish the august idea of the Holy Trinity, before Whom Heaven and Earth and those that are under the Earth bow down and adore. God marks the sparrow's fall. The hairs of our head are all numbered. As if to warn us to respect trifles, Saint James tells us not to despise small things, for if we do, we may fall by little and little. Our school-books prepared us early, by recording the fact that little drops of water, and little grains of sand, make the mighty ocean and the solid land. Towards the close of the last century there died a modest young lady whose holy fame has in this century swept the world with a flaming devotion to her; she is loved under the title of the Little Flower; and her way is the Little Way.

When first returning from France Nano Nagle had brought with her some silk materials which she had purchased in Paris. While living with her mother and sister in Dublin, she one day asked her sister, who was a pious young lady, to have the silk made up into a magnificent dress. But Nano was both edified and astonished when her sister confided that she had sold the silk in order to help a distressed family with the proceeds. I quote from the *Annals* of the Parent House: "This circumstance, together with the death of this sister soon after, wrought so powerfully on the heart of Miss Nagle, as perfectly to disengage it from the fashionable world, which she tasted so much of, and enjoyed until then. She has often said to her Sisters in religion, that it was this trifling occurrence which fixed her determination to devote the remainder of her life to God in the service of the poor."

Henceforth it would not be a question of how much or how little she would give. She will give all she can. Wordsworth expressed the idea neatly when he said:

Give all thou canst. High Heaven rejects the lore
Of nicely calculated less or more.

She will give all to the poor; she will give *herself* to them. She will go away from them, but Ireland like a banshee in gray tatters will keep shrieking in her ears till she returns to them again.

I will summarize the handicaps under which the rank and file of the Irish people struggled for existence at the middle of the eighteenth century, when Nano Nagle sorrowingly departed from their midst.

The native tenant was rack-rented by foreign landlords. Rack-rent means what it says. It was a rent which racked.

Perhaps the landlord lived abroad, and between him and the unhappy tenant there were several middle-men and agents, all of whom got their commissions, and the tenant in his swollen rent paid them all.

The native tenant was tortured by a being called the tithe-farmer. The collector had to get a tenth of everything for the Protestant clergy, so the Catholic people had to pay for the upkeep of a church and ministry with whom they refused to have any contact. The richer people could avoid the tithes, hence the brunt of the tax fell on the poor man who was constantly surrounded by sharks ready to strip him naked. In the maelstrom, poor Protestants suffered as well as poor Catholics.

The native tenant was bound to work on Catholic holydays of obligation or pay a fine. If he indulged in even the most innocent sports on a Sunday his Puritanical masters would fine him or put him for a couple of hours in the stocks. His Catholic church could not have a spire or a steeple. The landlords were enclosing more land for pasture so that the tenant had less for tilling: sheep and cattle were held of more value than the persecuted peasantry. If the tenant took refuge in boglands he paid an excessive rent for these too. He was fined, and whipped, if caught with a rod cut from his own tree. He must remain absolutely unarmed, and the law could have him searched for arms at any time. Public whippings were the rule; as an example, and to strike terror, such lashings were given on market days when the lashed were tied to cart-tails and dragged through the streets. It is said that the great Protestant patriot of Ireland, Charles Stewart Parnell, first pledged his love to the Irish people when he heard of such lashings from an old keeper on his estate who had witnessed them.

No Catholic could keep a horse of any value; if a Protestant bid a sum of about 25 dollars the Catholic owner had to part with his work-horse. No Catholic might move into the cities of Limerick and Galway, the last refuges of the native race. A reward was given for news of unregistered

Bishops, Jesuits, or Schoolmasters, and the Catholics had to pay for the rewards. Still, the Protestant Parliament of Ireland had to keep complaining to England of the growth of Irish Catholicism! Trade and industry were ruined and money was debased — the chivalrous Protestant, Dean Swift, smashed the scandal of the false copper coins and became a hero of the Catholics. Thousands were thrown out of employment and the dawn of emigration began — for Dissenters as well as Catholics. America was rising.

I quote from another scholar, Sir Philip Magnus, a brilliant young Englishman of our own generation of writers. His admirable book on Edmund Burke appeared a few years ago. Sir Philip writes: "The Ireland into which Burke was born provided a searching test for any man's faith in the existence of a divine plan behind human government. Ireland, during the eighteenth century, was the worst-governed country in Europe, although the English aristocracy which was established there displayed an instinct for beauty and distinction which has rarely, in these islands, been surpassed. The English made Dublin the second city of the Empire — a superb capital, whose stately buildings bear witness to this day to the taste and character of the men who dwelt in them. But the English did not restrict their presence to Dublin: they spread themselves over the entire countryside. In every Irish county English noblemen and squires were occupied in planting avenues, laying out gardens, and building pleasant Palladian mansions by means of Irish labour, on land which in many cases had reecntly been confiscated by Act of Parliament from its native proprietors, and which was to be supported in future on a mounting tide of Irish rents. While the dispossessed Irish swarmed in their cabins at the gates, the English conquerors, divided from the natives by a racial and religious gulf, developed a haughtiness and a pride of caste which was scarcely paralleled elsewhere. In many districts the actual owners of the soil were regarded by the mass of the people as tenants under a wrongful title; yet their manner towards the native Irish was comparable only with that adopted on the opposite side of the Atlantic by the cotton-planters of Virginia towards their negro slaves. The English in Ireland disported themselves like princes; they were the monarchs of all that they surveyed. They professed the most profound contempt for the natives among whom they dwelt, and brought the lash down carelessly on Irish backs at the slightest sign of disrespect. With the aid of a special *Penal* Code the Catholic religion of the vast majority of Irishmen was ruthlessly trodden underfoot. Since land was the main source of power, the object of the Code was to secure as quickly as possible the transference to Protestants of all land which remained in Catholic hands. Politically, professionally, socially, Catholics were excluded; their bishops were outlawed; their schools suppressed; their participation in industry limited by a law which forbade them to employ more than two apprentices in any trade other than that of linen-weaving. Such were the conditions in which Edmund Burke began to learn the grammar of politics and of Empire."

The above words, from a gifted Englishman writing on an Irishman, of Nano Nagle's own family, will help the reader to understand the pitiful plight of the peasantry delineated in the *Annals* of her Convent. The miracle is that the Catholic people managed to survive such evil times. Whenever a ray of hope appeared for them it was quickly lost in the prevailing darkness, as, for instance, when a high-minded Englishman, Lord Chesterfield, came as Viceroy in 1745, and began to remove some of the worst grievances of Catholics. His serviceable efforts were cut short by his early recall and his successors undid the good work he did. The pathos of such a narrative must have moved the mind of the late Pope Pius XI, vivid and colourful leader, when he said: "From my boyhood days my sympathy has always gone out to Ireland. When a lad at school, I came across a History of Ireland; and, although it was very sad and mournful reading, I read it with the greatest interest, so that my heart went out to Ireland. After some time I.

chanced upon a *Life of Daniel O'Connell*. I can well remember reading the speech he made in the House of Commons on his election for Clare; how he refused to take the
oath that was tendered to him, and how that oath was abolished. A nation that has suffered so much for God and
for Religion cannot but end happily and well. Since I became Pope I pray every day for Ireland."

While Philip Dormer, the noted Earl of Chesterfield,
was gracing Dublin with the amenities of what we know
as Phoenix Park, during his stay as Viceroy from 1745
to 1747, a less pleasant thing happened in the Irish Capital.
A certain Father Fitzgerald was saying Mass in an old
hayloft in the city, surreptitiously of course, in keeping
with the Penal hush-hush, when the rickety floor gave way.
The priest and nine worshippers were killed. Such a
sacrifice, in the presence of the Supreme Sacrifice, gave
the graceful and polished Earl of Chesterfield the gentler
idea of letting Catholics adore the Lord in safer surroundings. It was what we popularly talk of today as Tolerance.
Remember there was no repeal of the laws. Tolerance was
tolerated. The laws continued, intolerable. If the laws
of the Limerick Treaty had been put into force at the right
time there would have been no shameful tragedies, for then
Catholics would have enjoyed liberty, equality, and fraternity with their fellow Protestants in Ireland. Only the
All-Wise God of Destiny can explain the reason for some
of the subjunctives of Irish History. If, and if, and if
again.

Burke considered it the most debasing degradation to
rob the human mind of Education. Writing to a Peer in
Ireland he said: "While this restraint upon foreign and
domestic education was part of a horrible and impious
system of servitude, the members were well fitted to the
body. To render men patient under a deprivation of all
the rights of human nature, everything which could give
them a knowledge or feeling of those rights was nationally
forbidden. To render humanity fit to be insulted, it was
fit that it should be degraded. Indeed, I have ever thought

the prohibition of the means of improving our rational nature to be the worst species of tyranny that the insolence and perverseness of mankind ever dared to exercise."

Burke also wrote of the Penal scheme to an Irish gentleman, Sir Hercules Langrishe: — "You abhorred it as I did for its vicious perfection. It was a machine of wise and elaborate contrivance, and as well fitted for the oppression, impoverishment, and degradation of a people, and the debasement in them of human nature itself, as ever proceeded from the perverted ingenuity of man."

We can imagine Nano Nagle breaking her young heart as she planned to set out on what she thought was her unreturning flitting. She had asked herself all the questions. How could she help her people? Where would she get the means? For she had not yet inherited her fortune. If she did start a school, how could she escape arrest? If she did break the law how could her family escape? What right had she to expect them all to suffer because of her efforts? Why not leave things alone? Why upset matters and let further depths of hell loose on the whole Catholic nation? Was not the enemy mood of the hour an ugly one? How could her health stand the strain of opposition from every side, and the ever-haunting possibilities that must surely hang over her head if she dared even in one detail to defy the deviltry of powerful men before whom the nation nodded?

The most inspired rashness could hardly find an encouraging answer to any of these riddles. To and fro these questions would rove in her dreams, and holy Ireland would keep her in a divine discontent. Reverie would reawaken what the cold daylight of human reason dispelled. There was no peace at home. She might find some conventual calm abroad. And one must make a decision. To France she must go. It may be for years and it may be for ever. No — not for *ever*. The Timeless would see to that.

CHAPTER 6

IRELAND FOR EVER

NANO Nagle expected to find peace and rest in France. She found neither. The sights she saw during her short stay in Ireland continued to flash upon the inner vision of her soul. The dismal tragedies of home had penetrated so deeply into her sensitive mind that they could not be forgotten. Peace in a convent had been her dream upon leaving. But now it seemed as if the sheeted dead were rising in wraiths before her eyes to rush her home. The little children in their pleading thousands seemed to wave their love to her across the sea; with outstretched arms they seemed to ask her help. Disconsolate she will be if she resists their appeal.

What was now her true vocation? She thought she had already settled that. Not so. Doubts and scruples now agitated her mind. She could not get rid of her misgivings. Conscience kept piling up awkward questions, and jostling answers kept intruding, pro and con. The battle had begun. If she pleaded that any contact with the wicked world might merely drag her into its vortex again, the Lord could answer that His Grace was sufficient for her. If she wished to be charitable, but were afraid of the consequences, Saint John the Evangelist would tell her that "Fear is not in Charity." She could justly protest that the situation in Ireland seemed too hopeless for making any start, but the God of Hope could urge her along to help the native race with the words of Ezechiel the Prophet: *Oh, my people, and I shall have put my Spirit in you and you shall live, and I shall make you rest upon your own land.*

Yes, she could endlessly cross-examine herself with so many questions that her mind would eventually become a mirage of doubts and anxieties. She might even reproach herself with weakness and faintheartedness for deserting the poor little ones who were so closely joined to her in the Mystical Body of Christ. She heard them calling to her: *Will you also go away?* God was making demands on them. He would make further demands on her. Her fallen people were still an image of Christ fallen beneath the Cross, and she must at least make one effort to help in the work of the dear God Who loves the people, and Who wills their resurrection.

In writing of the beloved Saint Patrick reference is often made to "The Voice of Ireland." When Patrick left Ireland he seemed to hear the voice of the Irish echoing from the woods by the western sea, and bidding him to return and labour among them, and share with them the blessings of the Son of Light. In vision he saw the tiny hands of the babes of the Gael outstretched imploringly to him. By answering that mysterious *Voice* he accomplished a work whose fruits are by the Grace of God, today, extended by the Irish throughout the world. The Voice of the Irish rang in Nano Nagle's ears too. She could no longer endure her inner conflict alone. Human nature and health could not stand the battle with indecisions for ever. Mercifully for all of us there is the confessional. She now confided the problems of her conscience to a wise, prudent, and skilful guide of souls, a confessor of the Society of Jesus. She opened her whole mind to him. She had come to France to enter the religious life. That was her original intention. But now she was torn in the reverse direction. Home to work among the poor she felt strongly impelled. Once and for all what was it to be: retirement in a convent in France, or open crucifixion in the cause of Catholic Education in Ireland? Whatever it was, she would abide by his decision. "Go home to Ireland and teach the poor." That is how the good Jesuit Father instructed her upon God's Will. His memory and advice may well be held in benediction.

When Pope Celestine sent Patrick to Ireland a worldwide apostolate began. When a son of Saint Ignatius of Loyola directed Nano Nagle to go back home to Ireland, a world-wide apostolate of Christian Education began. For, apart from the work which she directly initiated, her influence and ideals inspired other generous souls to devote themselves and their fortunes to the reclamation and instruction of the poor. Directly, she gave Ireland two excellent teaching Orders: she introduced the Ursulines there; she founded the Presentation Sisters there. Indirectly there was another interesting link. Three years after Nano Nagle died, there was born in Dublin the heroic woman who also belongs to history — Catherine Elizabeth McAuley. Like Nano Nagle she too belonged to the realms of wealth and high society. Her relatives weakly conformed to the fashionable Protestantism of the day but the unconquerable Catherine, despite all the conformers' wooing and wheedling, was determined to hold fast to the Faith of the Holy Roman Church. She eventually gave to the service of that same Holy Church her own gracious self, her fortunes and inheritance, all for the uplifting and bettering of Christ's poor. She ensured that her good work would be permanent for she founded the celebrated Sisters of Mercy, who perpetuate her merciful apostolate through the years unto the ends of the earth. Mother Catherine McAuley's shining name is linked to my narrative because it was to the Sisters of Nano Nagle that she went to make her novitiate. And Nano Nagle's example inspired the philanthropic and benevolent Edmund Ignatius Rice in the founding of the Christian Brothers of Ireland. In the United States I believe the good Mother Katharine Drexel, who also gave up wealth and society in God's cause, regards Nano Nagle as a spiritual grandmother, for it was with the Sisters of Mercy that Mother Drexel began her training for the religious life when she founded the worthy Sisters of the Blessed Sacrament for work amongst the Negroes and Indians. Yes: the Jesuit confessor in France gave rise to many inspirations when he was inspired to direct Nano Nagle home to Ireland. Nano's faith had been tried and tested. Saint Peter in his First Epistle had long ago expressed a reason for such tests: "That the trial of your faith (much more precious than gold which is tried by the fire) may be found unto praise and glory and honour at the appearing of Jesus Christ." Gold regains its shining beauty by being tested in the fire, and faith is cleansed and brightened in its passage through the fire of trial. It was thus for Nano Nagle.

For the sake of comparison I mention again the popular name of Edmund Ignatius Rice, who also wished to devote his remaining days to religious seclusion on the Continent. One day he was speaking to a Miss Power, a friend of his, when a band of ragged boys passed by. "What!" she said, "would you bury yourself in a cell on the Continent rather than devote your wealth and your life to the spiritual and material interests of these poor youths." This salutary exhortation helped to hurry him along to his work of rescuing the wrecked youth of his own land; and the way of life adopted for his new community was a modified form of the Rule of the Presentation Nuns.

Nano Nagle promptly sacrificed her own wishes and her own will; she immediately followed the advice of her spiritual director and went home to Ireland to carry out her assured vocation of instructing poor children in the ways of Eternal Life. As Bishop Coppinger affectionately expressed it: "She returns again to Ireland to fertilise the vineyard — a salutary cloud! exhaled here by the Sun of Justice, borne by divine grace to a religious atmosphere, impregnated with the purest virtue, wafted back by charity to her native soil to diffuse an odour of sanctity, and dissolve in showers of beneficence."

Her equipment was sound; her humility was deep, her judgment was prudent, her virtue was deep-rooted, and though the size of her fortune was yet indeterminable, her hope could justify her in taking Christ at His Word when He said that we should lend, hoping for nothing again. So, herself and her all she loaned to the Lord. But she made it clear that nothing could make her come home except the warning of her directors that she might risk her own soul if she did not follow this vocation of helping to save the souls of others.

I mentioned how her father loved her so dearly and how he used to intercede with her mother to excuse the vigorous playfulness of the child. He had died while she was in France, and deep must have been her grief at the loss of him to whom she was attached beyond all telling. Her mother and sister had gone to live in Dublin, and there she joined them on her return from France. Her father's position and fortune would at this time have been a decided encouragement to her, so it looks as if her trials were to begin in one way and another.

Let a quotation from the *Annals* of her holy house convey some of her developing story: "She had therefore to encounter the censure of her friends, and the shafts of worldly prudence. She had to apprehend the sneers of ill-nature, and all that was disgusting, in the probable failure of her design. She had, together with all this, to bear up against the weakness of her frame, unequal, as it seemed to be, to her intended painful undertaking. The field was truly discouraging before her, but she reflected that it contained the *Evangelical treasure*, and at any risk she was determined to purchase it. *She hath considered a field and bought it.* She was deeply wounded at the sight of so many souls that were delivered up a prey to the miseries of ignorance; she saw the pulpits deserted, and the voices silent which should have thundered aloud with all their energy; she saw the confessionals as carefully concealed as the transgressions deposited in them: she was shocked to see the word of God thus chained down by injustice and the little ones crying out for bread, while there were none to break it to them: with such incentives nothing could deter her."

In critical and detailed analyses there has arisen the question as to where Nano Nagle's work for the poor began. The commencement in Dublin is a mooted question. Let the *Annals* of her own Convent continue her edifying story: "She remained some time with her mother and sister in Dublin, and during her residence there she commenced the work of God. She took a small room, assembled about thirty children, whom she instructed in the Christian Doctrine, and taught to read and spell. In this good work she was assisted by one of her sisters, who was as charitably disposed as herself. From her having afterwards declared that she was absolutely terrified at their wickedness, we may easily suppose that the vulgar world, in miniature, was delineated in this little assembly: oaths, imprecations, resentment, envy, and dishonesty were so habitual amongst them, that it confirmed her in the idea that they required her sole attention, and that without patience, prayer, and perseverance, she could never hope to make any lasting impression upon them. Some time after this, her mother and sister having died, she came to Cork, to reside with her brother, where, in secret, she recommenced her charitable exertions. She hired a room convenient to her brother's residence, in which she assembled thirty poor children, with a mistress to teach them. She daily taught them herself, unknown to her family: this was the opening of her mission of charity, and the first of *the Order* which, happily *for us* she instituted. One of her schools being discovered accidentally, her conduct was highly disapproved of, from the apprehension of the persecution which it might bring upon the family, and even upon religion itself, during that period of oppression."

Gerald Griffin, who was born about 20 years after Nano Nagle died, honoured our dear heroine with the tenderest words of his felicitous poetry. He thus invoked her — as would all who love her:

Is no waking reserved for our sleep of despair?
Oh, see! there's a shooting of light in the gloom,
And the spirit of NAGLE *replies from the tomb.*
Hail, star of the lowly! Apostle of light,
In the glow of whose fervour the cottage grew bright!
Sweet violet of sanctity, lurking concealed,
Till the wind wafts the leaf, and the bloom is revealed.

By the light of that glory which burst on thy youth,
In its day-dreams of pleasure, and woke it to truth,
By the tears thou hast shed, by the toil thou hast
*   borne,*
Oh! say shall our night know a breaking of morn?

I mentioned that Nano Nagle's educational valour helped to inspire Edmund Ignatius Rice in founding the Christian Brothers of Ireland. Gerald Griffin became one of their number, and his sister, Lucy Griffin, became a shining light among Nano Nagle's nuns. Two of the most hallowed graves in the city of Cork are those of Nano Nagle and Gerald Griffin, the gifted and gracious author who died at the age of 37.

Archdeacon Hutch, in his painstaking study of Nano Nagle's life, gave a frightful picture of the social and moral life of Cork, as it confronted her from the start of her heavenly crusade. He backed up his sad survey by quotations from contemporary records which make one shudder at the thought of poor Nano Nagle, always a lady to her fingertips, mingling in the midst of such revoltingly raw excesses. No doubt God made the country and man made the town; and let us hope that the offending scenes quoted by Archdeacon Hutch were confined to scattered mobs and factions, and bloods, and bucks, and ruffians, who were the exception rather than the rule, as they clattered swords and sticks for the fun of the thing. An alarming item he quotes is this one for October 20, 1765: "Several linen and cotton gowns were burnt on the backs of the wearers, by being sprinkled with *aqua fortis.*" And another one for December 31, 1769: "Rioting had become so common in this city that it was not safe for any person to stand at his door without some weapon of defence." Of course that date of December 31 might indicate that New Year's Eve is an excitingly terrific night through all ages and nations! But we are quickly dismayed when the good priest gives us other contemporary quotations for the background.

A writer in 1778 refers to the presence of sedan-chairs in Cork and naively hints that "these vehicles are extremely convenient for the followers of Bacchus, who has a great many votaries in this city." Just 60 years later, in 1838, Miss Nagle's cousin, Father Theobald Mathew, in this same city of Cork began his far-reaching war on the demon of intemperance, and, by the end of 1838, the ardent Capuchin had pledged nearly a quarter of a million people to total abstinence in the Counties of the South. "Here goes in the name of God" said Father Mathew, as he launched his blazing crusade to better the moral and social tone of his race, and the masses of the people responded to him as a saving apostle from on high, who brought happiness to their households, and who styptically healed those wounds that were menacing the life-blood of the nation, at the timely hour that he recruited his international army of temperance-lovers, and crowds of all denominations listened to him. The good Quakers were among his vanguard.

Manifestly Nano Nagle was treading on difficult ground, and she had to step warily among the pitfalls. Remember that she was ahead of the other reformers. Scattered throughout the city of Cork there were political clubs and meeting-houses; they were supposed to support social science, but convivial art often drowned the higher thought. City tradesmen formulated a remarkable drinking club open to those whose Christian names had *forty-five* letters; they met at a tavern where they spent *forty-five* pennies each, and each drank exactly forty-five glasses of punch, which produced *forty-five* toasts. The toasts included the *Glorious Memory* and a prayer against despotic rulers.

At the close of Nano Nagle's day the Orange Society had dawned. It was a secret oath-bound Society limited to Protestants: its object was really political: it tried to counteract the efforts of the United Irishmen who were trying to bind Protestants and Catholics together in Ulster for the common good of the country. The Orange Society served to drive Catholics all over Ireland in 1798 into an organization hostile to the Government. It helped to halt Home Rule for Ireland in 1914. It extended from Ulster to the United Kingdom and the British Colonies. It was named from King William III, Prince of Orange.

The Orangemen enrolled in lodges in the form of a secret society. Their original object was to maintain the Protestant Ascendancy. Their toasts became historic: take the commonest form where the Orangemen drink to "the glorious pious and immortal memory of the great and good King William who saved us from Popery, slavery, knavery, brass money and wooden shoes." Brass money refers to the finances of the Catholic Stuart King — James II, for whom Catholic Ireland vainly fought at the battle of the Boyne; and the wooden shoes refer to the French Allies of James and the Catholic Irish.

The last Catholic Stuart to compete for the Throne of England was Bonnie Prince Charlie who tried it in Scotland in 1745. His failure in the year '45 may still have, twenty-five years later, induced men in Cork to drink *forty-five* glasses of punch at a sitting, when *forty-five* pennies might go far, when the best brandy was about thirteen pennies a quart and the best claret nine pennies a bottle, when the Catholic Stuarts were in exile and no one sang their praises except some outlawed Irish Catholic poets and schoolmasters that dreamed their way from obscurity to obscurity.

Despite the grim outline of the age, Nano Nagle was not disheartened; and desperate diseases called forth desperate remedies. She had begun her medication of the young body politic by means of religion and education in unison. Here we can cull her own blissful words from a letter of hers. Other people's letters may be as interesting as yesterday's newspaper or an album of somebody else's snapshots, but here is a vital letter that may rank as *Chapter One* in the educational history of modern Ireland. From the soul it comes, simple and appealing. Miss Nagle wrote it to her beloved friend Miss Fitzsimons under date of July 17, 1769: —

Dear Miss Fitzsimons,

I am sorry Miss Coppinger cannot see the schools, as I think no one can have an idea of their use unless an eye-witness. As you wish to have a particular account of them, I will tell you how I began. I think I mentioned to you before that it was an undertaking I thought I should never have the happiness of accomplishing. Nothing would have made me come home but the decision of the clergymen that I should run a great risk of salvation if I did not follow the inspiration. This made me accept of a very kind invitation of my sister-in-law to live with her. When I arrived I kept my design a profound secret, as I knew if it were spoken of, I should meet with opposition on every side, particularly from my own immediate family, as, to all appearances, they should suffer from it.

My confessor was the only person I told of it, and as I could not appear in the affair, I sent my maid to get a good mistress and to take in thirty poor girls. When the little school was settled I used to steal there in the morning. My brother thought I was at the chapel. This passed on very well until one day a poor man came to him, to beg of him to speak to me to take his child into my school, on which he came to his wife and me, laughing at the conceit of a man who was mad, and thought I was in the situation of a schoolmistress.

Then I owned that I had set up a school, on which he fell into a violent passion, and said a vast deal on the bad consequences that may follow. His wife is very zealous and so is he, but worldly interest blinded him at first. He was soon reconciled to it. He was not the person I most dreaded would be brought into trouble about it; it was my uncle Nagle, who is, I think, the most disliked by the Protestants of any Catholic in the kingdom. I expected a great deal from him. The best part of the fortune I have I received from him. When he heard it he was not at all angry at it, and in a little time they were so good as to contribute largely to support it, and I took in children by degrees, not to make any noise about it in the beginning.

In about nine months I had about 200 children. When the Catholics saw what service it did, they begged that for the convenience of the children I would set up schools at the other end of the town from where I was, to be under my care and direction, and they promised to contribute to the support of them. With this request I readily complied, and the same number of children that I had were taken in, and at the death of my uncle I supported them all at my own expense.

I did not intend to take boys, but my sister-in-law made it a point, and said she would not permit any of my family to contribute to the schools unless I did so; on which I got a master, and took in only forty boys. They are in a house by themselves, and have no communication with the others.

At present, however, I have two schools for boys and five for girls. The former learn to read, and when they have the Douay Catechism by heart they learn to write and cypher. There are three schools where the girls learn to read; and when they have the catechism by heart they learn to work. They all hear Mass every day, say their morning and night prayers, say their catechism in each school by question and answer all together. Every Saturday they all say the beads, the grown girls every evening. They go to confession every month, and to communion when the confessor thinks proper.

The schools are opened at eight; at twelve the children go to dinner; at five they leave school. The workers do not begin their night prayers until six, after their beads. I prepare a set for first communion twice a year, and I may truly say it is the only thing that gives me any trouble.

In the first place I think myself very incapable, and in the beginning, being obliged to speak for upwards of four hours, and my chest not being so strong as it had been, I spat blood, which I took care to conceal for fear of being prevented from instructing the poor. It has not the least bad effect now.

When I have done preparing them at each end of the town, I feel myself like an idler that has nothing to do,

though I speak almost as much as when I prepare them for
their first communion. I find not the least difficulty in it.
I explain the catechism as well as I can in one school or
the other every day, and if everyone thought as little of
labour as I do they would have little merit. I often think
my schools will never bring me to heaven, as I only take
delight and pleasure in them.

You see it has pleased the Almighty to make me succeed,
when I had everything, as I may say, to fight against. I
assure you I did not expect a farthing from any mortal
towards the support of my schools, and I thought I should
not have more than fifty or sixty girls until I got a fortune;
nor did I think I should have a school in Cork. I began in
a poor, humble manner; and though it pleased the Divine
Will to give me severe trials in this foundation, yet it is
to show that it is His work, and has not been effected by
human means.

I can assure you my schools are beginning to be of service to a great many parts of the world. This is a place of
great trade. They are heard of, and my views are not for
one object alone. If I could be of any service in saving
souls in any part of the globe, I would willingly do all in
my power."

The Catechism referred to by Nano Nagle was one of
the most important among Catechisms. It was called "The
Douay Catechism — An Abridgement of Christian Doctrine with proofs of Scripture for points controverted.
Catechistically explained by way of question and answer."
The first edition was printed at Douai in 1649, and a late
edition in Dublin in 1828. The author was Father Henry
Turberville, a Douai Priest. There was a smaller edition:
"An abstract of the Douai Catechism, for the use of children and ignorant people." Archbishop Butler's very
popular Catechism came about the time Nano Nagle was
moulding her new Community.

Her letter reveals her customary characteristics — humility, modesty, energy, industry, unselfishness, patience,

and a childlike calm in the midst of what might be calamity, if the law came upon her secret schools. Her generosity and affection towards those children, who were to be the mothers of a new generation, show that she put into practice the message of Saint John — where are Charity and Love, God is there.

Her quiet courage may be evaluated from the fact that brave souls, who came long after her, were still fiercely carrying on this warfare for the rights of Catholic Education. I mention specially the patriarchal prelate, Dr. John MacHale, Archbishop of Tuam, who died in 1881 at the age of 93. Since the days of Saint Patrick no braver man ever wore a mitre than this true champion of Catholic Education, who was a bishop for 56 years. He was born in 1789 — about five years after Nano Nagle died. For his patriotism and his faith he was often cross-examined by the forces of Government. Once, on being examined publicly, he was asked where and how he had got his early training. He had of course gone to a hedge-school, an institution conducted in the open air, because no other place of education was made available by the law. From the age of five to fourteen this outdoor academy was his alma mater. But this is how the Archbishop described it, with unsparing scorn for his captious questioners. He said the school, in which he was educated, was planned by the author of the Universe, fashioned by nature; that its halls were most majestic; its dimensions magnificent; that the blue vault of heaven was its canopy and the desk on which he essayed to write was the bosom of mother earth; her lap, the seat on which he reclined.

Archbishop MacHale saw the reign of seven Popes and the installation of six Primates of all Ireland. He saw three rebellions, four famines and nine land agitations. He saw the battle for Catholic Emancipation, the battle for primary Education, the battle for true Catholic Education. He took part in the war against tithes and against proselytism. Many great victories were won in his time for Catholicism. With him, he had the great Daniel O'Connell, powerful in organization and powerful in Parliament. Yet, even after their heroic age, many victories had to be won before the masses of the Irish people came into their own. Think therefore how great must have been the courage of a delicate young lady, working single-handed for religion and education, in days ahead of such giants as Archbishop MacHale and Daniel O'Connell. I have introduced this historical note in order to stress the intrepidity of Nano Nagle. Something had to be done for Catholic Education. With a sweetly innocent confidence in God she went out and did it. Years later the great Archbishop MacHale brought the Sisters of Nano Nagle to his own Cathedral town of Tuam, the storied See of Saint Jarlath. He well knew the priceless value of Mother Nagle's educational principles.

CHAPTER 7

NANO NAGLE'S CHARITY TOWARDS THE YOUNG AND THE OLD

L IKE the tints that unite so pleasingly in the rainbow of
peace Nano Nagle's charity towards all the poor was a
blend of the tenderest tones.   It ranged from the prayer
for *daily bread* in the *Our Father* to the compassionate pity
and beauty of the *Corporal Works of Mercy*. She cultivated the minds of the children. She had care for their
souls. She prepared them to receive the Bread of Angels.
She clothed their cold shuddering frames. She visited
them, frequently fed them, walked with them, talked with
them and united them into what had become her holy
family of God's forlorn. No idle rhetoric is this nor rosy
romance. For her it was stark realism in bleak streets, and
hard work from dawn till dusk. Some there were in hidden haunts whose human shame in tatters and deterioration
kept them from partaking in the blessings of her schools.
These buried outcasts she would seek and clothe and teach,
for the Sun of God's Kingdom is meant to shine upon all
His creatures. The crushing laws of man had brought
them rust and stagnation and compulsory concealment.

I think Nano Nagle's mission of bestowing all she possessed on the poor, and of becoming a fearless mendicant
in their cause, may merit her the title of Angel of Charity.
She came to them as a happy pilgrim from on High at their
worst hour; her gentle voice was as music to them in their
unredeemed disorder; her smile was as a ray of love to
them when the hearts of so many were hardened against
them; her pity and benignity cast a consolation on their
hitherto sunless lives.

In her efforts to reanimate the common people she met
with many obstacles. The physical ones were grave enough.
Bishop Coppinger provides a feeling picture of her at this
moment: "How often have we seen her passing with steady

composure through the rigours of every season to tend her little flock? How often have we seen her after a well-spent day returning through the darkness of the night, dripping with rain, mingled in the bustling crowd, moving thoughtfully along by the faint glimmering of a wretched lantern, withholding from herself in this manner the necessaries of life to administer the comforts of it to others." Let us see the risks she ran.

Archdeacon Hutch says that, bad as was the social condition of Cork at the time, the physical state was, if possible, still worse. He quotes a paragraph from the *Hibernian Chronicle* for November 22, 1770, to this effect: "A correspondent observes, that since the lamps have been set aside in this city, a number of people have been drowned, who in all probability might have been saved, if that useful and well-appointed mode of lighting the streets had been continued."

In addition to the needless dim-out and black-out, further terrors assailed the pedestrian, as may be gathered from another newspaper protest of the period: "Our total indifference in this city to everything which concerns our public accommodation and credit, has become a subject of wonder; the day traveller runs the risk of being blinded from the screening of lime; he is often intercepted in his way by the lagoons of water which the obstructions of the public sewers retain in the streets; and if he be not rode over by the gallopers who charge along the streets, or run over by the cars which are whirled along with no less rapidity, he may felicitate himself, on his return home, upon the cheap terms of such injury as he may receive, in tumbling over a few of the many heaps of rubbish which principally occupy our public ways. If the traveller by night escapes drowning he has no reason to complain, for, what with the darkness of the lamps, and the naked and unfenced state of the quays, *to survive a night walk is a matter of family thanksgiving.* Every stranger who approaches this, the third city in His Majesty's dominions, does it at the peril of his life; and one of the least dangerous of the highways into town is now through a sort of canal of mud, and has been so for a long time."

This was quite a change from the fair city of modern Cork, with its attractive buildings and its progressive industrial and commercial centres. True, some people must have been making money there in Nano Nagle's time, for in her letter she describes it as a place of great trade. At that time 100,000 head of cattle were slaughtered there annually to supply the needs of the Royal Navy of Britain. Cork exported more than Dublin, except in linen. Dublin imported luxuries, but Cork exported the needs of life — beef, pork, butter, hides and tallow.

In Lent Nano Nagle visited her different schools each day to teach religious matters. Five successive hours she spent on this routine. She used to read the story of Christ's Passion during Holy Week and explain it in each case. At all times she eschewed the comforts of creatures and left herself so destitute in dress that, to the casual eye her rank seemed the rank of a beggar, and pitying souls were moved to proffer charity. This she received for her poor ones, thanking God for the alms and pennies, and praising His Holy Will for reputing her among the mendicants. He certainly rewarded the humility of the handmaid, for her work was growing, and this was her exaltation. Some of her friends accused her of misguided zeal. They considered her indiscretions shameful and her piety inconsiderate; they reproached her vehemently and constantly; but she was steadfast in her love for the little darlings. Surely, she felt, the common decency of humanity would protect her in such a ministration of mercy. The tongues of the worldly-wise ceased to wag and her work continued to prosper. She had the pure love of God in her heart and she could go anywhere. She did not allow herself to be turned aside by those smug people, who, as the *Imitation* says, seem to be somewhat "busied with vanities, and blinded with errors." At the tomb of Lazarus tears conquered death. Her pity for the poor would bring Christ to revivify them.

She had reached the children. But there were grown girls working all over the city. She sought out these also and instructed them. To protect the virtuous and reform the fallen — these were plans dear to her mind. Her charitable eye ran its loving gaze over the whole gamut of human life in this vale of tears; not in words, but in deeds; to give rest and refuge to aged women she built and endowed a house for them in Cork. So, if you seek her monuments, look around.

The reader may say that Nano Nagle could not keep this up for ever. Of course she could not. Her funds were being constantly drained. The pure spirit of charity is a lovely thing, but in this material world there must be material funds. Only God can afford to ignore material things. To heal some of the many wounds of life it is needful to have the good Samaritan's equipment of the oil, the wine, and the two pennies. Miss Nagle was generous and so were her friends. So too were the brave Catholics of Cork. Even if social life were lopsided, even if streets were unpaved or lamps unlit, the good people of Cork were not found wanting, and they rallied to their own saint in their own midst. But some systematic finances were needed. Enlarged work implied enlarged expenditure and enlarged income.

Nano Nagle's plan was a sweetly reasonable one. Let those of her pupils pay a fraction who could afford it. This would stabilize her work. It would also teach people to appreciate the advantages she had been freely advancing. Poor human nature, often strange and contradictory, is apt to set little value on what it can get for nothing. It tends to prize what has to be paid for. People are liable to grow tired of that which comes too easily to them. A little assessment may beget esteem for benefits which have been hitherto taken for granted. From the Old Testament we remember that unpardonable scene where God's own chosen Children of Israel in the wilderness spake against the Lord Himself and against their leader Moses; the ungrateful ones said: there is no bread

and our soul loatheth *this light bread*. So the Lord sent
fiery serpents in their midst to bring them to a spirit of
appreciation and thanksgiving. There is a simple saying
that we should be thankful for small mercies. It teaches
a lesson when people have to pay their possible part for
services received, and Nano Nagle's collection, from those
who could afford it, was a tiny one in proportion to the
rich benefits administered by her.

The totalising of pennies, the pennies of the poor, can
set mighty machinery in motion. They can man a movement or erect a basilica. Take Nano Nagle's fellow-
countryman Daniel O'Connell. His people were derided
as beggars by those who had helped to make them so. But
beggared as they were, they each cheerfully gave a penny
to set a significant movement in motion for their liberties.
The swelling total of the pennies gave O'Connell a fighting
fund that even frightened the smartly entrenched politicians who would mockingly try to dismiss him as "the King
of the Beggars," and whose names are mostly remembered
today because they attacked the great Catholic Tribune.
The pennies of Peter or the pennies of Patrick can lead to
a world of beatific achievement. The princely donations
of the privileged few have indeed established noble works,
but the mites of the multitudes largely rebuilt the Catholic
Church in Ireland.

By a house to house collection Nano Nagle totalised the
tiny offerings herself. Lest her motives should be suspected
she declined to take any more than 25 cents a month from
her subscribers. To hold on in slavery and penury to the
Catholic Faith, the people had surrendered political power
and civic existence, lands and property, wealth and distinction. Now that the daybreak had come they would not
mind surrendering a few pennies for a daring experiment
in Christian Education. Though she met with general success she also mortifyingly met with the few mean and
miser-minded who never support any good work, who
lurked jealously in wait for any possible failure so that
they might malevolently rejoice over the collapse of what

they refused to support, who calumniated the holy woman by wicked whispers that she ran her schools as a source of gain. No calumny could check her confidence, and her health was better than ever, though she was now working harder than ever.

She was thorough in all things. Since she must beg for the poor she was thorough in that too — persistent, uncompromising and unblushing, says her biographer. Insults, rebuffs, and snubs, often tested her patience and longanimity. To the mystical-minded, who knew her priceless worth, she was the Rose of Desmond, but to the casual world with its snap judgment, that only weighs external appearances, she seemed yet another tiresome beggar.

An anecdote is recorded to illustrate this. A certain gallant shopowner was regularly generous to her. One day he was not at home and a boorish shopman ordered her out. She meekly answered that she would wait for his master. The boor did not recognize her as she sat patiently for a couple of hours on a bundle of hides behind the shop door.

Imagine the merchant's confusion when he appeared and found that Miss Nagle, whom he venerated as the very image of womanly nobility, had been so shockingly insulted beneath his roof. According to the Book of Proverbs *a gracious woman shall find glory*. Nano Nagle found her glory in suffering humiliations for the Just Judge, who took good care to warn the selfish while He was here on earth, by presenting a verbal preview of what will happen on the Last Day to those who shut the gates of mercy on the poor that are His very own.

She went her way, uncomplainingly suffering from the heedless and the thoughtless; from those who judge the book by the cover and those who think all is gold that glitters; from those who are always on the watch to find out the faults and failings of others without ever doing anything useful themselves; from those who mistake bustle for work, and who therefore could not perceive the hidden value of her quiet toil. Nay more, in her fortitude she had worn the very soles off her unwearying feet, and only after her death did it become evident what agonies her relentless walking must have engendered in her final years. We may learn how oblivious she was to human comfort or precaution from a letter which she wrote to her friend Miss Mulally, in Dublin, on July 29, 1780:

"As you were so good as to desire to know how my eyes are that were so many months very sore, I thank God I got the better of them, and I must tell you how I was cured, though I believe few will try this recipe which had such a wonderful effect on me. On one of the coldest days last winter, and a most sharp, piercing wind (and I found nothing affected them so much as the wind), though I thought I might on account of them plead some excuse, yet at the same time it was not giving good example not to go down as much as others, I walked out to the school at North Gate; and, so far from any bad effect on them, I did not find them worse, but, I may say with truth, vastly better; and ever since, thank God, they have continued so. I think any little labours I have the Almighty has given me health to go through them; and if I did not make use of it in His service, He may soon deprive me of it."

To make the freezing wind a cure for sore eyes must surely suggest the heroic austerity of the saints. Not all walks of society could survive, if, for example, people stricken with pneumonia attempted to cure it by taking a stroll in the snow. But, God is wonderful in His saints, and there was supererogation in the sufferings of Nano Nagle. Her modest gentility calls to my mind the beautiful poem by Belloc on *Courtesy*. Our Lady's countenance remained calm in the midst of pain: *yet was her face both great and kind, for courtesy was in her mind.* I can never forget the dear Gilbert Chesterton, Our Lady's very Knight, delightedly reading to us this poem of his friend, as he loved to linger on its lines. It can be truly a psalm of life, especially the farewell: *For in my walks it seems to me that the Grace of God is in Courtesy.* That is how I think of Nano Nagle's graciousness and unbreakable courtesy. In this

our age we meet with a dismal tag called *self-expression*
which has often become another excuse for bad manners.
Miss Nagle's school of godly courtesy was conceived in the
older school of Nazareth.   She wished people to have their
liberty — but, as Saint Peter says, "not making liberty a
cloak for malice."

Now that we are convinced of the heavenly merits of her
external life the reader may ask what records there are of
her personal and private life.   The *Annals* of her Convent
serve to enlighten us: —

"For some time after she returned home she piously
conformed to the habits of the family with whom she
lived: she joined their parties at home, and with their
friends; but upon these occasions, when the sacrifice of
her inclinations and will was thus required, she previously most carefully discharged her duties of devotion
as well as her ordinary visits to her schools: no circumstance could ever prevail upon her to omit these. In
company she was always a subject of admiration and of
edification; her conversation was interesting, her address
dignified; there was no bitterness discoverable in her af-
fability, nor austerity to be seen in her gravity; she never
obtruded those harsh lectures, wherein pride, garbed under
the cloak of piety, is so apt to descant upon the failings of
others; her lessons were confined to her schools; in all
other places it was only by her example she spoke.   In her
presence detraction was confounded, because all knew that
the character of the neighbour was peculiarly dear to her
heart: all levity of expression was silenced when she appeared, overawed, as it were, by the lustre of her virtue.

Whilst others were employed at the card-table, she retired to her devotions without ever railing at their squander-
ing time.   She taught them, by this means, the incomparable
value of it.   By degrees she withdrew from all intercourse
with the world; she paid no visits but where charity conducted her; all other moments which were at her disposal
she employed in the exercise of compunction and prayer.

For the remainder of her life, she divided her time between the chapel, the school, and her apartments; at chapel, assisting every day at the Holy Sacrifice, her unaffected appearance was a lively transcript of her own perfect faith, and a new motive of credibility to all those who beheld her; so silent, so motionless, so absorbed in recollection was she! In her schools she was always laborious, patient, vigilant, and judicious; she studied well the dispositions of her uncouth pupils, and the degree of capacity possessed by them; her instructions were adapted accordingly.

She watched their countenances, which long experience had taught her to read, and she proceeded, or turned back, explained or repeated, as she found them impressed with what she said. During Lent, and when she prepared them for the sacraments, she instructed them for five successive hours every day without intermission. After her refection, which was both plain and frugal, she retired to her apartment, for the performance of her evening devotions: there, in converse with God, the *Great Teacher* of truth, she advanced in the science of the saints, and renewed her fervour for the ensuing day. In these heavenly communications she conceived the noble idea of perpetuating the good work she had begun. She had at this time a fortune at her disposal, and, seeing it could not be more usefully employed, she determined upon establishing some permanent institution for the education of the poor in this country. She met with several obstacles, and much opposition to her design; but those, at length, gave way to her zeal, and she was seconded by the active co-operation of those whom God raised up to carry on with her the good work."

We see now, how Nano Nagle decided that the work of God, which had flourished so far, must not perish. She wished to place it in the care of a religious community. How was this to be done? Religious communities were banned by the Penal Laws. In 1653, Dominican Nuns in Mayo gave their lives for the Faith in the savage Cromwellian persecution. In 1629, the brave *Poor Clares* ventured from the Continent to settle down in Dublin, at a time when the houses of the Friars were mostly closed. The *Poor Clares* had their convent raided by the Penal persecutors who dragged the nuns in their habits, barefooted, through the streets of Dublin to meet the lawgivers at Dublin Castle. They were told to leave Dublin but they managed to survive in secret near Athlone for ten years. In 1642 the invading heretics desecrated the convent and set fire to it. A body of Irish Catholic soldiers met the invaders who did this evil thing and put them to the sword. The *Poor Clares* still lingered in Galway, but after 1718 they were not allowed to wear the habit. At the beginning of the eighteenth century we are assured that there were no convents anywhere in Ireland except in Galway. By 1712 the Poor Clare Nuns decided to risk settling in Dublin but they were soon raided, and only through influence were they allowed out on bail, but the raid revealed that Archbishop Byrne of Dublin, and his Vicar General, had exercised their ecclesiastical functions in bringing the nuns to Dublin, so they themselves had to flee and function in hiding. The Mother House in Galway was raided too, and the nuns had to flee for a time. In 1698 Parliament ordered all Bishops and Religious to leave Ireland. Benedictine Nuns who had settled in Dublin during the reign of the Catholic King James II were dispersed when the Williamites came. In 1731 the Augustinian Nuns, who dared to settle in Galway, were raided by the Government authorities, and the Mayor of Galway reported thus: "The Sheriffs searched the reputed nunnery called the Augustinian Nunnery, and found none but servants therein, but discovered in seven rooms ten beds, in which, it was apprehended, the reputed nuns lay before their dispersal."

Perilous, therefore, was the spiritual vineyard of Ireland for Nuns in those days. They were in daily danger of imprisonment. Many had to flee into exile. The *Poor Clares* had been driven from East to West. And now Nano Nagle wanted to bring a religious Community into the busy and crowded City of Cork, not for cloistral contemplation either, but for open teaching. The cries for "Liberty of Conscience" had died long previously with the Earl of Desmond, and with O'Neill, the Earl of Tyrone. Who was she to expect such a privilege at this fated hour? "No one of Popish religion shall teach school." Had not that been made clear, over and over again? When Sir Richard Cox addressed the Grand Jury in Cork, in 1740, he said there were offending Catholic schoolmasters in the county. Clearly it was their business to bring them in to be dealt with. Cromwellian records had already mentioned these "Popish School Masrs who taught the Irish Youth, traying them up in Supersticion, Idolatry and the Evill customs of the Nacion." And the law was still on the look out for these ineradicable teachers. Nano Nagle was in her grave when an Act of 1795 brought some relief — "An Act for the Better Education of Persons professing the Popish or Roman Catholic Religion." If we have any doubt about her difficulties, the Protestant Historian, Lecky, will summarise the position of Catholic Education in the eighteenth century once and for all: he said "the legislation on the subject of Catholic Education may be briefly described, for it amounted simply to universal, unqualified, and unlimited proscription."

No doubt Nano Nagle could fortify herself with the armouring words of the divine Psalmist: "The poor man shall not be forgotten to the end: the patience of the poor shall not perish for ever." But what a battle!

God must have loved her a great deal to give her such grace and courage. Yes: He loved her infinitely. And she returned His love. He rewarded her with her wish. She consulted an eminent Jesuit, Father Doran, and also his nephew, Father Moylan, who was later Bishop of Cork. They strongly recommended her to try to establish an Ursuline community in Cork, as this would help to answer her educational prayers, and prove a benefit and a blessing to the people at large. On this decision she promptly acted. When duty called she was inflexible and undelaying.

Countless thousands of her race, who in the centuries

up to this, had given their lives for the truths she was teaching, surely interceded for her in her gallant struggles and besought, on High, the Lord of the Resurrection, that she might live and triumph and bring back what had been so long blighted. In the mystic links of this consoling Communion of Saints one incident can be introduced so that, from the one, we may learn all. In her letters Nano Nagle has referred to the Rosary and the Mass. These were the central points of Irish Faith in Penal Days. They still are. Over a hundred years before her, a great gentleman gave his life for these two foundational tenets of our holy religion. It was Sir John Burke, and his name is on the list of Irish martyrs whose cause of beatification is now advanced in Rome.

Rosary Sunday had dawned at his Castle in Ireland and the people were gathered in his Hall for Mass. It was the familiar story: the Mass in secret, the smuggled priest, the eager outlawed flock that craved the healing Sacrament of Penance and the Food of their souls in the Eucharist. This time somebody was to pay the price, and it was the charitable host himself. His Castle was raided at this identical holy hour, but Sir John was determined to save the priest and the sacred vessels of the altar. He was finally captured and sentenced to death. His wife, who was about to give birth to a child, visited him in prison, and at the last farewell on earth he told her that he wished this child to be given to the Dominican Order as an offering to God and His Mother, the Queen of the Rosary.

The child Eleanora Burke certainly corresponded to the wishes of her martyred father, for she became a Tertiary of the Order of Saint Dominic, and at an early age made her room in her mother's house a cell where she prayed and fasted. The "oldest existing Irish convent in the world" is to be found not in Ireland but in Portugal, and it was there that young Eleanora Burke from Ireland was the first to enter, and under the name of Sister Catherine of the Rosary to win the fame of great sanctity, so great that after her early death the people sought relics of her habit. Her father had given his life to the Rosary in one way: she in another. It was her special devotion. She was asked what *method* she followed in prayer. She said she knew nothing about *methods* and the only thing she could say was her Rosary — "one mystery of which was enough to occupy the longest life."

This was the spirit that Nano Nagle wished to bring to Cork, not in private but in public. It is only natural to think that her Irish precursors prayed for her success, victorious round the throne of God. The people in Ireland's valleys below kept a candle flickering here and there for the Blessed Mother too, as the following "Hymn to the Virgin Mary" suggests. It was written by Conor O'Riordan about the year 1750:

Queen of all Queens, oh! Wonder of the loveliness of
        women,
Heart which hath held in check for us the righteous wrath
        of God;
Strong Staff of Light, and Fosterer of the Bright Child of
        heaven,
Pray thou for us as we now pray that we may be forgiven.

She of the King of Stars beloved, stainless, undefiled,
Christ chose as His Mother-nurse, to Him, the stainless
        child;
Within her breast, as in a nest, the Paraclete reposes,
Lily among fairest flowers, Rose amid red roses.

She, the bright unsheathèd sword to guard our souls in
        anguish,
She, the flawless limber-branch, to cover those that lan-
        guish;
Where her healing mantle flows, may I find my hiding,
Neath the fringes of her robe constantly abiding.

Hostile camps upon the plain, sharp swords clashed to-
        gether,

Stricken fleets across the main stressed by wintry weather;
Weary sickness on my heart, sinful thoughts alluring,
All the fever of my soul clings to her for curing.

She the Maid the careful king of the wide wet world
    chooses,
In her speech forgiveness lies, no suppliant she refuses;
White Star of our troubled sea, on thy name I'm crying,
That Christ may draw in His spread net the living and the
    dying.

The unquenchable candle of the people and the flickering lantern of the daughter of the proud Nagles are the
early high-lights of our story. They will lead to a blaze
of light round the darkened altar as the next Chapter must
tell.

CHAPTER 8

NANO NAGLE BRINGS THE URSULINES TO IRELAND

OUR heroine has received her decisive instructions. Bring the Ursulines to Ireland. The project was difficult enough, judging by the prejudicial and bitterly obstructive times. But there were other problems. Where could Nano Nagle find fit subjects to volunteer for her meditated establishment? Communities on the Continent were not anxious to risk the perils and hazards of the land of bondage, for that is what Ireland then was. The French Sisters had dedicated themselves to teaching their own people, to living and dying in their own Convents. They could hardly be expected to leave all that they held dear, and to face the inhuman penalties of the Penal Laws in a strange country.

However, the rescue of Catholic Education in Ireland was at hand, and Ireland characteristically came to its own rescue. Four noble young women of Ireland came forward and placed themselves completely at the disposal of Nano Nagle. *Do with me what Thou wilt.* It requires liberal grace to say that, at any time, to God, and fully mean it. Without any reservations or conditional clauses these young ladies were ready for Catholic Action of the first order, and a Convent in Cork was their objective. They belong to educational history, so let us see who they were. Like Miss Nagle herself they came from distinguished families, and could have enjoyed social prestige and leisure in the world, but they gladly preferred to sacrifice themselves to the service of the Supreme Teacher of all nations.

First in this higher calling was Miss Fitzsimons, deeply devout and talented. Father Moylan met her in Paris and quickly enthused her for Nano Nagle's undertaking. Actually she had intended joining the good Sisters of the Visitation, but so receptively was her mind moved by the pressing need for God's work in her native land that she promptly became number one volunteer for the future Community in Cork. Her spiritual training in France was the prelude to training others at home, and for this she entered the Ursuline Convent, in Rue St. Jacques, Paris, in 1767. In religion she took the name of Saint Angela.

Next came Miss Coppinger to join the same House of the Ursulines in Paris, in 1769. She belonged to the noted family at Barryscourt, in County Cork, and was a cousin of the then Duchess of Norfolk — the former Mariana Coppinger of Cork, who married Charles Howard, the Eleventh Duke of Norfolk, the only remaining Catholic Duke in England. The name Coppinger, which is of venerable tradition in Ireland and England, is said to have come originally from Denmark. The family, to which our young novice belonged, was long distinguished in the public life of Cork — one of them having been Mayor of the City as far back as the Middle Ages; they were widely connected in France, hence Miss Coppinger's name carried weight at home and abroad. Another famous member of the family, Bishop Coppinger, will enter further into our pages. Miss Coppinger was devoutly attached to all that pertained to the extension of our holy Faith, and was readily won for the new Ursuline Community by Nano Nagle herself. She was given the title of Mother Augustine, in religion.

The illustrious Nagle family contributed yet another member. This was Margaret Nagle, a cousin of Nano. She accompanied Miss Coppinger to Paris, and became Mother Mary Joseph in the Ursuline Community.

In Paris, ahead of these two blue-blooded young ladies, was another — Miss Nano [Honoria] Kavanagh, who was closely related to the ruling family of the Butlers, Dukes of Ormonde, and was also closely related to Miss Coppinger. Miss Kavanagh had already set her mind on the religious life, so, when it was a question of God and Ireland, the historic name of Kavanagh was quick to respond, and she became the fourth member of the heroic little group under the name of Mother Ursula.

And now a word on the indefatigable Father Moylan, who was guide, philosopher, and friend to Nano Nagle, in all the problems that this complex project postulated. He was her zealous and co-operative agent in paving the way in Paris, where he was already well-known. He cut the Gordian knot of many a difficulty; but obstacles arose galore. His proposals at the Ursuline Convent in Paris must have necessitated infinite negotiations on every side. The plan awaiting consideration was one of the most difficult under Heaven, a foundation in Ireland. Unpropitious appeared the prospects. Doctor Moylan was forced to go through disappointments, delays, refusals, reversals, procrastinations, and seeming insurmountabilities. His patience, all the way, was akin to that of Job, and success came to him in the end, through his unfaltering confidence in the Lord of the Harvest.

Thorny hindrances may be expected in full by all those who set out to exert prodigal energy in the work of God. Doctor Moylan had luckily defeated such bafflings. The preliminaries were perfected, and the Ursuline authorities now were persuaded to accede to the wish that meant so much to him, and to Nano Nagle, and indeed to "the most distressful country." The four young Irish ladies in the novitiate in Paris were exemplary in their fervour, and went on persevering in the science of the Saints. So successful was their novitiate that they were a credit to God and country. Doctor Moylan would soon come back to bring them home to their own Convent, prepared for them by the benefactress of Cork.

Everything now looked hopeful for Nano Nagle. But alas! There is little plain sailing in the barque of Peter. Those who, in their curiosity, seek to know clearly the connection between the pain of this world and the Providence of God, must await their satisfying answer at the Ivory Gate. Meanwhile the accepted rule here is: no Cross, no Crown. In the unfolding of Nano Nagle's dramatic story,

many of her crosses are made manifest; she bore them un-
flinchingly and bore them alone.

The shadow of uneasiness creeps across our page when
we study the following quotation from the *Annals* of her
Convent: "Little did Miss Nagle suspect all this time that
these Ursulines were intended by Doctor Moylan for the
education of young ladies, and not to be devoted to the
only and great object which she had in view, viz: the instruction of the poor."

Of course it will be pointed out that Nano Nagle may
not have adequately acquainted herself with the Ursuline
rule in advance. She wished to specialise exclusively in
the ranks of the poor, whereas the Ursuline Order was
designed to teach children from other walks of life, for the
Christian leadership which the higher responsibilities of
their privileged state implied. But, as Shakespeare says,
by indirections we find directions out. Each step was leading to the establishment of her own Presentation Community, and God often leads us to a straight objective by
curving roads. She asked Him for one Order in Ireland
and He gave her two. And the two have so greatly magni-
fied His Name, in the education of all classes, that it would
take many books to detail the gifts and graces that have
happily accrued to their unswerving labours for God's
Kingdom, at home and abroad.

Here, I find it desirable to digress, in order to describe
briefly the Ursuline Order — which Nano Nagle providentially introduced into Ireland. I could not mention the
history of education without referring to the widespread
achievements of the Ursulines, which achievements began
with their remarkable Foundress, Angela Merici, now a
canonised Saint of Holy Church. Nor must we ever talk
about being *too old* when it comes to doing something useful for God and His creatures. Love is boundless and age
is an accident. For Saint Angela was over 60 years old
when she established her teaching Order, the work of her
fruitful life.

Angela Merici was born near lovely Lake Garda, in

Lombardy, in 1474. She was an orphan at ten, and consequently went to live at an uncle's home. Goodness was innate in her character, and her love of God found further incentives in the sanctifying Third Order of Saint Francis. The Christian instruction of children early became her absorbing apostolate, and she turned her home into a school, as the first step in her combat against juvenile paganism. The work grew, and other holy young women joined her in teaching the little ones. Her mission was assured, but in her humility she would only *direct* her group of associates who were known as "The Company of Saint Ursula." She and her friends continued to live in their own families, only meeting from time to time for spiritual conferences and systematic devotions. We see here that her story has a close similarity to that of her admirer, Nano Nagle. In 1535, when wild things were being done all over Europe in the wake of the revolting hysterics attending the *Reformation*, twelve Ursuline members met together in community, with episcopal approbation, and with Saint Angela as Superioress. Thus began the Ursuline Order, which spread rapidly through Italy, Germany, and France. In a few years it numbered many houses. It was founded at the acceptable time. In 1639 the Order came to Canada, and, in 1727, to New Orleans. The Ursulines pioneeringly laboured amid the Rocky Mountains, with missions for the Indians. I must mention how the great American champion of human liberty and lover of Education, Thomas Jefferson, esteemed the Ursulines. When he was President of the United States, in 1804, the Ursulines in New Orleans addressed a letter to him, in which they solicited the passage of an Act of Congress guaranteeing their property rights. In his reply Jefferson reassured the Ursulines, saying: "The principles of the Constitution of the United States are a sure guaranty to you that it will be preserved to you sacred and inviolate, and that your Institution will be permitted to govern itself according to its own voluntary rules without interference from the civil authority. Whatever diversity of shades may appear in the religious opinions of our fellow citizens, the charitable objects of your Institution cannot be of indifference to any; and, by its furtherance of the wholesome purpose, by training up its young members in the way they should go, cannot fail to insure the patronage of the Government it is under. Be assured that it will meet with all the protection my office can give it."

It is explainably human for people to have their names associated with the good works they execute. In her humility Saint Angela feared that her admirers might associate her name with her good work, so she conclusively prevented this by dedicating its title to Saint Ursula.

To explain further, the story of Saint Ursula is briefly this. She was the daughter of a Christian King of Great Britain. She was asked in marriage by the son of a great pagan king. She obtained a delay of three years to make up her mind. Meantime, at her request, she was given ten companions of noble birth. Each of the ten companions, accompanied by a thousand virgins, embarked in a ship. The eleven ships set sail for three years. The time came for Saint Ursula to return, but, when nearing the harbours of homeland, the wind arose and bore Ursula and her companions far from the British shores. By water they went to Cologne. They visited Rome in the interval. Finally they arrived back in Cologne, where they were martyred for the Faith by the Huns. This is approximately accredited to the third, fourth, or fifth centuries. The story has begotten great masterpieces in Art, and enjoys universal fame.

In 1604, a beautiful rich young widow bought a home for the Ursulines in Paris — in the Faubourg St. Jacques — and this was the Motherhouse from which Nano Nagle introduced the Ursuline Order into Ireland, for the continuation of her treasured schools.

We may now be admitted by historical retrospect into the inner circle of Miss Nagle's plans, which so far she had kept from her relatives. Her continued difficulties will still confront us. Only when her faithful little group of nuns will arrive in Cork — then and only then — can she feel sure of success.

When this worry will be over, the next trouble will begin. What will her family say when they hear that she has given her Convent a local habitation and a name, and thereby has made herself a greater felon than she already was, according to the punitive laws prevailing all over the Isle? Hitherto she had been founding schools, and her family had become reconciled to the fact. Providence had been kind to her. She had succeeded in escaping the labyrinthine meshes of the law in her outlawed role. She had convinced the timid that it was possible to set up schools, without disaster ensuing. Her wisdom, tact, prudence, and simple trust in her Maker, had brought her efforts to a miraculously safe outcome. Why go further? Why not leave very well alone? She was now indulging in the double crime of teaching and of smuggling Nuns into Ireland. Will the patience of her family stand her piling illegality upon illegality? Why tempt the Lady Luck?

To the general run of the cowed and brow-beaten population, resignedly inured to being penalised, and accustomed to accept their very existence as an illegality that was tolerated, the idea of bringing a teaching Order into their unanimated midst would seem a piece of sheer lunacy. But Nano Nagle kept her secret. People would be told her plans at the right moment — the moment of success, when that which had seemed a fancy had become a fact. She was too busy, seeking further candidates for her work, to be occupied with this or that irrelevant opinion of her increasing transactions. In the Summer of 1769 she had reviewingly detailed some of her thoughts, with heartfelt simplicity, in a letter to her close and trusted friend—Miss Fitzsimons, who was already in her second year at the Ursuline Convent in Paris: —

"As it is always a real pleasure to me to hear from you, I am much obliged to you for both your kind favours. In the first there was enclosed your note. I can't help saying that if I could be jealous at anything you did in my regard, it would be by your not writing in a more friendly manner, as be assured you can command anything in my power.

I cannot express how much I suffered on your account, as I was sure your uneasiness must be great at not hearing of the arrival of the young ladies I mentioned. They were to depart in the first vessel that sailed to Havre. When I wrote I thought everything was settled, but it has pleased God to order things otherwise, which in all appearance has turned out a fortunate occurrence, for by the delay there are two subjects more, such as one might ambition in every respect. I shall say nothing of their merit as that will speak for itself.

I am not acquainted with Miss Coppinger; I have seen her, but it is on the amiable character Fr. Doran gives her I depend, and I am afraid I shall not have the pleasure of seeing her again before she goes, as the measles are like a plague here. Though not always mortal, yet they are dangerous to grown persons, and Mrs. Coppinger told me it was the only disorder she dreaded for her daughter. She and the father are greatly pleased at her choice of life — they are so pious. I wished Mr. Shea was so well pleased at his daughter's inclination. He has not yet given his consent. He says it is a sudden thought. He does not know it long, though she has been thinking of becoming a religious more than twelve months. She is a person of incomparable sense and prudence, and it is not very probable she will change.

Miss Coppinger's parents won't let her go until her aunt Butler approves of her resolution, to which (by what you mention of her good intentions towards this foundation) she will immediately give her consent.

* * * * * * *

Had I only a proper person to begin this foundation, I think it has the prospect of surprising success.

I am charmed with the account you give me of the ladies you are with; I hope the same spirit will be communicated here. I think religious discipline would be too strict for this country; and I own I should not rejoice to see it kept up. I must say Miss Moylan's prejudice to take on here has made me see things in a clearer light than I should have done, and makes me accept the disappointment I have met with as a decree of the Divine bounty. All her friends are sorry she went abroad; and I must say, laying aside her own merit, this house would have a great loss in her, as she is of a family deservedly beloved. They are in hopes she is beginning to change. I wish it may be so. If she has so much zeal, she will never have such an opportunity of exerting it as here. [This Miss Moylan was half-sister to Bishop Moylan; she did join the community when it was established in Cork; she died in 1842, at the age of 90, having spent 72 years as a nun.] .

I must look on it as one of my crosses that the two ladies who were so good as to patronise this foundation were removed; but the Almighty is all-sufficient, and will make up this loss to us. I beg you will present them my compliments.

Fr. Moylan desires to be affectionately remembered to you. As he gave you an account of the building, I shall say nothing of it, only to excuse myself as to the house I built first. I never intended it for ladies. At the time I was sure I should get the ground at the rear to build on, and as it gave on the street I was obliged to have it in the manner it is, in order not to have it noticed as a convent. I shall refer you for that and many other things to my next, [this letter has not, alas, been preserved], which I hope the young ladies will be the bearers of, and believe me

Your ever affectionate Friend,

Nano Nagle."

What qualifications did Miss Nagle expect in her candidates for the new teaching community? First, virtue; next, ability. She wanted them to be constant in prayer and capable in teaching. To labour is to pray: by such teaching had the holy father Saint Benedict turned the wilderness of Europe into a garden of God. By prayer and teaching, a new Order would restore to eighteenth century Ireland the holy traditions of Catholic education, of which it had been divested so wickedly and so long, traditions that had made Ireland first flower of the earth and first gem of the sea.

Nano Nagle insisted on the best education for the children. To achieve this, she similarly insisted on the best education for the teachers. In the spring of 1770, a year before her community was smuggled into Cork, she wrote to Miss Fitzsimons in Paris, expressing her concern for the complete educational equipment of her future teachers: —

"It gives me a vast deal of trouble to find that these two young ladies that want to learn can have no advantage in that respect. If it would be permitted there to have anybody to teach them anything you thought would be hereafter an advantage to the house, don't spare any expense; you will be the best judge of that, and of everything else in their regard."

As an educational reformer Miss Nagle was far-sighted, strict, precise, and practical. To her, Catholic Education meant what it said: it was to be, at one and the same time, all that was truly Catholic and all that was truly educational. She wished her pupils to know their religion, to love it and live it. She wished their secular education to fit them for their duties in life, and to be as sound and progressive as any afforded elsewhere. Her good sense was virtuously balanced on the Golden Mean. This is shown in another letter to Miss Fitzsimons in 1770: —

"I hope you will act in regard to the young ladies as you think proper, and be sure I shall always approve of it. I must say I was desirous they should learn what was proper to teach young ladies hereafter, as there is a general complaint both in this kingdom and in England that the children are only taught to say their prayers."

She put her advice into practice at home, while waiting for her novices. She sedulously continued to take care of her schools and her pupils. This mild and modest school-mistress was also called upon to be a lively supervisor of her new buildings. As far as Catholic Ireland was concerned, building hitherto had been of a negative character. She was a pioneer in construction and in repairing the damages. She expected much, both in labour and in prayer, from her incoming novices, so she spared no effort in doing her part, by preparing for them a habitable abode. In dealing with others she was always sweetly reasonable and considerate to the core.

Slowly her educational system was taking root; the progress of her work may be described as the inevitability of gradualness. Miss Nagle gives us a widening glimpse of developments in another letter written to her cooperative friend, Miss Fitzsimons, who was still in Paris. The letter is dated from Cork, September 28th, 1770: —

"I am sorry it was not in my power sooner to tell you how much I am obliged to you for not standing on ceremony with me, and being so good as to write to me so often of late, though I could not answer your kind favours as punctually as I wished to do. I believe you'll attribute my silence to the real cause, which is want of time.

I can't express the joy I had to hear of Miss Kavanagh's resolution, and that she had joined you. It was what you ambitioned this long time past. If once we were fixed, the object in view is so great that I dare say many would follow your and her example.

I had little reason when I first thought of this foundation to expect the success it has already met with. I must say, every disappointment we have had the Almighty has been pleased to make it turn out to our advantage; though my impatience made me very often not submit to His divine will as I ought.

I believe we are indebted to your worthy friend for this young lady's determination to come here. We are

happy, I think, in having one of the Sisters. I am not surprised at what you mention to me in regard of Mr. Kavanagh, for he and his lady, by some conjectures of their
own, were sure Miss Nano [Kavanagh] intended coming
here. As for my part, I could not say anything that gave
the least notion that she was so inclined; nor did I flatter
myself by what the clergyman then told me of her that
she would; and I must do her brother and sister justice,
they did not seem at all angry with her for it. I dare say
she will be of great service to her by her prayers.

I cannot tell you how eager Fr. Doran is for your coming over soon, as he foresees they will every day be starting
some new difficulties on account of the French lady, which
is already the case, and was made an objection when Miss
B. got leave to come. He wrote to his nephew [Fr. Moy-
lan] the many reasons that made it so necessary to have
this establishment begun as soon as possible, as he and I
are sure, by the character you give of this lady, that she is
one of those modern religious persons who think every in-
convenience is such a cross that there is no bearing it. She
that makes such a sacrifice for the good of souls will have
fortitude to make light, I hope, of not having everything
settled as comfortably as it ought to be.

One could not imagine in a house so lately built that the
walls would be as dry as they are, nor can one judge of
those till they are plastered, for when the plaster dries immediately, it's owing to the walls being so. Had I not seen
it had this effect upon it I could not have believed it. You
will find it will be very habitable this winter, which I did
not think it would be; and when you are settled there I
shall be to blame if I do not get every necessary that is
thought wanting, as there is nothing in my power I shan't
endeavour to do.

I hope you will be so good as to excuse in the beginning, all, and consider we are in a country in which we
can't do as we please.

By degrees, with the assistance of God, we may do a great deal."

The remainder of the foregoing letter is regrettably missing.

The available portion enlightens us on the ever-perceptible points of Miss Nagle's exemplary character. She wants her teachers to show a cheerful sense of sacrifice: let them not consider every casual instance of lack of personal comfort as an insupportable set-back. The big sacrifice, borne welcomingly, will bring blessings that counteract the irritating tribe of petty miseries. She rejoices in the fact that God's purpose is always good. She modestly indicts herself for at all doubting the Divine Design, and concludes with renewed trust therein. The meiosis of her expression is a heavenly delight: "we are in a country in which we can't do as we please"! God bless her innocence and equanimity! Why, the magistrates were bound to send herself and her nuns to jail, to fine them, and finally transport them, and wipe out her convent utterly! She had a narrow escape from this alarming fate. I will later describe how the limbs of the law tried to trap her.

Pope Pius the Seventh referred to our holy heroine as "Honora Nagle, an opulent and noble lady of the Kingdom of Ireland." This description manifests itself all the more, as our chapters portray her many-sided story. Her opulence had dispensed itself in countless ways among the poor, but there are even greater and more permanent manifestations of it to come. She was noble in thought, word, and deed. Her flickering lantern, by God's protective Providence, had guided her through night, and storm, and darkness. In the words of the Old Testament she could truly say: *Thou art my lamp, Lord: and the Lord will lighten my darkness.* She had built one house already. The Lord will come and dwell here in His Real Presence. Her opulence and nobility had been spending themselves here, and consequently, within a year the altar lights will glow inside these walls.

We have reached the year 1770. Nano Nagle is now about 42. She is on the eve of completing the first part of her great work. No storm will quench the Lamp she has lighted.

Her Ursuline adjutants came and flourished like the palm-tree in Jericho. But there are intervening branches of the account that await exposition in another chapter.

CHAPTER 9

NANO NAGLE BREAKS THE PENAL CHAIN: THE MORNING STAR HAS RISEN

THE controlling hand of the Lord was discernably ruling and guiding Nano Nagle, and He rewarded her confidence by seeing that she wanted for nothing, as she emerged from success to success. Delay there might be, but not defeat.

The time had come to tell her family about her newest venture. She went in person to tell it. It was now easier to break the news, since her plans were a decided success. And, since everything was a success, the family reaction was more favourable than it might have been, if things had turned out to be a failure. She broke the news gently. One may call her an apostle of quiet and calm. Peacefully she did all things, both great and small. There may be some maladroit mortals who, in doing even the smallest thing, make the largest noise. Miss Nagle did the biggest things without even the smallest noise.

It is the Summer of 1770. Her family are away in England, at the beautiful old Roman town of Bath. Thither Miss Nagle went on a visit. But it was not to seek the social graces for which Bath was famous, nor to refresh her frail frame with the healing chalybeate waters, which had made Bath the Mecca of those fashionable mortals who were stricken with creaking or gouty limbs.

Of course she could feel at home among many friends in Bath. It was here that her cousin Burke had many admirers; it was here that his splendid fellow-countryman, Doctor Christopher Nugent, took care of Burke's health; it was here that Burke fell in love with Doctor Nugent's daughter, Jane, whom he married. She was a Catholic, and it was perhaps to please her religious feelings that Burke refused to be called to the Bar — for he could not be called unless he first took an oath in denunciation of the Pope. By this year, 1770, Burke was making history in one way, Nano Nagle in another. Burke had just published the greatest of his early writings — *Thoughts on the Causes of the Present Discontents*. His championship of the American Cause resulted in his being made Agent in London for the Colony of New York, in 1770. Nano Nagle had come to Bath, in 1770, to tell her family of her battle against the present educational discontents at home in Ireland: she had made the first breach in the thick armoury of the Penal Laws.

In July, 1770, Miss Nagle wrote the following facts from Bath, to Miss Fitzsimons — her cherished Ursuline associate in Paris. There is what one might call a lavish economy of expression in this direct letter: —

"You thought I came here for my health. As you are so good as to interest yourself in my regard, and I was afraid it might make you uneasy, I beg to assure you that, thank God, I never was better, and it was not to take the waters I came, nor have I tasted them.

"I came to see my brothers; and be assured it was with much ado I could prevail on myself to pay them this visit.

"I did not acquaint you with this tour, as I wavered so much with myself, that I may say till I was in the ship I was not sure of coming — it was so much against my inclination to leave my children; and only to serve the foundation I never should have prevailed on myself.

"Our friend, I have reason to think, spoke with a prophetic spirit by what has happend, for my own family would never have the opinion they have at present, nor ever interest themselves as they do for its success. You must have been surprised when you heard that they knew nothing of it. You heard what was true; the young lady who told you was the first, my sister Nagle says, who told herself; and though she did so she could hardly believe her.

"You don't forget that I wrote to you when I began my schools my own immediate family knew nothing of it; so the same method I was resolved to take now, as I was sure they would be the first to oppose me. I never said one word to them till I saw things had such a prospect of succeeding, which I was sure I never could have persuaded them of, if they did not see it.

"It gives them all great pleasure that I should be the means of promoting such a good work, and my sisters-in-law are as eager to get good subjects for it as we could be. I hope you will approve of my manner of acting, as the less noise made about affairs of this kind in this country the better.

"Mr. Keating got a letter from Dr. Butler, [then Catholic Bishop of Cork], on which he came to speak to me about his sister, and says as we must be of such service to the kingdom, if we had the Protestants' consent for the establishment he would be better pleased she was among us, as she could do more good there than anywhere else; on which I told him before my brother and sister, that had I consulted my own family I should not have had a school in Cork, which they said was true."

* * * *

The Venerable Archdeacon Hutch, in his nineteenth-century study of Mother Nagle, makes the following comment on the foregoing: "From the concluding portion of this letter it is evident that Miss Nagle was meeting with opposition from a quarter whence she had least reason to expect it, viz., from the Bishop of the diocese. One ought naturally expect that the prelate would have been zealous in promoting a project likely to prove so beneficial to the flock committed to his charge. But, *oft expectation fails, and most oft there where most it promises.* And yet we need hardly be surprised at his opposition to Miss Nagle's projects; for though a bishop, Dr. Butler had little, if any, of the episcopal spirit. An aristocrat by birth, he was haughty in his manner, worldly in his tastes, and unaccustomed to control himself, as subsequent lamentable events fully prove. Opposition from such a source was in itself a strong indication that while Miss Nagle's work was favoured of Heaven, it met with the disapproval of the enemy of souls."

The good priest, who penned the above sharp criticism, did it apparently in order to clear the air, historically speaking. For Dr. Butler was Bishop of Cork from 1763 to 1786. This means that he was Miss Nagle's Bishop throughout the entire time that she was moulding and perfecting the wonderful work to which she sacrificially gave the finest and fullest years of her life. Archdeacon Hutch implies that she did not have much of a friend in her Bishop, a fact that may have added to her unrecorded crosses. Ireland is the Land of Destiny, and Destiny might have given her for guidance a Prelate with the blazing Apostolic fire of Archbishop John MacHale, who would fearlessly bless and back her work for Catholic education, offering no quarter, consultation, or compromise, to the vicious and conceited bigots that arrogantly strove to keep a venerable Catholic nation in enforced ignorance. Or Destiny might have given her a Prelate with the heavenly strength of Archbishop Croke of Cashel, the bold and determined democrat, who would give his life for his people, who laboured for faith, education, and traditional ideals, and whose name is unforgettably enshrined in the national scriptures; for the people do not forget their friends. But Destiny seemingly did none of these things for Miss Nagle in this instance. She accepted, and did not complain. The fact that she battled her way, mostly alone, must only serve to enhance the glory of her victory.

The final story of Bishop Butler may be now narrated, solely to illustrate the noxious spirit of the time. The reader has heard a good deal about the Penal Laws, in theory. Let us now hear of them in practice — just to show that Nano Nagle must have been sometimes near to the jaws of death. In the genealogical section on her, it has been mentioned that Bishop Butler gave up his Bishopric when he inherited the title of Lord Dunboyne, on the death of his nephew, Pierce Butler. Despite all Bishop Butler's hopes to keep the title of Lord Dunboyne alive, it died with himself in 1800, and was not revived till 1860 — in the person of Theobald Fitzwalter Butler. Bishop Butler was over 70 when he inherited the title, and his aberrations in changing his religion naturally shocked his flock, who needed pastoral care then more than ever. Nobody ever leaves the Catholic Church for intellectual reasons; and it was not believed that it was the love of truth that led Dr. Butler to exchange the Roman Pontifical for the Book of Common Prayer; for the scruples of his conscience never permitted him to officiate in a Protestant Church, and only rarely did he attend a Protestant service.

Nay more. It is said that, while the aged Lord Dunboyne was driving along a country road, a woman rushed out of a cottage, praying for a priest for somebody who was dying within. "I am a priest," said Lord Dunboyne, as he entered the cottage and heard the confession of the penitent who was *in articulo mortis*. From this moment it is said that he inwardly followed the Catholic Faith. This leads to the real point of our story.

When Lord Dunboyne died, after holding the title for fourteen years, his will was contested by his sister, Mrs. Catherine O'Brien Butler. And here enter the slippery and tortuous methods of the Penal Laws. Was Lord Dunboyne "a relapsed Papist" when he made his will? If he were "a relapsed Papist" (what a forensic title!) then his will was invalid. For anybody returning to Papistry simply could not make a will! And matters were further complicated by the fact that Lord Dunboyne had willed his properties, in County Meath, to a Catholic College — that of Maynooth, which had been established five years before he died. The case made legal history, as well as canonical history, involving the Seal of Confession. It came before Sir Michael Smith, the Master of the Rolls, in Dublin, in 1802. Its complexities brought imprisonment to an innocent priest.

God was very kind to Lord Dunboyne at the last, for He gave him the grace to send for his friend, Father Gahan, who received the aberrant Prelate back to the bosom of the

Holy Roman Church; he had confessed his sins with every sincere sign of repentance, and abandoned Protestanism. Legally, he now merited the disabling description of "a relapsed Papist."

Lord Dunboyne's sister, in contesting the will, had Father Gahan hailed before the Court. Penal ferocity was now going to lay siege to the Seal of the Confessional. Father Gahan was a celebrated Augustinian, who did wonderful work among the Catholics, in Dublin, in those grim penal days; and he was charitably filled with sorrow when his friend Dr. Butler fell. Actually, Father Gahan, and the Catholic Archbishop of Dublin — Dr. Troy, had told Lord Dunboyne not to will those estates to Maynooth College. They well knew the prevailing spirit of the law; and the time was an angry one against Catholics.

Father Gahan was painfully and repeatedly cross-examined as to what was the religion of Lord Dunboyne at his death. He demurred. He said his religion forbade him to disclose any information on this point; that his knowledge, if any, arose from a solemn and sacred confidence in the course of his ecclesiastical duty, nor was he bound by the law of the land to answer. The Master of the Rolls said there was no privilege allowed, and he overruled Father Gahan's protests. Father Gahan still refused to answer. He was held guilty of contempt of court, and was thrown into prison. The seal of the Confessional has never been broken. The might of Penal tyranny could not smash it. That which is told to one man and to God in the Sacrament of Penance is always confidentially safe. Priests have allowed themselves to be broken rather than break that holy Seal of Silence. The sainted Father Gahan was one more hero of its inviolability.

After much ado Lord Dunboyne's will was solved. Maynooth College was represented by a great Protestant lawyer of the period — the immortal John Philpot Curran. A compromise was effected, and about half of the benefit of the will was given to the College — the income being used for a higher course of ecclesiastical studies in "The *Dun-*

boyne Establishment," as it is known to this day. Brilliant scholars from this learned institution have risen to the fore-front in the ecclesiastical world in many lands, through all the years that have elapsed since the stormy period we have just described, when the professing of Catholicism cried for the courage of martyrs.

The narrative of Bishop Butler makes the guiding Providence of Mother Nagle stand out remarkably. She accomplished her work in spite of the worldly temerity that confronted her and that might have held others back.

There is yet another note in this story, on which the modern Catholic reader may meditate, while giving thanks for the blessed privileges of our own era. When the saintly Father Gahan died, in 1804, he was buried in the grave-yard attached to a Protestant Church in Dublin. For there were no Catholic Cemeteries. Penalism pursued Catholics to the grave.

I have stressed the historical setting in the foregoing narrative to exemplify the ghastly wicked temper of the thing called the law. The reader may readily imagine how tragic it would have been for the sweet and gentle Miss Nagle if she were ever dragged into the quagmire of cross-examinations, that awaited Papists who tried to outwit the foul Penal Code.

It has been already mentioned that Nano Nagle's evangelical ardour sought spiritual solace for the souls of the negroes. She had a consuming zeal for bringing the blessings of education to everybody. Irrespective of race or colour, she wished the Light, that enlighteneth every mortal, to shed its beneficent beams on the outcasts that sojourned afar, in the sorrowful valley of shadows.

Here she seems to have been animated by that spirit which the Angel of the Lord communicated to the Apostle, Philip, in the touching scene that is outlined in *The Acts of the Apostles.* On the road going down from Jerusalem, Philip, by divine inspiration, met a man of Ethiopia, an important official of great authority under Candace, the Queen of the Ethiopians. This official was returning from

Jerusalem. As he sat in his chariot he was reading the exalted words of the Prophet Isaias. The Spirit of God urged Philip to go near and join himself to the chariot. Philip ran to the Ethiopian, whom he heard reading the words of Isaias the Prophet. Proposing to him the vital question that is asked by all thorough teachers, Philip said: *Do you understand what you are reading?* Like an apt pupil the Ethiopian answered: *How can I, unless somebody should guide me?* So he asked Philip to sit beside him. The Ethiopian was reading the beautiful passage where the Prophet tells of Him, Who was led like a sheep to the slaughter; of Him Who, like a lamb silent before the shearer, opened not His mouth.

The dusky Ethiopian showed the grace of interest, and he begged Philip to inform him. Of whom was the Prophet speaking? Then Philip taught him, explaining to him the scriptural meaning, and preaching Jesus to him. They went along till they reached some water in that desert way. "See, here is water," said the Ethiopian, "and what is there to hinder me from being baptized?" "You may," said Philip, "if you believe with all your heart." Answering in those words, for which the Christian world is ever ready to lay down its life, the Ethiopian declared: *I believe that Jesus Christ is the Son of God.* Then did Philip baptize his newly-taught convert.

A corresponding love of missionary teaching must have actuated Nano Nagle when she wrote the following letter in the year 1770: —

"I am sending boys to the West Indies. Some charitable gentlemen put themselves to great expense for no other motive. These boys being well instructed, and the true religion decaying very much there by reason of those that leave this country knowing nothing of their religion, made them lay this scheme, which I hope may have the desired effect.

"All my children are brought up to be fond of instructing, as I think it lies in the power of the poor to be of more service that way than the rich. These children promise me they will take great pains with the little blacks to instruct them. Next year I will have pictures for them to give the negroes that learn the catechism. I must beg you will be so good as to buy me some dozens of the common pictures of that sort for them. I forgot to speak to Miss N. to send them to me by the first opportunity."

To represent as fairly as possible the historical setting of the period about which I am writing, I may add a note on the foregoing letter. When Cromwell and his marauders had ripped Ireland to pieces, about the middle of the seventeenth century, there was one final form of utter cruelty which was inflicted on the ruined and defenseless Catholics. The widows and orphans of Ireland were hunted down by the Cromwellian soldiers and sent as slaves to the West Indies. The unholy merchants at Bristol did an iniquitous business in exporting Irish slaves to the West Indies — men, women, and girls, who were sent to toil and die in the sugar plantations there. The Commissioners of Ireland, under the so-called Cromwellian *Commonwealth*, gave orders to those same nefarious merchants in Bristol, enabling them to go to the governors of Irish garrisons, who were to hand over to them the Irish prisoners of war they were holding. If the impoverished, found anywhere, could work, they too were seized, and so were the women of marriageable age if they had no visible means of support. The point therefore is that there were some of the children of Nano Nagle's own race already in the West Indies, awaiting her little missionaries. She was resolved to miss nothing in the scope of her charity to the poor at home or abroad.

Continuing the quotation from her letter to France written early in 1770, we read: —

"I am glad she [Miss N.] is liked by the ladies where she is. Had they known all she suffered for this foundation as well as I do, it would make them pass over many imperfections they may see in her. I am confident her intention is good. I run no risk in giving directions about her to a person of your piety and sense, as you may be confident that had I known the Fille St. Joseph was a Jansenist [the prevaling pessimistic and rigoristic heresy was Jansenism] I should never have sent her there.

"I hope you will act in regard to the young ladies as you think proper, and be sure I shall always approve of it. I must say I was desirous they should learn what was proper to teach young ladies hereafter, as there is such a general complaint both in this kingdom and in England that the children are only taught to say their prayers. As for spiritual matters, I am sure the nuns will take good care of that.

"I must beg the favour of you to present my compliments to the Superior, to your mistress and to your former one. My best wishes attend them and the young ladies. Had I the happiness of being looking at you, I should imagine you were laughing at me, to think I fatigue myself in the least. I can assure you I never thought there was the least trouble in acting in regard of the schools.

"Do not be uneasy about my health. Nobody can enjoy better health than I do, thank God. I must say I suffered a great deal in mind, which for a time I thought would have hurt my constitution, but it did not in the least. I am afraid you will all be tired of me, I may live to be so old. That is what is most to be dreaded. [Fourteen years after writing this, she died, alas, at the early age of 56]. I beg you will believe me with the sincerest esteem, your most affectionate friend,

Nano Nagle."

Her friend Father Moylan was delayed, by family mourning, in going to Paris to bring home the new Community. Her letter from Bath, in the Summer of 1770, to Miss Fitzsimons, also reveals the reverential estimation in which she held Dr. Moylan, about whom I am later giving amplified information. Miss Nagle wrote: —

"Though I did myself the pleasure of writing to you lately, yet I do so now again, as a letter I received from our worthy friend [Father Moylan] makes me acquainted with the sudden death of his sister-in-law. She was a most amiable person, and I am most sincerely sorry for her.

He says he is resolved to leave Cork in about twelve days, if the ship be ready and the wind fair. I always admired his zeal, and this is a great instance of it, to leave his afflicted family and tender father, all whose trouble for the death of his eldest son this shock revives, for if anybody ever died of grief his daughter-in-law has.

"Yet notwithstanding Fr. Moylan's fortitude to leave his friends in this situation, if his father, who is old and sickly, should fall ill, it won't be in his power to depart as soon as he expected; nor can I imagine it possible he will let him go, as he can hardly leave him out of his sight in this his urgent affliction."

Father Moylan was delayed longer than he would have wished, owing to his father's health; but, in the Spring of 1771, he set out for Paris to bring home the exclusively native Community, who were now spiritually and scholastically ready for their trying future in the Land of Doom — which the word Ireland is said to mean.

More difficulties, the reader will say. Yes. We have by now grown accustomed to the sorrowful mysteries that keep repeating themselves along Nano Nagle's path; we have become used to the presence of the Cross, as it casts the lengthening shadow of its embracing arms so affectionately over her prospering enterprises. The constitutions of the Ursuline Order enjoined that a *professed* nun should be at the head of any new foundation that was being opened.

Who was now to be at the head of these four young Irish aspirants, that were to make their profession in Cork? Would some Sister from the Ursuline Community in Paris volunteer for this duty? Not so. Previously, when Miss Nagle sought volunteers from France, and they were not forthcoming, she daringly discovered her own volunteers and sent them to be trained in France. This time she needed one French volunteer, and she was again disappointed.

But nobody can blame the French Sisters for their refusal to go crusading in Ireland, where deadly laws were biting at the blessed bonds of human nature itself. Nor is it the business of the biographer to scrutinise the motives that made them prefer the calm of their Gallic cloister to the uncertainties of the Hibernian whirlwind. God help the Nuns of France anyway, for, not many years later, the whirlwind of their own French Revolution uprooted them from their shores; though the cries of Liberty, Equality and Fraternity were bellowed on every blast in France, the Nuns had to seek these vaunted Freedoms elsewhere. And where did some of the Nuns find a home, above all places? In Ireland, in Cork, in the very Convent for which Nano Nagle had been fondly and vainly seeking a Superioress from France, a little over 20 years before! Lovingly did the Irish Sisters give their hospitality, and with gratitude did they repay the generosities which the French had accorded them at the time the Irish Community was being moulded in Paris. But I must not here linger any further on the turnings of the historical wheel of fortune, as regards the French refugee Nuns.

Dr. Moylan knew that there were many noble Irish women in French Convents, here and there; hence he turned to the Ursuline Convent at Dieppe, in Normandy, where one of his own people rallied to the call for the old land. Mother Margaret Kelly this was, a native of Ireland, who had spent most of her life in France, where she had found spiritual peace and happiness. Though she was deeply attached to France, she agreed to loan her holy services to Ireland and help to save the day for Nano Nagle, who was herself helping to save so many souls at home.

When Father Moylan served in a parish in Paris he enjoyed the favour of the Archbishop of that great diocese and was marked out for rapid ecclesiastical promotion, but he chose to leave all in order to serve his own people at home, despite the gloom and despair of the times. He was now fortunate in finding an Irish Nun in France, who would oblige him by putting Ireland first, as he himself had done. For the time being, Mother Kelly would take charge of the four young Irish Nuns, till the time came when one of themselves should be qualified to head the new foundation in Cork.

On the way, Dr. Moylan and his charges stopped at the Carmelite Convent of Saint Denis to visit the Princess Louise, daughter of King Louis the Fifteenth of France. The Princess was a novice in that Convent — which by the way was almost exclusively Irish.   Dr. Plunkett who was then a Professor in the Irish College in Paris, and later Bishop of Meath, describes this Carmelite Convent which the devout daughter of the reckless King Louis had selected: "The Superior of the Convent, the mistress of novices, in a word the whole *ètat major* are Irishwomen, and such as do honour to Ireland by their virtue, understanding, and prudence."   It was the King's custom to visit his daughter frequently there, and on one occasion he asked each Nun what her family name was.   They were all Irish, and the merry King Louis amused them all, as he humorously observed: "Here I am in the midst of my Irish Guards!" We have already seen how many gallant Irish officers served him well in his armies.   The King's daughter was specially in the care of two Irish Nuns, Mother Creagh, the Prioress, and Sister MacMahon. Mother Creagh's father was a Limerick gentleman who was an official of the Stuart Kings in the Palace of St. Germains, wherein we have already traced the prominence of the Nagles.   Sister MacMahon was the daughter of an Irish officer in the service of France: she was a lady of great holiness and of perfect manners, and was given the task of converting the French King's daughter into the ideal Carmelite Nun.   So beautifully was this done that the Royal Princess extended her everlasting affection to her Irish teacher.

We see therefore why Dr. Moylan and his company were so graciously and affectionately welcomed by Princess Louise, who said she wished she had *their* vocation. As she bade adieu to the young teachers, she encouraged them still further in their worthy life by saying that "she would be glad to be at the feet of an Ursuline in Heaven." The little party stealthily sailed from Havre, and great must have been the gratitude of each, when Dr. Moylan succeeded in smuggling them into the Cove of Cork, on the Feast of the Ascension of Our Lord, May 9th, 1771.

It was not the fair and resurrected Ireland of today that met their eyes. The Cove of Cork, later called Queenstown, and now familiar on the Irish map as Cobh [Cove], was then but a mere clump of huts, where a few fishermen eked out a wretched existence. No graceful Gothic Cathedral lifted its pinnacles of piercing piety to the Irish sky, as in our time. No church bells pealed; for penal proclamations silenced them. In our own day we hear people sometimes quoting the emotional words of the returned exile: *And doesn't old Cove look charming there?* Now, yes. In our own happier era I have entered the Harbor of Cove in Summer days when all looked a real delight; I have entered it too at sunset, when the lights twinkled from the terraces, and the twilight wrapping the hills glowed in a haunting revelation. But not so charming was Cove at the period of which we are writing.

No doubt, Dawn on the Hills of Ireland must ever be reckoned a dream divine, at any time. But evil men, by the prolonged and vengeful Penal Code, had left scars, and sores, and degradation, imprinted on the very face of the countryside. A few healing concessions may by this time have been made to the wealthier Catholics, but the *poor* Catholics remained absolutely unthought of, in their affliction and subjection. Not till the nineteenth century did the wrongs of the Irish poor begin to be righted. Miss Nagle was a century ahead in her care and thought of the lowly and neglected. In her God-given *Insight* she was ahead of others in seeing that the penal scheme, so abortive and sinister, was now about to collapse in final failure. She knew that nothing violent ever lasts. Filled with sublime hope therefore she welcomed and greeted her newly-arrived Community. She was enlivened by the same secure hope that animated a Christian Scribe of Ireland, six hundred years before, when he wrote in one of our venerated extant treasures, *The Book of Leinster: "The Destiny of our virgin Erin is at all times greater than man can tell."*

Nano Nagle was bringing spiritual and educational happiness to her people, as certain as the sunrise — with which they hopefully loved to emblazon their national banner.

CHAPTER 10

NANO NAGLE TRIUMPHS OVER THE FORCES OF REPRESSION, SUPPRESSION AND OPPRESSION

THE reigning demigods of the Cork Corporation decided to let slip the dogs of war on Nano Nagle and her newly arrived Nuns. A superabundance of cursed Penal processes, and entrapping enactments, gave them a wide choice of charges wherewith to harass the daring virgins, who were now relighting the vestal fire of Catholic Education under the very eyes of the civic fathers. The Cork Corporation of 1770 was very different from the Corporation of 1920 — when Ireland was on the eve of renewed nationhood, and the Lord Mayor of the City, Terence Mac-Swiney, focussed the sympathetic eyes of the world on Ireland by gallantly giving his life, after a period of two and a half breathless months on hunger-strike, to defend those ancient principles of Freedom which he demanded for himself and his people. Brave unto death, Lord Mayor Mac-Swiney denounced cowardice as want of Faith in God.

Faith in God was the key to Nano Nagle's bravery, and cowardice was entirely absent from her composition. Celestial courage was her characteristic. Even if the Cork Corporation were exclusively Protestant, and even if it were infected by a horrible hatred of the Catholics, she was not going to quail. Like all Corporations, at all times, these municipal magnates were appointed to give good government to the city. This they forgot. Ruffianism became rampant. Chicanery came in. The lights went out. But what did it matter to the Cork Corporation, so long as their own personal position and private interest remained immune? If the air were well seasoned with bigotry, so much the better for the sleek civic satraps, so much the worse for the pauperized Papists.

Strangely enough, the lofty aldermen were jealous of some few of those despised Papists. Despite disabilities, some of the Catholic tradesmen and provision merchants were rising to considerable success, wealth and importance; by their patient industry they were rivalling some of the privileged pets of Protestantism. This was evident, and annoying.

In numbers too, far from being extirpated, the Catholics of the city outnumbered the Protestants. Not long after Nano Nagle was born, a census showed there were about three thousand Protestant families, and about six thousand Catholic families, in the City of Cork. Strangely, too, the Faith of our Fathers was growing, in spite of the plethora of Penal preventions.

About 1703, there were four *registered* priests in the City of Cork; there must have been many who were unregistered. In 1729, the Catholics of Cork did a most audacious thing — at a most ruthless hour of the Penal hurricane. They built two Chapels, one in the North of the City, one in the South. Quite capacious and substantial structures they were, and frequented by considerable congregations. A writer, who saw them, will oblige us with a description, which is a tribute to the people's Roman and Petrine endurance: —

"One Sunday morning I stepped into one of their mass houses, and a spacious one it was. The priest had just finished the celebration of Mass. There were several elegant carriages standing before the door when I entered, and a prodigious crowd of people in the street — as motley an assemblage of human creatures as I have ever seen."

Like the old lady who kept repeating that she had a horror of spiders and the Pope, the Cork Corporation gave vent to a few screams at the uneradicated and restored evidences of the Vatican in their midst. They thought the laws by now should have driven Papists to the catacombs, utterly underground, but here they were again at the surface; Papists in their suburbs and in the very hub of their little universe.

The women who were going to teach Popery must be checked. No stately courtesy or chivalric magnanimity towards ladies could make the magistrates falter. There was a Statute suitable to the occasion. It was the Ninth of William the Third, Chapter 1, Section 8. It bound the Mayor and the magistrates to send the Nuns to prison, as a preliminary to transporting them, and it bound them to abolish the Convent. If the Mayor and his magistrates failed to carry out the law they could be fined 500 dollars each, and rendered incapable of ever being Justices of the Peace again.

Whether through bigotry, or alarm, or both, the Corporation officials convoked a Court of *D'oyer Hundred,* and its business was to expel the Nuns. Criminal trials could be held under the writ of *oyer and terminer*: the Old French words meaning to *hear* and *determine.* The word *oyez* still lingers in our courts; and the division of a County, called the *hundred,* is still in use in the State of Delaware.

Our historical grief it is that no verbatim record remains of the aldermen's portentous pondering. Archdeacon Hutch quizzically comments that we may assume the speeches were as lucid in argument, and as finished in point of rhetoric as aldermen's speeches usually are. Anyway the Penal Laws prevented any Catholic from belonging to the Corporation, so the Protestant magistrates had the field all to themselves. They decided, with one dissenting voice, that Miss Nagle's Convent should cease to exist. But the dissenter saved the day. It is a blessing of God to find in any extravagantly solemn public body a man with a sane sense of humour. Such a man on this occasion was Alderman Francis Carleton. He had all the characteristics that we praise so much in our era. He was broadminded, fair, liberal, non-persecuting, and tolerant. He had a happy faculty for healthy ridicule, and he was gifted with the saving grace of a medicinal humour.

The Irish well know how to kill a thing with fun. They are amongst the world's most merciless satirists and humorists. As Padraic Pearse, the founding father of the modern Irish Nation, expressed it, laughter is the crowning grace of heroes. With heroic laughter did Alderman Carleton alight upon the pomposity of his fellows, who sat in ominous judgement upon a few virtuous, peaceful, and well-bred ladies. He said that the mighty Protestant Constitution could not possibly be reeling or tottering from the fact that a few pious women had decided to live under one roof in order "to teach poor children, drink tea, and say their prayers." He poked fun at their false alarms in thinking that the Pope might steal in person upon the entrenched Protestants and pour fire and brimstone on the Orange Ascendancy. Indeed, when we look back on the disturbances of the eighteenth and nineteenth centuries, we realise that the Popes had plenty of sorrows and troubles of their own: Pius the Sixth was a prisoner of the French; Pius the Seventh was a prisoner of Napoleon; Pius the Ninth, in protest against the open robbery of the Papal States, became the prisoner of the Vatican.

There were many salient points that Alderman Carleton could raise against the repressive agenda of his comrades, as he tried to put them at ease by banter and badinage. He could point out that the Penal Laws were already over 70 years in force and that they had failed to crush the Catholics. He could point out that the Statute of King William the Third was now an outmoded piece of legal vengeance, for here were the Catholics in their midst in greater numbers than ever. Why not decently admit that the Catholics had won in the shocking contest against legalistic tyranny? Furthermore these women would prove themselves good citizens by their campaign of social and educational reformation. And why not be business-like, and keep in Cork the money that would be otherwise spent in education in France? For the Catholics would always find a means of circumventing statutory condemnation of their Creed. Sooner or later the coterie of ruling Protestants would have to cry halt to this coded savagery against their Catholic fellow-citizens. The sooner the better. These women would hurt none. They would help all. Was it not laughable for grown men to be scared of a few girls? And so on.

Luckily for Nano Nagle the Corporation surrendered to the sanity of one just man, who was sixty years ahead of his time in showing that Catholics should be set free. But do not think that civic tolerance saved Nano Nagle and her Nuns from living in constant terror of the Penal Laws. She herself was prudence personified in her wary goings-out and comings-in. Her work came first and foremost, and, in order to devote all her energies to it, she was dove-like in her peaceful procedure. Needless controversies and clashes are a physical and mental tax, and merely leave respective rivals the wiser in their own conceit.

The reader may like to know how the Catholics generally fared in Ireland at the year of which we are writing. There was a corrupt Parliament sitting in Dublin. Bad as this was, it was even suspended for fourteen months by the Viceroy. The Viceroy was Lord Townshend, one of the most unscrupulous rulers that ever tried to govern Ireland. He was so attacked that he had to resign in 1772. One Catholic concession was wrung from his regime. An Act allowed a Catholic to get a long lease of fifty acres of bog-land, which had to be at least four feet deep, and a mile away from the nearest market town! The tenant could fertilise this sodden and boggy waste at his own expense. If it were too quagmirish to keep up the four walls of a hut, the tenant could lease half an acre of dry land that might stand a structure. This was the concessionary limit to which the overmastering oligarchs would go. To which strange small mercy the Catholic peasant no doubt responded with a proverbially fervent *Glory be to God.* Within a few years, the Catholic merchants, who were beginning to do well on the unprohibited provision trade, received a serious set-back. England passed the Embargo Act which prevented the exporting of salt meat or similar provisions, so as to keep supplies from going to the warring American Colonists on the one hand, and to make food cheap for the British Army on the other. Such were the ups and downs of the Irish Catholics in their stride towards victory.

Since Cork is the constant scene of Miss Nagle's work, I add a few historical details on this city — so pleasantly situated by the River Lee. Cork is said to have grown up round a monastery founded by Saint Finnbarr in the sixth century. Today, as a town with a flourishing University College, its motto is summarised as: *where Finnbarr taught let Munster learn.* Cork has played many an important part in Ireland's tumultuous story. It was sacked by the Danes and burnt by the Black-and-Tans. It was the capital wherein the McCarthys, one of the oldest and most noted Irish families, held ancient sway, for they were the Lords of Desmond. After King Henry the Second of England tried to take possession of Ireland in the twelfth century, Cork became a storm centre between the invaders and the invaded. The English Settlers tried to hold the city against the native Irish, age after age. The Settlers had a hard job keeping an eye on the alarums and excursions of the unyielding Irish.

The ancient chronicler, Holinshed, tells us that the English, who occupied Cork, had "to watch their gates hourlie, at meals, from sun to sun, nor suffer anie stranger to enter the citie with his weapon, but the same to leave at a lodge appointed." Another chronicler, Camden, adds that the city was "so beset by rebellious neighbors as to require as constant a watch as if continually besieged."

Nearly three hundred years before Nano Nagle's day, Perkin Warbeck landed in Cork and started his rebellion against King Henry VII of England. The Mayor of Cork was hanged for supporting the Pretender Warbeck. When King John visited Ireland, in 1210, Cork was one of the twelve counties which he formed — his power being recognized therein. In the time of Cromwell, 1649, Cork city only escaped a general massacre of the inhabitants by surrendering to the Puritans the moment Oliver himself arrived at its walls, not on one of his visits but on one of his visitations. It is said that Cromwell ordered the bells of

Cork to be melted for his war effort, saying that "since gunpowder was invented by a priest" he thought "the best use for bells would be to promote them into cannons."

In 1690 Cork went through another fierce struggle in the war between two Kings of England, James II and William of Orange. John Churchill, who became the first Duke of Marlborough, besieged Cork and won it for William after a deadly contest. The reader will see why so many ancient buildings were ruined after the repeated raids of rivals, after recurring rebellions, wars, and insurrections. Memory alone preserves some of Cork's old structures. Its two Cathedrals and its University College are of the nineteenth century. And Shandon Church only dates from 1725 — the fane that is unforgotten, owing to Father Prout's lyrical ecstasies on *The Bells of Shandon.* Blackrock Castle marks the place from which William Penn set out for America. In her journal, Queen Victoria paid her praise to the comely delights of Cork Harbour which is girt with green hills.

This is but a faint recital of the storied part played in Irish History by the centuried city of Cork. It had witnessed the physical battles of knights and mercenaries. In our narrative the city is the constant locale for the moral battles waged by Nano Nagle; here she wrought lasting victory for Catholic Education. Here, with undeviating devotion she toiled, day in, day out, morning, noon, and night, for the consecrated cause to which she had decreed her life from her early twenties, until Death, which was for her but the kiss of the Lord, drew her to the City of God.

Documentary evidence will emphasize Nano Nagle's daring and original methods. It has been already revealed that she did not consult the Protestant authorities about founding her Schools or her Convent. Full well she knew that she would be refused. So she told nobody. Not even her own family. By subtle secrecy she achieved her objective; and wondering eyes suddenly met with her schools, her teachers, her Nuns, already in action as living realities.

God alone she consulted on the initiation of her work and on its manifestation to men.

To show how different she was, I introduce a remarkable letter from another source. This letter was written twelve years after Miss Nagle had so meritoriously defied an evil law by founding a Convent in Cork. This letter was written by a Catholic Bishop to a Protestant Bishop. The writer was Doctor Plunket, to whom I have already referred in his scholastic connection with France. He was now Catholic Bishop of Meath. The year is 1783, a year before Nano Nagle died. Bishop Plunket wished to get a licence for opening a Catholic School in his own diocese. For this he had to get the permission of the Protestant Bishop of the same diocese. The approach in such cases almost implied the use of *Blarney*. There were cases where it might entail abasement and grovelling to win concessions from the condescending. All cases demanded tact, diplomacy, with the wisdom of the serpent breathing through the dove of simplicity. The social and ecclesiastical gulf that separated the Catholic Bishop from the Protestant Bishop in those days was no mere matter of remote or distant differences. It was not a hermeneutical question of Consubstantiation, Impanation, or the Parousia, that caused current agitation. It was a ready question of a vital thing called a Catholic School, which was sacred as life-blood to Catholicism, which was anathema to contemporary Protestantism, and denied thereby.

The Protestant Bishop was a powerful official among the privileged minority. At his back were the omnipotent forces of Government and Landlordism. His control extended to the utterly unprivileged majority, the Catholics, who were called upon to pay extorted contributions to his church, inside the door of which they could not in conscience put their foot. The Protestant Bishops' flocks were well-to-do. The Protestant Ministers thrived on the money wrung largely from the Catholics who were almost already drained of resources by trying to pay unjust and killing rents to the landlord. Sometimes a man owned almost an entire town, and his fat rent-roll enabled him to lord it over his subdued tenantry. It enabled him to ride with his retinues in great state to his Protestant Church, which seemed a sort of theological annexe or justifying append-age to his mansion. The landlord buttressed the Protestant Church, and the Protestant Church buttressed the land-lord. The surrounding serfs buttressed both with money. These serfs in the main were Catholics: deeply attached to their religion, they were forced to greet their God generally within mean muddy edifices that matched the dilapidation and degradation of their own unsightly dwellings. The Protestant Churches were fine structures, and their Min-isters looked correspondingly prosperous. The Catholic priests barely kept body and soul together as they strove to serve their loyal people unto the last.

It was only as late as 1869 that this wretched situation was amended and remedied by a great and good English-man, William Ewart Gladstone. He saw that the privileged position of the Protestant Church in Ireland inflicted in-justice on an entire nation. He decided that it must be dis-established for the common good. After a protracted and bitter fight the wise and enlightened Prime Minister Glad-stone succeeded, and henceforth the Irish Catholics were spared the spectacle of an endowed and State-established Church in their midst, to which they had been compelled to contribute at the point of the sword, by violent collectors, by soldiers and police.

The letter in which Bishop Plunket, the Catholic Bishop of Meath, beseeches the Protestant Bishop for legal per-mission to open a Catholic School, is dated July 10, 1783. It runs as follows: —

"My Lord,
    The Roman Catholics of the diocese of Meath wish to avail themselves of the indulgence of the legisla-ture, which, by a late Act, allows under certain re-strictions, persons of their persuasion to instruct youth in this kingdom.

I am called upon by them humbly to request your Lordship will be pleased to grant licence necessary for that purpose. A school so situated as to be under the eye of their ecclesiastical superior, would, they assure me have a particular claim to their confidence; be better calculated than any other in this district could be to answer the end of such an institution; and is what they earnestly desire.

Concerned as they are, that they address themselves to a prelate of a liberal and enlightened mind, they doubt not but your Lordship will, on this occasion, concur with the wisdom and humanity of Parliament in diminishing one of the most painful grievances they have laboured under for a series of years. To so discerning an encourager of everything that tends to promote public and private happiness in this neigh-bourhood, I need not observe that a numerous and respectable school, authorized by the law of the land, having your Lordship's sanction, would, by attracting strangers, by diffusing civilization, and by giving ad-ditional employment to industry, be productive of substantial advantage to Navan.

On my part no attention should be wanting to guard against abuses, which, if I could not prevent, I should be the first to complain of. I should make it a capital object of my care that the Roman Catholic youth of this diocese should be taught to revere the civil con-stitution of their country; and that their affections should not be estranged from it by any unfriendly principles whatever.

No steps have I taken to forward this business, nor shall, until acquainted with your Lordship's inten-tions.

May I then presume to hope, my Lord, that you will grant to one Roman Catholic, or more, if necessary, qualified as the law prescribes, a licence for teaching in Navan. A line on this subject from your Lordship, with which I beg I may be honoured, shall regulate my conduct.

In the meantime, it is with particular satisfaction, I embrace this opportunity of assuring you, that I am, with great respect, my Lord, your Lordship's most obedient and humble servant,

P. J. Plunket."

The reply of the Protestant Bishop is illuminating. It was sent from Dublin, two weeks later. Here it is: —
"Sir,

Upon my return to town a few days ago from the county of Wexford, I received the favour of your letter, and I must beg leave to postpone giving you an answer to the application which you have made to me, until I shall have some conversation with you upon the subject, which I shall be particularly glad to have, as it will give me an opportunity of becoming acquainted with you — a circumstance which I am certain (from your general character) will always give me pleasure.

I am, Sir, your most obedient and very humble servant,

H. MEATH."

We do not know what happened after that. We do know that a request was not automatically followed by a permit. We do know that, as late as 1814, a request made in circumstances similar to the above, was not acceded to, and a license was refused because the schoolmaster in question loved his country so much that his reputation for patriotism was distasteful to the consulted powers.

All the more astonishing therefore was Nano Nagle, who, as she confesses, asked nobody for a licence. She observed that the Catholic Bishop, of her own diocese of Cork, said he would be better pleased if she had the consent of the Protestants. But what official Protestants gen-

erally thought of Catholic Education can be gathered
from the following shocking proclamation, dated about
thirty years before Miss Nagle set up her Catholic Schools:

"George II, by grace of God, of Great Britain,
France and Ireland King, Defender of the Faith.

Forasmuch as we have received information by the
petition of the Lord Primate, Lord Chancellor, Archbishops, noblemen, bishops, judges, gentry, and
clergy of our Kingdom of Ireland, that in many parts
of the said Kingdom there are great tracts of land
almost entirely inhabited by Papists, who are kept
by their clergy in great ignorance of the true religion,
and bred up in great disaffection to the Government;
that the erection of English Protestant Schools in
those places is absolutely necessary for their conversion."

Another point arises. Nano Nagle had already practically finished all her good work at the time that Bishop
Plunket besought the license to which I have referred.
Bishop Plunket had the advantage of an Act of Parliament
which was giving some relief to Catholics at the time he
wrote. It had just then been passed. It allowed Catholics a
little liberty in buying and selling land. The act forbidding
the celebration of Mass was repealed. So was the act which
ordered priests to register. So also was the act which had
ordered Catholic Bishops where, and where not, they could
reside. Catholics were now allowed to live in Limerick
and Galway. Catholic schoolmasters were permitted to
teach — under careful conditions as shown above. Catholics could become guardians of children. Previously,
Catholics were presumed guilty of all robberies committed
in the country. By the new act of Relief they were not
so presumed. And a Catholic could now own a horse
which was valued for more than 25 dollars: previously
a Catholic could only own a horse which was worth less, or
perhaps *worthless*.

To their eternal credit, at this time, a patriotic group of Protestants let the world know of their pleasure at the modification of the laws against their Catholic neighbors. At the old home of Hugh O'Neill, in Ulster, they met. Led by the sublime soul, Henry Grattan, they passed the following resolution in the year 1782:—

> "As men and Irishmen, as Christians and Protestants, we rejoice in the relaxation of the penal laws against our Roman Catholic fellow-subjects; and we conceive the measure to be fraught with the happiest consequences to the union, and prosperity to the inhabitants of Ireland."

But, by the time these few privileges were given to Catholics, Nano Nagle had well-nigh completed the grand work of her life and placed it on a permanent basis. She, who strove exclusively in the shadows, was spared to see signs of the sunshine. She weathered the hampering and harassing of the old revengeful code which classed her worthy acts as illegal. She survived long enough to see her divinely favoured accomplishment passing from illegality to legality. The God of battles could now cite her in those words taken from the tenth chapter of The Acts of the Apostles: "Thy prayers and thy alms are come up for a memorial before God."

Educationally lost, her people had been like sheep without a shepherd when snow shuts out the sky. I may here apply to Miss Nagle the chaste words of the inspiring Catholic poet, Alice Meynell: "*She walks the lady of my delight, a Shepherdess of Sheep.*" She had gathered the white flocks of the young innocent ones unto her, and she was not going to lose hold of them.

CHAPTER 11

-NANO NAGLE AND THE POOR: SHE FOUNDS THE PRESENTATION SISTERS

ALL continued to go well with Nano Nagle. Her Ursuline Nuns moved into the habitation, which she had prepared for them, on the 18th of September, 1771. An act of agreement between herself and the Nuns was duly concluded. By her own wish the Convent was placed under the protection of powerful patronage; under that of the Blessed Virgin Mary, the Mother of us all, and under that of Saint Joseph, the Patron of the Universal Church. Mass was said and the schools were opened, but the Nuns dare not yet wear the religious habit. Only eight years after they arrived in Cork did they dare to do so. By appearing in secular dress they hoped to make their schools seem secular schools. The Statute, under which the Cork Corporation could have expelled them, used the term "religious persons." As "religious persons" the Nuns were in constant danger of being prosecuted. The term of condemnation sounds strange!

When the Community resolved to wear the habit of their Order, even Nano Nagle herself was taken aback. In all ways she walked circumspectly, for the days were evil. She remonstrated with them for their rashness, even though they had only taken a lesson from herself in openly resisting malicious laws! Imagine having to worry in the Island of Saint Patrick about wearing a religious dress. The Nuns attempted the continual wearing of the habit. They pleaded to Miss Nagle that the habit even helped them to bear with the cold weather! She wittily hinted that Father Moylan might make it hot for them. When Father Moylan came upon the scene, and saw them wearing their habits, he naturally was amazed at their heavenly imprudence, for even the harmless habit of a Sister might call down a widespread persecution. He urged them to go slowly, but he agreed to their extra cautious use of the habit. The Lord, Who decides wherewith we shall be clothed, Who robes with inimitable plumage the birds of the air, and Who clothes the lilies of the field, saw to it that the Ursulines were not waylaid in their holy habits. From that time on they wore them, "and carried on their religious ceremonies with as much solemnity as if they had been sanctioned by the laws."

A *Chapter* was held in 1775, and the Convent was now so fully organized that the Irish Nun from France, Mother Margaret Kelly, having completed her four-year task of being guardian angel to the rising Community, returned to her adopted land. To succeed her as Superioress, the Sisters elected Mother Augustine Coppinger, who had left her own beautiful family estate, near Cork, to teach the Catholic children of her own same city. The Ursulines were on the high road to lasting success in Ireland. The efforts of one wonderful woman, Nano Nagle, had started them and maintained them. If she had done nothing else but this, she would still stand out luminously on History's page, still deserve the reverence and benediction of the entire English-speaking world; for endless have been the fruits of the work done by her Ursuline friends. But great are the other deeds of Nano Nagle that yet await our exposition. We marvel as they unfold.

The year 1775 is an apt date for American readers to remember, for it is proudly connected with the Independence of these United States. It was also the year when Nano Nagle started a tremendous new work in Ireland, a work that was duly extended to the United States about 80 years afterwards. Yonder in London her great-souled cousin, Burke, was making the year 1775 memorable also: in the English Parliament he made the rafters ring with matchless passages that have passed into the abiding treasure-house of the world's greatest literature, as he passionately championed the cause of the American Colonists.

Nano Nagle, the active and affectionate lady of grace in the City of Cork, was now 47. To the poor she turned her loving eyes more earnestly and more thoroughly than ever. Her saintly and gifted Ursulines were admittedly doing wonderful work. For Nano Nagle, however, there was yet another educational world to conquer. That educational world pertained exclusively to the poor. That world, she decided, must have a special religious society attending wholly to its care. She was not a woman of words, but of deeds, and forthwith she took steps to supply the needs of the hapless poor. Her heart was on fire for them. There was genius in her quiet simplicity as she devised ways and means of serving them. She was saving her own soul, but she was also saving the souls of countless others. To a true Catholic there is no limit to which personal sanctity and charity may not go. Higher and higher Nano Nagle went, till after her profitable life she reached the Face of God in the world of the Blest. Only nine more years of her productive life now remained, and yet we find it difficult to estimate justly all the lasting good that she accomplished during that final short span. The poor, the poor! She yearned to reform them, and make them spiritually and temporally happy in the Grace of God. That was her undying aim. As the trusted friend of the orphan, the outcast, and the destitute, she freely spent herself without rest.

Her Ursuline Convent had fructified and become stabilized. Its members increased, and so did their labours. They instructed children of all descriptions; all who came to them were refreshed by their care. But there were still further large fringes of society that Nano Nagle was resolved to reach. By their rule the Ursulines were enclosed. They could not reach the sick and the poor beyond their walls, nor could they go to instruct the poor at home. These were the extra works that Nano Nagle devoutly wished to be done, corporal and spiritual works of mercy as commended and commanded by our Redeemer.

Being a wise and thoughtful woman she knew that her

Ursulines could not reach out to any work beyond the scope of their rule. Rules are rules, and no order can exist without them. Only by the scrupulous keeping of rules can any order survive. The Ursulines kept to theirs; they worked splendidly within their precise sphere, and Nano Nagle was satisfied. But she was not satisfied on the question of the unreached and unattended poor, whom she, in her distinct way, vowed to reinvest with moral and social dignity and decency.

In the meantime she continued to live in a small house in Douglas Street, Cork. In this humble house she had first received her Ursulines when they arrived home from France. They had now moved to the large and spacious dwelling which she had constructed for them at her own expense. They tried to induce her to live there with them, but quietly she declined, and humbly she lived on in the original temporary dwelling. Daily she went forth to supervise, and serve, and teach in her poor schools. While she was out on her consecrated errands, the Ursulines often removed her bed to an appropriate apartment in their capacious dwelling. They would have felt blessed to dwell under the same roof, with a saint of God. But she went her heavenly way in her own small house, where a great work was soon to be born. She naturally would visit her Ursulines, and enjoy recreation with them; every Saturday evening she used to teach Christian Doctrine to their young ladies. But her heart was more than ever pouring out love to the poor: these she must and will instruct.

Towards the close of the year 1775, therefore, she laid the foundation of the worthy and venerable Presentation Order. From the very birth of the Christian Church there have been holy women, ready by a myriad means, to serve the Lord of Love. They stood by Him on the Hill of Calvary, faithful unto the last, when no man remained thereat, except John — the dreaming poet, beloved, the Saint of God's love. The tireless Saint Paul says: *"Help those women who have laboured with me in the*

Gospel." Even in the dark night of eighteenth-century Ireland, Nano Nagle found no difficulty in gathering round her some of those holy women of her Isle, who longed right then to labour for the Gospel among God's poor.

Miss Nagle had already gone to vast expense in building a Convent for the Ursulines. It seems miraculous that she still had enough of her own money left to endow an adequate building for her new Community. The Divine Architect of the Universe must have again blessed her generously, for, in this same year, 1775, she was able to start her new building. Here at last was to be brought to fullest reality her mind's dearest dream; here was her hope, her home, her treasure; for this she had prayed and yearned; here she would be Christ's hostess to the homeless, and here at last she would breathe forth her loving soul to the good God, Who had enabled her to do so much in so little time. In the parliament of men neither she nor her good works had any legal existence. But what of it now? Her hopes were set beneath the Heart of Christ, and though her years were advancing, she *was* successfully winning the hearts of all the people through the Holy Spirit of Enlightenment.

In addition to her need of walking cautiously amidst the circumscribing laws, she also had to go with gossamer tread through the delicate maze of what we call human feelings. Her pious resolve was to wipe away all tears from the eyes of the poor, to soothe their sorrow, to ease their children in their crying and their pain. The carrying out of her good intention caused poignant sorrow to herself. We cannot escape being confronted with human feelings till we finally rest with Him who reigns as Alpha and Omega in the harmony of the Heavenly Jerusalem. Nano Nagle started to build her new foundation quite close to the Ursuline Convent, which she had erected but a few short years before. This was an occasion where even the human feelings of her friends played an unexpected part in worrying her. There is plenty of room in this marred world for every kind of good work. How

much room in each case? That is the question on which
finite mortals may as neighbours disagree.

Miss Nagle's new Convent was arising in such close
proximity to that of her Ursulines that the fact became
a source of uneasiness to them. Their human feelings are
understandable. Two good works may be so closely located that *this* may injure *that*. The Ursulines could not
regard their work as being yet fully settled and secure.
Would Miss Nagle's interest be now divided? Hitherto
they received her whole care. Would even half her interest sufficiently assure their future? Reflecting on such
concerns, they felt that the serenity of their tenure was
disturbed by misgivings. Genuinely feeling that the interests of their existence were seriously involved, they decided to communicate their concern to Father Moylan,
who had been their sincere Raphael, and protector, from
the inception of this enterprise. In all things he was a
fair and faithful friend to them and to Miss Nagle. To
adjudicate and arbitrate on this delicate proposition he
required surpassing wisdom. But such are the decisions
that men are heartbreakingly called to make, even in the
holiest and most peaceful spheres. From the text it has
already appeared that Father Moylan was instinctively
sympathetic to everything connected with the Ursuline
cause. And Miss Nagle was obviously indebted to him
for his having so gallantly shepherded her Ursulines home
to safety.

He now took a definite view on this agitating matter.
He automatically sympathized with what he considered
the justifiable anxieties of his favourite Ursulines. It was
nothing new to Nano Nagle to meet with disappointments,
either from within the household, or from without. Her
self-denial, humility and patience are already constantly
evident to the reader. If, at times, her cup was overflowing, she consoled herself by reflecting that the cup of her
Redeemer had been likewise. She had pledged herself to
taste of His Chalice, and of His alone. Father Moylan
made friendly but firm remonstrances to her. She re-

mained equally friendly and firm in her intention. Clearly a crisis was evolving.

It was now many years since she decided to dedicate herself solely to the Christian instruction of the poor. She had not changed. She would not change. Her heart and soul were unalterably set in making a new foundation, exclusively adapted to the needs of teaching the unprivileged. She felt the cry of the Crusaders that "God wills it." No arguments could prevail upon her. Even the persuasion of her dearest friends could not turn her aside. When she made up her mind she was deeply definite and strong. Be her friends sweet or severe in admonishing her, she recked not of their displeasure at her purpose, either way. Should she please the Creator or the creature? She had long ago pledged herself to please her Creator. Should she serve the privileged or the unprivileged? She had long ago pledged herself to serve the unprivileged. The former were generally sure of attention; the latter might be forgotten. She was adamantly resolved that they must not be forgotten — those neglected ones that hover helplessly in the vague periphery of human society, untaught and unfed, through no fault of their own. This unfortunate fringe was as sacred to her as the fortunate.

She therefore went on apace with the construction of her newly-commenced Convent. In the little old and ascetical dwelling which had been destined to cradle two different communities, she continued to pray and struggle during those days of eventful transition. To form the nucleus of her salutary Society for the instruction of God's poor, she chose from among her self-sacrificing associates two devout ladies who were eager to give their time, their toil, and their lives, to the heavenly cause that animated her, and which animated them with comparable zeal. In their character they evinced every mark that foretold success in the onerous life that awaited them.

But when would her pathway be untroubled? Father Moylan thought he had left her assenting to withdrawal. But Miss Nagle's motto in all things was *Excelsior*. Higher up had gone her new walls. Father Moylan became painfully aware of the fact. She was not retreating but advancing. It was an awkward moment for him, and it invoked his direct intervention. He came upon the building-ground and felt driven to tell her expressly how much he disapproved of her defiant endeavour. With absolute respect she listened to all he felt impelled to say. She was meek, modest, and calm at his sentence. Silence is indeed an unanswerable answer. Father Moylan was proceeding to extremes: he said he would order the workmen to throw down those walls they had just put up. He told her to betake herself and her new companions to the other end of the city. There she would be sufficiently separated from his cherished Ursulines, to whom he felt her adjoining edifice was an encroachment on their rights.

It was now her turn to speak. She gently said she would comply with his wishes. She would even go further away than the other end of the city. Mildly she agreed in every detail. But Miss Nagle's assent to his request was as disarming as her previous declining. She sweetly added that if she were only displeasing him and the Ursulines, and that if she must consequently be banished from the place which she loved so dearly, then she would never try to establish her new work in Cork, but rather would she go to some other part of Ireland, where she would be, not oppressed but encouraged, in her efforts for the poor, who absorbed her whole heart and soul.

Her heavenly humility must have melted Father Moylan. True, he had a perfectly jurisdictional and canonical right as Parish Priest of Saint Finnbar's to question or investigate her undertakings, especially if he thought that her recent actions would in any way affect the interests of Religion adversely. As pastor he had his rights and obligations. On the other hand Miss Nagle, as a disciple of Christ, humbly felt that, if she were not received in one city, she was free to enjoy the evangelical privilege of going to work in another. Luckily for all, the pastor did not wish her to shake the dust of Cork off her shoes. He made up his mind he must not lose the disciple, whatsoever the delicacies of the situation might enjoin, for he knew in his heart that she was a treasure to his own town, a destined treasure to his race, and to humanity at large. Had he not all along declared that she was guided by the Spirit of God? Did not the increasing volume of her unselfish work now betoken the mark of the Most High? So he permitted her to proceed with her charitable designs. He decided that there would still be room enough for all the good works they were all sincerely trying to do. Later that year, 1775, Father Moylan was made Bishop of Kerry, and nobody in Cork missed him more than his friend Nano Nagle.

The Dove of Peace folded His wings over the walls of contention, and a blessed silence brought the complication to an end. Saint Joseph, the Carpenter, must have appreciated Miss Nagle, for he quickly gifted her walls with a roof, and her new Convent was appropriately opened on Christmas Day, 1777.

Again her early associates belong to the Catholic History of Ireland, hence their names merit mention. First there were Miss Fuohy and Miss Elizabeth Burke. They were natives of the City of Cork, and were appropriately endowed with the gifts and graces needed for their new calling. Miss Nagle, being a perfectionist on the subject of Catholic Education, went to endless pains and expense to see that these young ladies were thoroughly trained for teaching. She liked to do all things well. On January 25, 1775, she wrote another chapter of her meritorious history when she led her companions to join her in her small house, which was simple as the house of Bethlehem; her humble house from which she had launched her Ursulines to greater developments; her humble house which had become the incunabula of her two far-reaching works; her humble house which would serve her for a few more years till her new Convent became her permanent abode, in 1777. On Christmas Eve, 1775, the modest Community was joined by another holy young woman, Miss Mary

Anne Collins. She exemplified all the virtues of Miss Nagle herself, whom she had long followed as a model of Christian character, and in whose footsteps she was long spared to walk with fidelity.

Christmas Eve, 1775, therefore was the date that Miss Nagle and her three devoted companions began their novitiate together. It was a significantly symbolical hour in which to start the cradling of a new work for God and His poor. Her lowly house was a fitting accompaniment. There was at hand a wealth of inspiration in the words of the Midnight Mass to encourage them. The four faithful souls, who were on the threshold of revolutionising Christian Education in Ireland, could find in the Mass of Christmas Day an unending beauty of Literature revolving round the Truth which was born into the world on that day, the Truth of the Teacher to whom they were preparing to consecrate the rest of their existence.

The Psalm at the *Introit* of the Midnight Mass seemed to ask the question of the mad Penal hour: "Why have the Gentiles raged, and the people devised vain things?"

The *Prayer* was appropriate to the lifting of the darkness: "O God, Who hast brightened this most holy night with the shining of the true light, grant, we beseech Thee, that we may also taste in Heaven His joys Whose mystical light we have known on earth."

The *Preface* betokened the Light too: "From Thy brightness, a new light hath risen to shine on the eyes of our souls, in order that, God becoming visible to us, we may be borne upward to the love of things invisible."

The *Offertory* of the Daybreak Mass suggested the Eternal and Unchangeable: "God hath established the world, which shall not be moved: Thy throne, O God, is prepared from of old; Thou art from everlasting."

The *Communion*, in its quotation from Zacharias, brought a lovely note of Hope: "Rejoice greatly, O daughter of Zion, shout for joy, O daughter of Jerusalem; behold thy King comes, holy and the Saviour of the world."

The *Introit* of the Third Mass on Christmas Day had

its message for a budding Community of teachers: "A child is born to us and a Son is given to us; Whose government is upon His shoulder; and His name shall be called the angel of great counsel." The *Gradual* of the same Mass continued the tone of brightness: "A hallowed day hath dawned for us: come, ye Gentiles, and adore the Lord; for this day a great light hath descended upon the earth."

Finally, the *Introit* of the Mass within the Octave of Christmas, had its exquisite melody from the *Book of Wisdom:* "While all things were in quiet silence, and the night was in the midst of her course, Thy almighty word, O Lord, came from heaven, from Thy royal throne."

There was not much opportunity for the glory and panoply and compelling majesty of the Catholic Liturgy in Cork, in an unpretentious little house, on Christmas Eve in the year 1775. Such a beautiful thing was viewed as illegal and outrageous by the presiding Puritans of the time. The reflection is meant to evoke gratitude from us in our twentieth century, when we can enjoy the high noon and plenitude of our lovely Liturgy. Nano Nagle and her young teachers bore the spirit of that Liturgy in their hearts. For them it was hardly yet the break of day. In the quiet silence of the night they began their prayerful vigil. There they started their elevating work 168 years ago. By now it has brought Beauty into the lives of countless children all over the world.

CHAPTER 12

THE SUCCESS OF NANO NAGLE'S NEW SOCIETY: SHE IS PROFESSED AS SISTER SAINT JOHN OF GOD

IN the modest house in Cork, where they began their novitiate on Christmas Eve, 1775, Nano Nagle and her three other holy companions lived a life of the utmost sanctity, the utmost asceticism, and the utmost privation. Their present as well as their future life was a strenuous one. Their present and continued practices of devotion were in keeping. They gladly gave themselves up to earnest prayer and self-denial, in the manner typified by Him Who walked our earth as the Way, the Truth, and the Life.

It was a period of penitential preparation for them. Francis Thompson, ever inspiring in Catholic Poetry, talks of "the cloistered penance of the seed." The idea is apt. We watch the seed put into the brown earth in Springtide. The farmer covers it over with the new-ploughed clay. We wonder what will become of that seed. It lies penitentially buried in Mother Earth, which is still cold from the Winter frost. God's Spring sunshine warms it. Lost from view for so long, the little seed shows signs of new existence at last. It bursts as a bud of Spring, hopefully, from its imprisoning furrow. It has been hidden from all, save the Eye of God, in the cloister of the earth. It now certainly begins to bring forth fruit worthy of penance, as we watch the tiny bud arrive to the rich fullness of Summer's fruition; after an absence of many cold dawns within the soil, the seed has come to young green growth, divinely sprung from its penitential cell.

It was now the period of cloistral penance for Nano Nagle and her associates. Their preparation was the prelude to fruitful services towards the poor in the years of religion that were dawning. Her own heart was keeping time with the sad hearts of the poor. To the Heart that beats ever steadily with Love for all mankind, she had recourse for the protecting title of her new Society. To this she gave the name of *"Sisters of the Sacred Heart of Jesus."*

We come to the Summer of the year 1776. It is the month of the Sacred Heart. Rich red roses and the soft Summer air always make this month of June a dream in Ireland. June 24, 1776, was a radiant Summer day in the life of Nano Nagle, when she and her three companions received the holy habit of her new Society. For them it was verily the day which the Lord hath made.

The name which she took in religion was meaningful, and noteworthily expressive of her healing mission in life. She became Sister Saint John of God. John of God was born in Portugal — a few years after Columbus discovered America. He became a healing wonder of the Sixteenth Century. He was granted a vision of the Infant Jesus who bestowed on him the name of John of God. His mortifications and public penances were so vivid that alarmed worldlings called him mad. He traversed the streets, calling to God for Mercy, and calling mankind to God. Blessed John of Avila suggested to him to stop the lamentations and find another way of atoning for his past life.

So John of God very practically gave himself to the service of the sick and the poor. He even carried on his shoulders, to his healing hostel, those who could not walk — a therapeutical Saint Christopher. Heavenly guests had visited him from early days, and, significantly, the helpful Saint Raphael had appeared in personal converse. An admiring Bishop made John a special habit to wear. There was a reason. John used to exchange his own cloak with beggars. This distinctive habit would stop him. Aptly enough it became the habit of his Order.

Charity was the watchword of John, as it was of Nano Nagle. His first two companions, who were formerly bitter enemies, were converted by his example of Charity. His Charity was unending. It extended to all the poor, to widows and orphans, to fallen women, to poor students. God miraculously watched over him. This was evident when John walked through the fire at the Grand Hospital in Granada, when he rescued the inmates from the lapping flames, through which he passed unscathed. For thirteen years his saintly services towards impaired humanity kept mounting up, until the hour of Destiny called him home to the Divine Physician, after an illness that arose from his trying to save a drowning man. The powers of the land buried the humble John with the pomp of princes. Pope Leo the Thirteenth made Saint John of God the Patron of hospitals and of the dying.

This was the doughty Patron chosen by Nano Nagle, who curatively walked in the light of his redeeming example, and was henceforth known as Sister Saint John of God. Of her companions, Miss Fuohy became Sister Joseph; Miss Burke became Sister Augustine; and Miss Collins became Sister Angela. "From this year," say the *Annals* of her Convent, "we may date the founding of the Presentation Order." It was the year 1776. The *Annals* add that Miss Nagle went no further than wishing her Sisters to form a *Congregation*.

Three words here merit attention: *Society, Congregation,* and *Order*. In the laws of the Church they are of course used precisely and definitely. In the conversation of the people they are sometimes used indistinctly or indefinitely; or all three are mixedly used for one idea. When a number of Catholics associate under a religious rule, under proper ecclesiastical approbation, for the salvation of their own souls or to work for the good of other souls, this is called a Religious *Society*. If this *Society* exist under the approbation of the Bishop of the Diocese, or of the Pope, and the members, bound to the observance of the rule, make *simple* vows only, it is called a Religious *Congregation*. If the Congregation is approved by the Pope, and the members are allowed to make *solemn* vows, the *Congregation* is called a Religious *Order*.

Mother Nagle's Sisters began as a *Society*. When their Rules were approved by Pope Pius the Sixth, on September 3, 1791, they became a *Congregation*. By the Bull of Pope Pius the Seventh, on April 9, 1805, they were raised to the rank of a Religious Order.

At the present day the Presentation Sisters rank as a Congregation, *juris pontificii*.

In Miss Nagle's eyes, the great duty of her Society was to work for the poor, the charitable education of the poor. Clearly, it was not the rank of the Society that preoccupied her chaste and humble spirit, but the worthy work to be done by the Sisters. In this ideal she seems like the frank realist, Saint Jerome, who wrote: "Bishop, and Priest, and Deacon, are not titles of merit, but names that bespeak work." Or, again, when Saint Jerome said: "The glory of a Bishop is to provide for the need of the poor." So it was with Nano Nagle and her Sisters. She was, unremittingly, the hard working servant of God, providing for the poor. She wished each of the Sisters to be the same. One of the most glorious things recorded of her is that she knew every attic in Cork. She traced the abashed poor to every pitiable corner. From their shrinking existence she drew them into the light, by the attraction of her charity. The vows made to serve the poor, by herself and her companions, were carried out to the minutest detail. The radiance of her own enlivening example brightened the hard pathway of all.

The *Annals* of her Convent furnish a record of her unfaltering service that has inspired thousands. No exhortation to watch and pray seemed necessary in her case, for prayer and vigil were the obvious badge of her innermost life. Frugality, parsimony, and severely exacting works, were the outward demands proposed for herself and her associates. After meals, that barely met subsistence, they hastened to their enduring toil in the classrooms. The physical state of many of those poor children that met their merciful eyes may be gauged from the grimness of the poverty-stricken age. Heavenly forbearance, and the sacrifice of the Saints, seemed necessary on every hand. All around, the sociological scene invited the sweep of many a new broom, as may be imagined from the depiction of the period, on whose prevailing murkiness we have already expanded.

When life's labour was ending, each of those happy Sisters, after deeds well done, could recite with the Psalmist: "I have waited patiently for the Lord, and He listened to me and heard my prayers." As they looked around on a cruel world, which had become congealed with indifferentism towards the poor and ill-clad, a world which thought it tragical-comical that nice young ladies should waste their good lives on wayward waifs and strays, a world of withered dreams, a world that was itself troubled in its sleep, they could join with the Royal Psalmist in talking to the King of Kings:— "To Thee have I lifted up my soul: in Thee, O my God, I put my trust; let me not be ashamed; neither let my enemies laugh at me: for none of them that wait on Thee shall be confounded."

The lives of the Sisters posited the daily conquest of human desires, human inclinations, human tendencies, and human contradictions, which could only be met, as they were, by lives of inner sanctity. For it required the great grace of a very special vocation to persevere and triumph in their efforts for the amelioration of human misery, and for the patient amendment of the social order — that was patently revolting and awry. By downright application to their merciful mission, they succeeded in doing splendid work in the three poor schools which they were by now conducting, and to which they gave their daily care incessantly.

The close of the year 1777 brought renewed consolation to Mother Nagle. Her second Convent was completed, that which was to house her very own Community, that which was shadowed by sorrow when it was half built, and that which was now irradiated by the joy of the poor as it opened its welcoming doors to them. All doors are traditionally opened in Ireland at Christmas, as the people feel that Jesus, Mary, and Joseph, themselves, may pass the way, in the guise of some poor souls seeking shelter. The Irish have plenty of Scriptural authority for it in practice, for, has not Christ in person said that, if you receive the least of His brethren, you receive Himself?

On Christmas Day, 1777, Mother Nagle opened her new Convent in honour of the Child Jesus. Characteristic in her love for the poor, she entertained fifty beggars to dinner on that blessed day of the Nativity. She fondly waited on them, cheered them by her charity, and set an example that was followed every Christmas.

In this tender work, she was carrying out the precepts of Christ Himself, as outlined in the Fourteenth Chapter of the Gospel according to Saint Luke. Christ therein warned guests not to seek the highest place but the lowest, at the feast; for those who exalt themselves shall be humbled, and those who humble themselves shall be exalted. He also gave instructions about the guests that are to be bidden to dinner or supper. It is not friends, or brethren, or kinsfolk, or rich neighbours that are to be called by the host, but the poor, the maimed, the lame, the blind. Such a host shall be blessed, for these poor ones cannot recompense him. And Christ Himself promised that the recompense shall be awarded at the Resurrection of the Just. Thus it was that Miss Nagle, the high-born maiden, took the lowest place of all, in order to wait on the lowliest as the servant of the Most High.

Though the Penal gloom hung with Puritan pall over Christmas, the day of days, Mother Nagle brightened the lives of the destitute with the happy spirit that was surely born of the *Venite Adoremus*. There were no bells to ring out the chorus of the Angels, for the Penal Laws would not have it, but the music of her words and the sympathy of her deeds, as she moved among her guests, must have made melody to God's poor, whom she was the first to serve in that unhallowed and unmerciful eighteenth century, with all its callous Penalism making for the wilful neglect of the impoverished Catholics. Christmas had once been suppressed by Act of Parliament, but it would never die in the hearts of the poor.

Nevertheless, even if there were no bells to "ring in the Christ that is to be," there were signs of the times that heralded happier omens for the Irish Catholics. The next year, 1778, Luke Gardiner, who afterwards became Lord Mountjoy, brought about a concession to the long-outraged Catholic majority: he introduced a bill before the Irish Parliament which repealed portions of the Penal Laws.

In future, Catholics could purchase property. Previously, a Catholic father had to surrender his whole estate to a son, if that son became a Protestant. This law was cancelled. Previously, a Catholic father had to pay for the education of his son, if that son became a Protestant. This law was also cancelled. The *Test* Act was repealed. This Act had prevented any Catholic from sitting in Parliament. Nor could any Catholic vote in an election for a member of Parliament, unless the voter took an oath to say that the truths of the Catholic Faith were false. This same oath had to be taken by any Catholic seeking civil or army office: added to this, the Catholic had to pass the "sacramental test" by going to Communion in a Protestant Church on Sunday — if he wished to hold office. These fettering decrees were now happily abrogated. By another concession, Catholics henceforth could lease land for 999 years. The Penal Laws had been falling into disuse. But they could be called into use at any moment when it was felt necessary to coerce the Catholics; and this coercion happened from time to time. Catholics could only feel at ease when the threatening terrors were officially wiped off the Statute Book. Some of the humanitarian erasing of the Penal Code was therefore done, in 1778, in the hope of conciliating Ireland, because Britain wanted to fortify herself against the United States of America — already recognized by France.

Mother Nagle discerningly saw, all along, that Penal fury was weakening and collapsing. Hence she hastened to perfect her own good work, which, she knew, would have wider and wider opportunities as the harsher atmosphere mellowed.

Fortunately there is an original letter of hers preserved by the good Sisters of the Presentation, at Mount Saint Joseph, Newburgh, New York. This rare relic reveals her undiminished zeal in the apostolate of education for the poor. It was addressed to her friend Miss Mullally, in Dublin, who, with her friend, Miss Corballis, was devotedly struggling to teach poor children, and whose school was familiar to Miss Nagle when she herself lived in Dublin. The letter was written from Cork, on August 21, 1777 — about the time that the Foundress was busy with the final stages of the new Convent, which is referred to, herein:—

"I waited for this opportunity, or I should not have so long deferred acknowledging your kind favour and telling you the pleasure it gave me to hear that your and Miss Corballis' health was better. I hope it is so well restored that you are both able to go on with all your pious occupations as heretofore, with that spirit of zeal which the Almighty has, I think, given such a blessing to and success as to have your schools be useful to such a number of poor children, and I hope the increase of the charities you get will enable to add daily to the good you do.

It gave great joy to your Sisters and to me to find that you and Miss Corballis were so taken with the Rule of the Sisters of Charitable Instruction. [These were Mother Nagles' own Sisters, dedicated to the Sacred Heart of Jesus.] We ardently wish that yours and your companion's health were so well reestablished as to begin it yourselves, as I am sure you will not find any persons more capable, if that is not the will of the Almighty. You may rely on us that every assistance in our power we shall give towards having an establishment of this kind in the Metropolis, not that I think they were so much wanting there, only that the good they would do would be more universally known and extend them in other parts of the kingdom.

I am building a house, and when it will be fit to inhabit, I believe young ladies that have fortunes will join us. We have been under many disagreeable circumstances since we began, too tedious to mention. Yet, with the divine assistance, I think I have reason to imagine in a few years, when we are fixed, it will succeed very well. We have received one young lady of great merit, who has a fortune to support herself. Her vocation was so good she would not wait until we were settled in a more comfortable manner than at present.

The bearer is a great friend of mine. She is acquainted with all our Sisters and good to the poor children. She is very desirous to see yours, which you will oblige me greatly to show her.

All our Sisters unite in assuring you and Miss Corballis of our most sincere regards, and begging your good prayers, believe me to be, with the greatest esteem, dear Madam,

Your most humble and obedient servant,

Nano Nagle."

June 24, 1777, was the gladdening day of Profession for Mother Nagle and her three associates. They pronounced their simple vows in the presence of Doctor John Butler, Bishop of Cork. Mother Nagle was nominated Superioress by the Bishop. Thenceforth, until the year 1793, when Pope Pius the Sixth approved of the Rules of the *Order of the Presentation*, the Nuns took annual vows; "they did so in private," as the *Annals* of their Convent tell.

Mother Mary of Saint John of God had now devoted the wealth of her purse and the work of her fruitful days completely to the charitable instruction of the poor children of God. Twenty years previously, when she was struggling with her unpretentious schools, nobody could fortifyingly credit her with a hope of success. On the whole, Bishops and Priests could then have given her little encouragement, for they themselves were faced with the relentless menace of Penalism, and they dreaded the thought of intensifying the already unbearable persecutions which were directed against the entire Catholic community. Nobody could blame them for generally holding back; they were discreetly and patiently waiting for the more murderous frenzy of the Penal Code to subside. With miraculous success, Mother Nagle did the thing that seemed impossible to all. God had chosen her for a very special work, and she succeeded in doing all things through Him Who strengthened her.

There is a beautiful prophecy of Saint Malachy which says that Ireland shall one day stand forth in her might and be fresh in her Beauty like the Rose. Prophetic determination of this kind must have actuated Mother Nagle, as she started out, with her new Institute, against all odds, to brighten the face of her nation and of her people, by instilling education into the minds of the masses of Ireland's children, and by dispelling the enemy called ignorance from their midst. Her own beautiful face must have smiled and shone with happiness on that June morning of her Profession, when, after twenty years of crucifying continuance in all her many efforts, she saw that her Convent, her Schools, and her Sisters had come to prosper, proceed, and reign.

There she stood triumphant, a fair flower among her kindred, whom she had led to the gates of the Morn. Her own pure heart was warm with love for the Sacred Heart of Jesus, to Whom, athirst, she had dedicated her parent house and its first fruits. The new Feast of the Sacred Heart of Jesus had been approved by Pope Clement XIII in 1765, at the time that Mother Nagle was struggling with her early schools. Her new Convent and her new Institute were among the first to be set apart in honour of the Heart that loves all mankind, the Heart to whom a later Pope, Leo the Thirteenth, solemnly consecrated the whole human race. The Spirit of her tender devotion to the fond Heart of Christ may re-occur to our minds as we meditate on many of the graceful thoughts that arise in the Mass for the Feast of the Sacred Heart.

Appropriately suggesting themselves are the words of the *Introit:* "The thoughts of his heart to all generations: to deliver their souls from death and feed them in famine." The words of the *Prayer* urge us all: "O God, who, in the Heart of thy Son, wounded by our sins, hast deigned mercifully to bestow infinite treasures of love upon us; grant, we beseech Thee, that as we offer Him the faithful service of our devotion, we may also make worthy reparation."

In the *Epistle* for the Mass on the Feast of the Sacred Heart, Saint Paul has a prayer for us all: "That Christ may dwell by faith in your hearts; that being rooted and founded in Charity, you may be able to comprehend, with all the Saints, what is the breadth, and length, and height, and depth: to know also the Charity of Christ, which surpasseth all understanding, that you may be filled unto all the fulness of God."

In the *Gradual* of that Mass are the words of Saint Matthew: "Take up my yoke upon you and learn of me, because I am meek and humble of heart, and you shall find rest for your souls."

The words of the *Offertory* bring us thoughts of the One Heart that is sure to soothe us, when all others fail: "My heart hath expected reproach and misery, and I looked for one that would grieve together with me and there was none; and I sought one that would console me and I found none."

The *Secret* concentrates on this constant note of Love: "Look, we beseech thee, O Lord, on the unspeakable charity of the Heart of thy Beloved Son: that what we offer up may be in your sight an accepted gift and the expiation of our sins."

The *Preface* bids us give thanks to God: "Who hast

willed that thine only-begotten Son hanging on the Cross should be transfixed with a soldier's lance, so that the opened Heart, treasure-place of divine bounty, might flood us with the torrents of compassion and grace, and that that which never ceased to burn with love for us, should be repose for the devout, and to the penitent should open the shelter of salvation."

The *Postcommunion* can conclude our thoughts on the Sacred Heart: "May Thy holy mysteries, O Lord Jesus, give us holy fervour; that by it perceiving the sweetness of Thy most loving Heart, we may learn to despise earthly things and to love those of Heaven."

So read some of the glorious thoughts of the Mass for the Feast of the Sacred Heart, as ordered for universal use throughout the Catholic Church in 1929, by the late Pope Pius the Eleventh. In the holy spirit of this Feast did Mother Nagle proceed with her successful work in Ireland over a century and a half ago. In the Isle of Saints she was a pioneer in many pious causes. Among them was her public devotion to the Sacred Heart of Jesus.

CHAPTER 13

MOTHER NAGLE'S GOLDEN RULE WAS TO SERVE AND TEACH POOR CHILDREN

WHAT rule of life would best enable her Sisters to teach the needy children? That was Mother Nagle's next compelling concern. She was always thinking of the spiritual and mental happiness of the children.

A child's needless tear is a blood-blot on the earth. Such was the thought of the great English Convert, Cardinal Manning, the lover of the people, who himself said that he rejoiced to claim blood relationship with the Irish — whom he called the "faithful race." Among the faithful race of Ireland in the eighteenth century there was no greater angel of consolation than Mother Nagle. As her salutary work unfolds we perceive its ever deepening concentration on the needs of the forlorn and unprivileged children. Wherever squalid suffering reared its ugly head, she was there with her holy hands raised to bless, to help, and to give.

She too, as her life and letters show, regarded the unneeded tears of children as stains of blood on our fair green earth, which the Father primally gave us in its virgin freshness, but which human selfishness flawed with sickly sores so soon. The poor did not have many friends to solace them in their sorrows at the period which is being described. Mother Nagle stands out, all the time, in the solitary grandeur of her generosity, shining across Ireland's troubled story like a beacon light from the dawn-star that undoes the darkness on the uplands of our Isle. There are lines from Lady Dufferin's popular poem that serve to illustrate the salient point about Mother Nagle — as the rare friend of the forlorn:

> "I am very lonely now, Mary,
> For the poor make no new friends,
> But, Oh, they love the better still
> The few our Father sends."

Mother Nagle was one of the few friends to the father-less. She cheerfully kept increasing her sacrifices for all God's children in necessity. Few were their friends. But, for that matter, few were the friends of God who were ready to do so much for Him, in the person of his poor, as Mother Nagle was evermore prepared to do, in her intensified self-denial and devotion to His commands. Readers may recall the incident from the life of the daring and super-sacrificing Saint Teresa, when God asked her to redouble her sacrifices, if she were to be His friend. In her true brilliancy, the Saint observed to her Friend and Father: "No wonder then that your friends are so few."

Illimitable was Mother Nagle's love for her Lord and Friend. By her sufferings and labours for Him, the evils of ignorance were undone, and the ungodly age was reformed. No self-satisfying boundary did she ever set to the range of her hopes for redeeming the youth of her race. As one is, so one does. Full generously she lived for God, and full generously she worked for God. For her, a holy life was a whole life, and a whole life was a holy life. There was no stopping, no interval, no inter-mission in her Charity. Her pure eyes feasted on the hard road before her, and she knew the Beauty of all Beauty awaited her at the end.

Immeasurable in return was the love of her people for Mother Nagle, whom the all-seeing Father sent to His children at the clamant and critical hour, when all doors appeared closed against them. By her multiple good deeds she increasingly led them to dwell in the tabernacle of His Kingdom. As she lived, so she taught: as she taught, so she lived: the Charity of Christ was her life: the Charity of Christ was her lesson. In her loving kindness, and in the performance of her good works, she was tranquilly guided by the Gospel.

It would be trite to say she was a woman of Prayer. Prayer was the very essence of her life: there was so much in her work that nature could not do: full well she knew how to ask God to supply, by the help of His Grace, those gifts which her human nature needed to carry out the series of good works that she so liberally achieved. Afar off, and yet ever near, the Lord visibly understood her thoughts. His Presence is manifest in her superhuman undertakings.

Day and night, the Angels of allotted vigil could report to God the increasing good works of her busy hands and of her profitable life. Work on, and on, for the poor of God. Her unending motto this was. In mind and voice she was ever with God. Far beyond the appointed measure she rendered to Him her offerings of sacrifice, as she trod the hard and rugged ways of salvation, in the edifying fervour of her charity. To combat the evil that separates souls from God she set the example of goodness that joins them to Him. When Christ said "Learn of Me," she took Him strictly at His Word: correspondingly she wished both Sisters and children to be "taught of God."

The Rule, which Mother Nagle and her first companions followed, had been prepared for them, in Paris, by the Curé of Saint Sulpice. In her letter, which is quoted in this chapter, she refers to the Curé of Saint Sulpice as having been Superior-General of the Sulpicians. But, from the Sulpician records, it appears that the Curé, whom she mentions, must have been Father John Joseph Faydit de Tersac, who was Pastor of Saint Sulpice, from 1777, till his death in 1788.

Something may be said, interconnectingly, of Mother Nagle's association with the worthy Fathers of Saint Sulpice, who had so ably helped to reclaim Paris to God. She must have known them from her early days in Paris. The Church of Saint Sulpice was evidently the scene of her conversion from the world to God, on that morning long ago, when she saw the people thronging its doors for early Mass, as she rode in adornment in her stately carriage through the pavements of the Faubourg Saint Germain. Those who have studied the life of the beloved Father Olier will not forget the Faubourg

Saint Germain. When, in 1641, he took charge of the Parish of Saint Sulpice — which embraced the whole Faubourg Saint Germain — it had the negative reputation of being the most wicked and vicious parish in the world.

For Nano Nagle there was magnetic edification aplenty in the life and work of the renowned Father Olier, who, like herself, died comparatively young, after having accomplished wonders in the domain of spiritual, moral, and educational reclamation. He could have enjoyed the attractions of a court chaplaincy, but he preferred to promote the work of God among the people.

The evils in the Parish of Saint Sulpice were said to be so rooted that they defied reformers. But, when Father Olier took charge, he soon effected reforms in the wilderness of sin. He and his priests made a point of personally knowing the souls that were committed to his cure and care. The poor were taught. Neglected servants, all the benumbed and benighted among the poor outcasts and the beggars, were sought and instructed in the Eternal Truths. Orphanages were built for the forsaken children; houses of refuge were opened, wherein young girls were reformed. Free schools were established for girls without means. Even the teachers were reformed as well as the taught. It is significant that the celebrated educator, Saint John Baptist de la Salle, was a pupil of Saint Sulpice, and that he founded his first school in Father Olier's parish.

Father Olier knew how to deal with the rich also, by inducing them to use some of their wealth in charity towards the poor, and by teaching them that religious perfection was as requisite for them, in their way, as it was for the priests, the nuns, or the indigent. Coldness or opposition from high places did not dismay the Sulpician Founder. He did not fear to check the worldly. To the Queen Regent, Anne of Austria, then ruling over the destinies of France, he spoke boldly and honestly. He denounced her worldly Prime Minister, Cardinal Mazarin,

for selling holy offices, and for impiously trying to insinu-
ate unworthy candidates into Bishoprics. Father Olier's
influence went far afield, and he is credited with converting to Catholicism the King of England, Charles II.

This brave priest in his timely work was surely an
example to Mother Nagle: for he, too, had gathered the
forgotten and destitute to his own home and taught them.
He was derided, just as she was, for this earnest rehabilitation of the outcast. But the scoffers were converted to
imitation of his good works. Father Olier had turned
the most wicked parish into the most exemplary parish.
The resulting and abiding devotion of the people therein
must have later manifested itself to Miss Nano Nagle on
the morning she was converted by seeing fervent worshippers waiting at the church doors for early Mass.

There were discernibly many features in the Sulpician
ideal to attract Mother Nagle into communication with
the good Fathers in Paris. For every Sulpician is bidden
to be animated by zeal for the glory of God, and for the
sanctification of the students; and to be an example of
detachment, self-sacrifice and poverty; and to teach mental
prayer and the Christian virtues to future "teachers of all
nations"; and to inculcate in all, a love of piety, learning,
regularity and dignity.

Similar ideals no doubt commended themselves to
Mother Nagle for her Sisters in their sphere, and she was
apparently eager to seek a code of discipline that would
combine and enshrine some of these governing virtues:
she, the perfect lady in all things, sought the most perfect
means of bringing out every grace of Christian refinement
in pupils that would grow up to be a holy leaven in the
family and in the world — pupils who would, by steady
example, proclaim to others that "the Kingdom of God
is within you." For her Sisters she sought to create a
School of the Lord's service, founded in the Peace that
comes of Order. In that service she wanted no minimizing:
the needy, crying to be filled, were ever present round them

as the Four Winds of Erin, and so there was never any shortage of work for her Sisters.

Mother Nagle stood as a daring pioneer at the gates of the day. She had all the responsibilities of the pioneer. So much depended on these early steps to combat the ignorance inflicted on her people. As far as the luckless Catholics were concerned, ignorance was the only thing, in their regard, which was *protected* by the law. Mother Nagle's task it was to light upon methods and rules that would most effectively and organizingly help her to defeat this superimposed ignorance. The work which she was now doing, made her the pioneer of Convent Education in Post-Reformation Ireland.

The work of a woman was a novelty in the field of Education at the time: what was Catholic and national, in that field, lay in the hands of heroic hedge-schoolmasters.

Nano Nagle stood out in Ireland as Mary Ward did in England. This courageous English lady, related to many of the old noble Catholic families, wanted to do a great deal for the Catholic Education of girls in the seventeenth century, and she compels our undying admiration by her victory over so many gigantic troubles. Like that of Mother Nagle her presence was a startling rarity in educational work; and her methods were more startling than some of the startled could brook. Also, like Mother Nagle, she started young: at 24, she opened schools, for both rich and poor, on the Continent of Europe. Having already seen the admirable work which the Jesuits were doing for the education of boys, she accordingly wished to do the same for girls. Her exertions met with praise and opposition. But it was mostly opposition, because the appearance of a woman so openly on the educational field was deemed arresting and revolutionary.

The tradition of the times mainly regarded nuns as dwellers behind walls; as cloistered souls who said their prayers, and performed acts of charity which were consonant with their cloistered state. It was disturbing for some to witness a new group of Nuns going out in the open, in order to reach human souls that might be otherwise unreachable. Why should they enter publicly into the domain of education for women? For this was all considered novel and strange, something hitherto untried.

It was however accepted that Mary Ward could do good by her challenging enterprise. The Jesuit Fathers, ever afire with educational zeal, had supported her from the start. On examination of the scope of her Institute, the illustrious Theologian, Suarez, held that its aim, organization, and methods, were without precedent. Popes, and Prelates, and Princes had praised her work, but still it was called in question. The brave woman was allowed to plead her own cause before the Congregation of Cardinals appointed by Pope Urban VIII to examine it. Her "Jesuitesses," as misunderstanding opponents called her Nuns, were suppressed in 1630. But her work was not lost. It was revived; and its rule was approved by Pope Clement XI, in 1703. In 1639, Mary Ward returned to her native shores, with a letter of introduction from the Pope to the Catholic Queen of England, Henrietta Maria. Mother Ward's work, like that of Mother Nagle, after divers trials, succeeded unto great fruitfulness. From the inscription on her grave in England, we read that "to succour the poor, and rise with them, was all the aim of Mary Ward." Her cause of Canonisation, like that of Nano Nagle, is warmly promoted: these are two of the most remarkable educational reformers among women in the English-speaking world, in the earlier Post-Reformation period, that await the Church's seal of sanctity.

From the thrilling story of Mary Ward it will be seen that Mother Nagle and her Sisters, operating in more varied and controversial spheres, were also very unusual pioneers, as they proceeded with their searching and sublime work in the City of Cork in the Eighteenth Century. And, at all times in this story, we must bear in mind that Mother Nagle was always hedged round by the intricate impediments of the Penal Laws, which she was constantly surmounting. Her efforts were to graft on recipient young minds the loving and gentle manners of Christ: legal spite, the meanest maintainable, was availably lurking round the corner to thwart her at any moment in her innocent mission.

By her exclusive concentration on the education of the needy, and by her sociological attention to the miscellaneous wants of the unprivileged, Mother Nagle stands out as an especial pioneer. Women, in our twentieth century, are noted and numerous in the wide fields of education and sociology. In the obscured Catholic Ireland of the eighteenth century, when bare existence itself was considered enough issue — without the introduction of educational and sociological uplifting—Mother Nagle maintains her place alone.

It was mostly in the nineteenth century that women began to merit and receive recognition in the public arena. Florence Nightingale, the English philanthropic author, who by her heroic work in the Crimean War, just after the middle of the nineteenth century, had become the foundress of military hospital-service, only died in 1910. In the field of letters, Jane Austen completed her work in the early part of the nineteenth century, dying at the age of 42. Of the nineteenth century also were the Bronte Sisters — Anne, Charlotte and Emily Jane: these were of Irish origin. To nineteenth-century Literature belong the novelist George Eliot (Mary Evans Cross), and the poetess, Elizabeth Barrett Browning. Glancing over a long list of authors in a book on nineteenth-century Catholic Literature, one notices the names of a few women — Louise Imogen Guiney, Alice Meynell and Adelaide Anne Procter.

In the eighteenth century, well before the names of noted women came into prominence, it was a highly remarkable and revolutionary thing to find Nano Nagle, the noble-born gentlewoman, appearing in the public streets as a moral, educational, and social reformer. Viewed from any angle, her entry was conspicuous. Later generations of women, who fought for the rights of female education, had effective organizations and some liberal public opinion to back their campaign. In Miss Nagle's case we may say that she had to wage her holy contest alone, against a powerful, corrupt, and coercive Parliamentary system, which seemed to negate every effort at Catholic Education. She victoriously broke through those unjust laws which her cousin, Burke, stigmatized as being the most wicked in history.

Long after Miss Nagle passed away, the revolt and the battle which she had begun, against educational and social injustice, had to be pursued with rising resolution. In this connection there are the words of the illustrious English scholar and Convert to Holy Church, Cardinal Newman. A hundred years after Miss Nagle's death, the world-famed Cardinal wrote a letter to Dublin, to Father Gerard Manley Hopkins — who now happens to be the most studied and discussed poet in our generation. Speaking of Ireland, His Eminence said: "The Irish Patriots hold that they never have yielded themselves to the sway of England and therefore never have been under her laws, and never have been rebels. If I were an Irishman I should be (in heart) a rebel." So much may be said on the question of Miss Nagle's defiance of ungodly and anti-educational laws.

A nation's children are its sacred trust, and with these, in a forgetful and icy age, Mother Nagle wisely began. Well-meaning but unpractical rainbow-chasers, in the educational and sociological spheres, may spend their days holding committee meetings, looking "before and after, and pining for what is not." Not so Mother Nagle; she always saw what was to be done, and straightaway she did it. She had a clear practical mind, as is seen from her work. She had a warm heart, as is seen from her love for the children. Her affection for the little ones may be expressed in the sheer beauty of the words of the President of Ireland, Dr. Douglas Hyde, in his prayer for children:

"O Lord, O God, take pity on this little soft child.
Put wisdom in his head, cleanse his heart, scatter the

mist from his mind and let him learn his lessons like other boys. O Lord, Thou wert Thyself young one time; take pity on youth. O Lord, Thou, Thyself shed tears; dry the tears of this little lad. Listen, O Lord, to the prayer of Thy servant, and do not keep from him this little thing he is asking from Thee. O Lord, bitter are the tears of a child, sweeten them; deep are the thoughts of a child, quiet them; sharp is the grief of a child, take it from him; soft is the heart of a child, do not harden it."

Child Welfare is an absorbing programme in our twentieth century. It was a precious and practical matter for Mother Nagle in the eighteenth century, and she lit the way for many who followed in her holy highway to serve the underprivileged. The child that Christ long ago set in the midst of them would seem to confront the world with children's needs, yesterday, today, and forever. As we approach the middle of this twentieth century we hear the distinguished President of the United States, Franklin D. Roosevelt, saying, on the question of children's needs:

"Democracy must inculcate in its children capacities for living and assure opportunities for the fulfillment of those capacities. If anywhere in the country any child lacks opportunity for home life, health protection, education, or moral and spiritual development, the strength of the nation and its ability to cherish and advance the principles of democracy are thereby weakened."

In the century before last, Nano Nagle was engaged in just such spiritual, social, and educational developments as those mentioned.

To teach the Truth and carry out Christ's commands of Charity; to harness words to actions; to substitute something of the Eternal Loveliness on Earth in the place of bitter disorder; to find one perfecting Rule for doing a thousand good things for God; these were some of the extensive objectives to which Mother Nagle set the driving power of her blessed spirit, as each bead in the final decade of her life's chaplet slipped speedily through her busy fingers.

To Miss Mullaly, her scholastic co-worker in Dublin, Mother Nagle wrote from Cork, on October 30, 1779:

"It gave me much pleasure to find that your journey back agreed so well with you. I hope it will be an encouragement to you not to slip any good opportunity to see your friends here, which would give them so much pleasure.

I am much obliged to you for going to see my sister [Mrs.] Ffrench. She mentions to me that she was sorry it was not in her power to pay you any compliments as she was not in lodgings of her own. I am sure she would have been happy to improve her acquaintance.

I am glad to hear Miss Bellew is so well disposed to do what you desire. I hope the Almighty will direct what is most to His honour and glory.

As to the rule I was so desirous to get, which was that of the *Grey Sisters*, I believe it is not what I have got: they call it *Hospitaliers*, and call the rule the third of Saint Francis. They make the three religious vows for life. More than half the year they fast on one meal, and the rest of the year abstain from flesh on Mondays and Wednesdays. They have of late been dispensed with saying the great Office, and only recite that of our Blessed Lady; but they have such a number of other prayers that I should imagine they can have but little time to attend the sick. This is the rule they follow at their great monastery at Nancy, in Lorraine, and where I believe the young woman died who was sent from Dublin. By what I can judge of it, I am afraid if it had pleased God to spare her life to come over, she would not have succeeded in that Order in this kingdom; so Divine Providence does everything for the best. They must be of a robust constitution to be received into it.

Doctor Moylan wrote to the superior of an Order that is called the *Hospitaliers* of the Order of the *Brothers de Villeneuve*. She is a particular friend of his, and tells him she would send him the book of her rule and constitutions only it is absolutely forbidden by their Superior-General to show it to anyone; but she writes in what it consists, which are the works of mercy, spiritual and corporal. They have different houses for their charities, which are most useful. There are some houses where they take care of the sick; others where they instruct orphans; others where they have boys as well as girls, but separately; others where they take care of old men and women; others where they receive as pensioners the daughters of citizens and young ladies of distinction. They have, also, houses of penitents; and in some places, she says, they are of great service to prisoners. She says she was honoured in the employment wherein she found most solid consolation. . . .

They make three vows for life, as other religious do, and there is a fourth they make, which is to serve the poor until death.

In the houses where they take pensioners they are obliged to have a school for poor girls on account of inspiring the young ladies with charitable feelings towards them, and that they should see their wants. The Nuns in these houses instruct women in their religious duties.

The education they give their young ladies is quite different from that of other convents. When they know well how to read, write, and work; when well grounded in their religion, then they are employed in going through every duty proper to manage a house, and are made good housewives. The young ladies brought up with them are generally very notable as to worldly affairs.

As to their obligations in other things they are just the same as we have in our constitutions. We are obliged to most of their charities; but we prefer the schools to all others.

The *Curé* of Saint Sulpice, who made our rule, was the Superior-General of this Order; and by what I see there is very little difference, only we make no vows; and my opinion is, it is that which renders them superior to others, seeing that in the world it is not known they make vows for life. [Mother Nagle evidently meant that she and her Sisters did not take *solemn* vows; they had already taken *simple* vows, in 1777.]

You and your director, from what you have told me of him, seem to be enlightened from above, and will judge which is best of the two rules for this kingdom. Until I have your opinion I shall say no more on the subject.

I am very busy preparing to fill up our new house, and if it is the Divine will to send you any good subjects to keep up your school you may rely there is nothing in my power that I shall not do if they come here. Though I know myself so incapable, yet they will see good example from our Sisters, and their time will be well employed.

They beg, I will assure you, of their sincere love, and of mine, to Miss Corballis, and believe me to be,

Dear Madam,
Your most affectionate friend,
Nano Nagle."

It will be seen from her letter that Mother Nagle was eager to perform countless charities, but she was especially eager to carry out her charitable work in the schools, in preference to all other good works.

The Supreme Teacher pronounced some memorable words about the urgent needs of the little children, as recorded in the Gospel: "Whosoever shall receive one such little child in My name receiveth Me." And again Christ said: "Take heed that ye despise not one of these little ones." These Gospel precepts formed the most pressing portion of Mother Nagle's work. She strove and prayed that hard-hearted men might suffer little children to come unto Him, Who, on earth, laid His Divine Hands in protective blessing upon the young innocents.

Catering to the wants of the poor, in body and soul, and attending in particular to poor youth: that was the way Mother Nagle and her Presentation Nuns were improving the social order in Penal Ireland. To her may be· applied the words which Padraic Pearse put into the mystical drama on the Little Boy, Jesus: "Among the children it was that I sought you, and among the children it was that I found you."

CHAPTER 14

THE GROWTH OF MOTHER NAGLE'S WORK: THE VINEYARD, THE VINE, AND THE BRANCHES BEAR HOPE

THE PRINCE of Life was enriching Mother Nagle, His saintly courtier, with further blessings of success. Each step was now bringing her nearer to the Mount and the Court of God: it was consoling that each step was also bringing greater growth to her spreading work. By her side, when she began, about three years ago, were three Sisters — *omne trinum perfectum.*

The mystic number had now blissfully doubled. The foundress and her six associates were busily progressing, happy spiritual family that they were.

When Christ told His followers to go forth and teach, He set no limits of geography or time. To the ends of the earth, and to the end of the world, His followers must keep going, teaching the Truths that alone can save the human race. Serenely attuned to the guidance of the Gospel, Mother Nagle wished her Sisters to go forth and teach everywhere. No bourne of land or race could confine her charity, and, wherever her own race was scattered, her enthusiastic Sisters faithfully followed; the Voice of the Irish called her back from France; her devoted Sisters have responded to the Voice of Ireland round the Seven Seas.

When Mother Nagle beheld her work on a permanent basis in Cork, she immediately desired to extend it to Kerry. Welcoming it there, in Saint Brendan's See, was the good Prelate who had mercifully allowed the construction of her Parent House, in Cork, to proceed according to plan — the Parent House that became a Fount from which the works of Mercy and Charity were to flow in a continuative stream. To her revered friend, Bishop Moylan, in the Kingdom of Kerry, the Foundress had her first recourse as a giver of those gifts which her Society then alone could give. To Kerry she had pledged her first foundation, but it was from her Home in Heaven that she saw the pledge finally fulfilled. And it was meet and just that the first foundation was in Beauty's Home, Killarney.

Six years before her early demise, she was busying herself with plans to present her Sisters to Kerry. Here is a letter which she wrote to her friend, Miss Maria Teresa Mullaly, who was conducting a school in Dublin: it is dated from Cork, on the Feast of Saint Michael, in the year 1778:—

"Dear Madam,

This is a pleasure I have longed for this sometime past, which was to acquaint you that, as Dr. Moylan mentioned to you about two years ago, I had a desire that some establishment should be made to keep up the schools for the poor children.

Not finding any person here inclined to undertake such an affair, made me at last consent to the Doctor's request, and last Christmas I took in three persons to join me in this good work. What made me defer it all this time was finding myself so improper a person to underteake it; but the Almighty makes use of the weakest means to bring about His works.

I am about to send two out of the small number we have to Dr. Moylan, (then Bishop of Kerry), as he is very impatient to have them, and in my opinion they are very proper to make a foundation in Kerry, as they have great zeal and talents, and every virtue proper for it.

I send you the rule which they follow (it is called of *The Sisters of the Charitable Instruction of the Sacred Heart of Jesus*) by this most respectable clergyman, Father Shortal, who is most zealous for its success, and will give you a particular account about it.

I could wish that we may unite in this Society, and am confident that the great God will direct you to what is most to His glory, and beg you will believe me to be with the greatest esteem,

Madam,

Your most humble and obedient servant,

Nano Nagle."

Miss Mullaly visited Mother Nagle, in Cork, and saw for herself that a branch of the new Society would be eminently suited to the work of teaching the poor in Dublin. Whenever Mother Nagle was asked to cooperate in saving and teaching the children, she promptly made unconditional surrender of her services to God: with alacrity she pledged all that she had to give. Fortified by the promises of her influential friend, Miss Mullaly therefore returned in happy mood to her little school in Dublin. In the Winter of the year 1778, Mother Nagle wrote her the following letter from Cork:

"Dear Madam,

I could not slip this opportunity without assuring my dear Miss Mullaly the pleasure it gave me to hear she arrived safe, and to assure her the trouble it gave me that I could not have more of her company whilst here, being every day more sensible of the advantage I should have reaped from it.

The hurry I was in at the time made me neither think of many things which I should have been glad to have had your opinion on; my thoughts were so much taken up about my nieces preparing for this voyage, which, thank God, was a lucky one, as they had a passage of only thirty hours, and if I did not send them by that ship they would not have gone this Winter, as none of the Bristol traders has sailed since, and I would not have ventured them in this bad weather to sea. (The nieces were the children of her sister, Elizabeth Nagle, who was married to Robert Ffrench, a member of an old aristocratic family in Galway: the girls were being quietly ushered to the Continent to receive the Catholic Education that would fit them for their future place in life, since bad laws prevented them from being educated at home.)

I had a letter from my sister Ffrench since they departed, wherein she tells me that Mr. Ffrench had hurt his leg, which prevents him leaving Spa (in Belgium) at the time they intended, and as I have not heard from her since, I am afraid it is worse, and that they won't be at Cambray when their daughters arrive there.

I am sure she (Mrs. Ffrench) will mention to me what answer the lady you wrote will make; which, if pleasing, I shall lose no time in communicating to you, as I was very much distressed since the young woman that lived with me, since my niece went, left this.

I have a gentlewoman that I really was resolved to take this sometime past, when fixed in the new house; but not till then — one is so much wanting at present, and the rule orders us to have them on trial for some months. She attends the schools; and I hope I shall have no reason to repent of the choice I have made, as my first motive was Charity, hearing of the great distress she was in through a lawsuit, and an extravagant brother who spent part of her fortune. She has had the best education this kingdom could afford, and has many useful talents, with great patience and humility in all her misfortunes. She seems at present to rejoice in all she has suffered, as it has placed her in so happy a state. She takes much delight in teaching poor children. I hope that some part of what is due to her will be recovered.

All our Sisters assure you of their most affectionate respects. We all unite in begging you will be so good as to present our best compliments to Miss Corballis. You cannot imagine how melancholy we were at night after you left us, as our recreation passed in speaking of you; and be assured you were not forgotten by us in our prayers. I hope you think of me in yours, as nobody wants it more than she who is, with the highest esteem, dear Madam,

Your affectionate friend and humble servant,

Nano Nagle.

Postscript:

It gave us all a vast deal of trouble to hear that you have been ill since you went to Dublin. I hope it was not owing to any cold you got on the road. I had a letter from my sister since I wrote this letter . . . .

She does not mention one word about what you wrote to Miss Bellew, nor what I wrote myself to her, only that she had received all the letters I wrote to her. As she was not there near as soon as I expected, she got a good many from me. It was the day after her daughters' arrival I heard from her; and she tells me they all dined at Sir Patrick's, where there was a great deal of company. (Sir Patrick Bellew, a member of a most distinguished Catholic family in Ireland, was a generous helper of the first foundation of Mother Nagle's Sisters in Dublin: he was a first cousin of Mother Coppinger, who was one of Mother Nagle's earlier Ursuline associates.) It was from there she wrote to me, by which I can imagine the hurry she was in, and not having an opportunity to speak about your affair prevented her from saying anything of it to me. In my answer I begged she would use all her influence with the lady, (Miss Bellew) which I am sure she will. I hope in her next I shall have some account of what will be done. Adieu."

Mother Nagle was therefore planning to make her two first foundations in Kerry and Dublin. As the Divine Artificer did not spare her to see either of these convents built, reference will be made to their rise, in an appropriate page, elsewhere in this story.

On the Feast of the Nativity of Our Lady, in the year 1780, the first election was held in Mother Nagle's Convent, and it was a natural tribute to her leadership that she was promptly re-elected as Superior by the "private suffrages" of her Sisters, and confirmed in her office by Father Nicholas Barron.

She was never disappointed in the hopes so cheerfully evinced by her Community. Gladly they followed, wheresoever she led. Their lives were ascetical beyond compare. Hard work, meagre food, poor clothing, the bare necessities of life — there were the lot chosen by the refined lady, who once lived so fashionable a life in France. Her multiplied sacrifices were courageously shared by her new associates, who, inspired by her captivating example, had turned their backs on worldly fortune and on the comforts of life, who had bravely left father and mother, friends and home, to rescue the remnants of their Catholic nation from loss of Faith, by means of spiritual training imparted within humble classrooms, by means of prayer, penance and devout edification.

Diligently aware of the fact that Christ bade us to have compassion on His brethren, who comprise the poor of every age and condition, Mother Nagle turned her attention to the crying needs of aged women, in a world so misshapen by social neglect. These poor creatures, unattended and forgotten in the morasses of misery that lurk in the rear of garish cities, seemed to peep from the corners of their destitute hinterland and ask if it were anything to all these who passed by. "Some pious drops the closing eye requires." But who would shed a tear over their last agonies? Who would see that they received the Viaticum for the journey from which there was no returning?

To harbour the harbourless, Mother Nagle built an Alms House near her Convent: there, the poor old ladies could be eased in the evening of their bleak lives, and finally ushered forth in prayer and peace to the Elysian haven of their God. In our casual lives we may comfort ourselves with the banal utterance: "It is so easy to forget." Placing herself unforgettingly in the Presence of God, Mother Nagle always found it so easy to remember the unremembered: for these unhoused and aged ones of the Lord, Who was Himself born homeless, she furnished the House of Alms, and generously endowed it from her own finances, so as to ensure its services to a most forgotten hem of human society. This work has been followed with fidelity by her Sisters: they keep their spiritual tryst with the

Angel of Mercy, who wills a serene old age for the orphans of the storm.

Nor did Mother Nagle's encircling charity halt here: she greatly desired to establish a house of refuge for those unfortunate women retrieved and reformed from the infamy and degradation of the streets. Society blotted these wretched ones with shame. Then society was ashamed to own them, and so left them to their shame. If they had a place of shelter, could they not be taught that the God of Purity designed their bodies to be the Temples of the Holy Ghost, and that they were a little lower than the Angels? Mother Nagle decided that they could be weaned from their malpractices; the All-Pure Mother of God, whom we invoke as "Refuge of Sinners," would help to shelter them from the ways of evil, and the same All-Holy Mother whom we invoke as "Our Lady of Good Success" would help them to earn support by honest daily toil.

It is indicative of Mother Nagle's charity and courage that, though a relentless world looked upon those poor creatures as so much useless flotsam and jetsam, who were blown blightedly through city streets, she herself felt that no part of God's creation was so worthless that it did not deserve to be recovered for the dear Redeemer. She was filled with the love of Him who pitied and sanctified Mary of Magdala. Little dream there was of Social Welfare, or Social Reform, on the part of the governmental system of the time; but Mother Nagle was ahead of her time, and in tune with Eternity. Some see only the world's meanness, others only see its majesty.

To Mother Nagle, as to Burke, Life meant the Sublime and the Beautiful. Putting the fallen on their feet, there was pathos in her compassion and practicality in her plan. She saw to it that the reclamation of the froward and the wayward was accomplished by teaching them the ways of virtue, by housing them, by feeding them, and by finding them work to keep them out of temptation's trap.

In the cycle of social misery there was little that escaped Mother Nagle's loving eye. The moment she saw an ailment she was eager to effect a remedy. Some might be satisfied to extend a spinal shiver of sympathy. But she spent herself and sacrificed herself to carry out a cure. It may be easy to sing the carol of that model Saint, Good King Wenceslaus. "Yonder peasant, who is he, where and what his dwelling?" The lines ask a pointed trio of social questions. These were the very similar and very practical questions that Mother Nagle asked in Ireland, and that she very practically answered, from her first-hand experience, while the ruling gentry were carousing in a way that led to the extinction of their class, oblivious to those afflictions of the poor that cried to heaven for vengeance. It was not ichor but deviltry that flowed in the veins of the prevailing gods, as they strove to leave the people ignorant and hungry.

Statesmen, warriors, politicians, and national patriots of the period have all been honoured in song and in story: books and the eulogies of oratory emphasize their fame. Mother Nagle has not yet recognizedly come into her own. She, who saved her people from the degradation of enacted ignorance, showed that her nation was a chosen one of God, and through her Presentation Sisters she proved herself divinely instrumental for furthering the destined mission of the Irish race throughout the earth.

Something may be said on the providential growth of Mother Nagle's work. It kept growing, despite legions of obstacles. Though her people had been almost ploughed under by the Elizabethan and Cromwellian terrors, the spark of God was still alive in them. The fiendish forces of hell and Penalism, synonymous things, were ebbing and waning. Blood, sword, rack, dispossession, transportation, scaffold, eviction, massacre — despite this tragic litany of things there was still hope for the survival of a Catholic nation. And Mother Nagle conclusively proved that there was hope. Virtue was the intrinsic nature of her life. Deep down, virtue was the inner nature of her people. To God, she was virtue pleading for virtue: the daughter of God stretching out her hands for the sake of the friends of her Father. In the most complete and unfeigned humility she went her road, and the Finger of God pointed the way for extending her gospel of Charity.

Sacred Writings are filled with stress on the growth of the good and the decay of the bad. The barren fig-tree is useless and merely cumbers the ground. Rather must we be like healthy vine-branches, grafted on to the fruitful Vine, which is Christ. The Father gives growth to the lilies of the field in their engaging loveliness. The Lord of the Harvest blesses with growth the wheat, the corn, the crops. The grain of mustard seed grew, and waxed unto a great tree that gave shelter to all the Father's feathered throng.

If the fig-tree be in danger of failure, Christ bids that it be fertilized, with richer soil around it, to ensure its growth. His conversation was shot through with this note of growth. We even measure the seasons by rules of growth and fruitfulness. When the fig-tree and all the trees shoot forth verdantly, then we know that Summer's growth is at hand. One might well note that Mother Nagle's character may be compared to a Summer's day.

Christ pointed to the morsel of grain in the ground that bringeth forth much fruit. We are bidden to bring forth fruit worthy of penance. He blest and multiplied loaves and fishes for the hungry hearers. We are told that the Father is glorified by His creatures bearing much fruit. Go and bring forth fruit and see that your fruit shall remain — so is repeated the message of growth in the Gospels: it echoes through them like a fugue of fructification. Of Mary's Son, in Nazareth's city, it is written: "And the Child grew and waxed strong, full of wisdom: and the grace of God was in Him."

Paul and Barnabas bade the pagans turn to the God Who gives us good, Who gives us rain from the heavens, and fruitful seasons, filling our hearts with food and gladness. And in *The Acts of the Apostles* growth is also stressed for the Church: we are told that the Lord added daily to the Church the souls that were to be saved. Nature, the Church, God — all give us the message of growth.

Mother Nagle's work, that grew at God's Will, was one more inspiring story among the many that report the growth of the Sower's Kingdom. It was one of the few stories of heavenly growth that could be recorded of her own nation in the eighteenth century. All around her were things stunted and stagnant. It was a crime to teach; a crime to have a Convent; a crime to wear a habit; it was death to do these things. Mother Nagle survived and succeeded in doing them. She even succeeded beyond all her hopes, aspirations, or intentions. The words of the Prophet Isaias are quoted in her regard: "And thy people shall be all just, they shall inherit the land for ever, the branch of my planting, the work of my hand to glorify me. The least shall become a thousand, and a little one a most strong nation: I the Lord will suddenly do this thing in its time."

Mother Nagle began alone. At the present point of her story, in 1780, she had six Sisters. She had one Convent. Today her Convents are in the hundreds. Her Sisters are in the thousands. Her work grew by the grace of God.

So swift and marvellous was the growth of her work that Pope Pius the Sixth spoke of it in these terms, a few years after her death: "We feel and acknowledge that this is the effect of the boundless Providence of Almighty God." And for the Presentation Sisters the Pope breathed a prayer: "We beseech our great and good God to give success and increase to this new undertaking."

From the windows of her lovely Irish home, in days gone by, Mother Nagle had gazed on the immemorial oak trees that waved through the arches of the Templars' Church on her father's estate, the Norman Church that had been ruined by heretical despoilers. The oak tree was now going to be an appropriate symbol of the Presentation Sisters. Mother Nagle had planted a tree that was to be strong, firm, sure and secure. The winds of Time would not uproot it. Beneath the foliage of its branches it would be safe to shelter.

Ireland gave her its holy soil for the tree. God gave the increase.

CHAPTER 15

MOTHER NAGLE'S GLORIOUS DAY IS FAR SPENT: IT IS TOWARDS THE EVENING OF HER LIFE

THE whispering shadows of Life's mystic evening were closing in upon the earthly exile of Mother Nagle, and the sanctified career of Ireland's noble daughter was about to end. "After this, our exile, show unto us the Blessed Fruit of thy Womb, Jesus." So do we, children of mortality, pray to the Mother of God, chastened by the assurance that we never know when our exile may end. If ever any child of God merited, by her love and her work, the Beatific Vision beside the Throne of Mary's Son, it was manifestly Mother Nagle. Only through the medium of the Church's most exquisite prayers and hymns may we endeavor to express the heavenly delicacy of the soul which God gave to this angel of charity, who had so healingly moved among the poor, during those thirty fruitful years that we have been attempting to sketch.

As a bride of the Lord herself, she had devoted to the Church, which is the Bride of Christ, three decades of blessed toil. She had not uselessly lodged within herself those talents which God had given her, or wasted those material fortunes with which He had endowed her birth. Not empty-handed was she going home to the Eternal Bridegroom. Though her stay on earth had by no means reached the Psalmist's chanted span of three score years and ten, yet were her days filled to overflowing with works of charity; her fleeting years were replete with the effecting of those commands that her Master communicated in the Sermon on the Mount. The Wise Virgin was she, who watched and tended her Lord's household unto the last. In exchange for the goods of earth He gave her the riches of Heaven.

Her life was assuredly the giving back of Beauty to God. With Beauty in abundance He had dowered her life; she had used it to bring Beauty into the lives of others, and, untarnished, she returned the gift unto Him, within the City of God.

No wonder the *Annals* of her Convent refer to her as "Miss Nano Nagle, this eminent servant of God, the honour, the glory of this house, and of her Order, and the true benefactress of her country." No wonder they record that "the evening of this great woman's life was the most brilliant part of her career." As a Religious, her virtues shone out more luminously than ever.

There was much in her life that was hidden in Christ; there were mystical communings with her Beloved Spouse, and nameless acts of Love that were hidden from human ken; there were propitiations and generosities that only the pen of the Recording Angel could present direct to God. This is all summed up in simple sentences that tell how she gave seven hours a day to the class-room, and yet managed to find four hours, in her unwearying round, for prayer and contemplation.

Observers may say that all these good things are at all times true of all God's good ones, or that the life of one good soul seems like the life of any other. Are they not all meek and mild, and good and kind, and doing and praying, and loving their neighbour and loving their God? Only a detailed study of the distinctive books, that are written on the distinctive lives of the many distinctive Saints can help to answer such queries. As our friend Chesterton put it: "A Saint is a person very much like the rest of us — only very different". Each human soul is an individual creation of God. We are assured that star differs from star in glory, and that in the Father's House there are many Mansions. And we are satisfied that Mother Nagle was a star that dwelt apart, in the history of Catholic Ireland, and in the history of the Catholic Church. She became the mother of popular education, as Catholics know it, in the English-speaking world. That in itself is unique.

Into the Vineyard of the Lord some come early, and

some come late. Although those who came late, in the Parable, received the same reward as those who came early, Nano Nagle did not make this a precedent, or an inviting excuse for being late herself. She was called early and she came early. Early hours and late hours did she keep, in attending to every aspect of the vast work she undertook for her Saviour. Acceptingly she bore suffering, and, in the patient continuance of her course, she never complained. Resignation was her ally; murmuring she treated as an arch enemy.

There are divers distinctive characteristics about Mother Nagle and her work. As a young laywoman she introduced a noted Religious Order into her country, and as a Nun in middle life she gave rise to the first teaching Order in Ireland, since Luther broke loose in Europe. The Order which she founded, and the branch of the Ursuline Order which she introduced into Ireland, were both thoroughly Irish. All these good works she did in the face of outrageous laws that tried to forbid her.

Thirty years of undiminished toil, in so many blessed fields of action, took a terrific toll on the fragile life of God's good servant. The onerous duties of teaching, catechizing, governing, and administering, were weighing her down. No wonder that the frail frame began to falter under the penances, mortifications and abounding austerities, to which she kept subjecting it, even though the willing spirit was ready to go on to realms of limitless suffering. Any available records can give but scanty hints of her abasement and abnegation in humbly meeting the wishes of her Crucified Lord. He preached to her from the pulpit of the Cross and she listened attentively. The pierced Side of Christ and His Sacred Heart had fullest meaning for her. So also did Mary's heart that was seven times wounded.

It was only after her death that the Sisters discovered those severe evidences of physical suffering that were brought about on her limbs, by the unrelaxed austerities of the Foundress, to whom bodily comforts were but minor consideration. Kind towards others, she was severe upon herself: her own disciplinary subjections seemed fashioned after those of Saint Paul, who felt that it was important to preach to others, but also felt that it was vital to keep one's self in check, resolutely mastered by mortifications. The multiple marks of suffering which the Sisters found on Mother Nagle's mortal remains are ample record of her penitential perseverance. Nor can any appreciation, in praise of her character, lay the writer open to the charge of over-much panegyric: the compelling facts of her life preach sufficient tribute to her innate goodness, and to her immeasurable achievements.

Gentle as the breezes that lisped through the green grass in her native meadows, pure as the spring-flowers that blossomed by the sunlit hedgerows of her countryside, Mother Nagle advanced with fond footsteps, unto the last, through the city streets, that now had known her ennobling presence for over thirty years of life's shifting scene. There was nothing dour or harsh about her reforming zeal. Her approach was affectionate. For her, Love was the ful- filling of the law; to the very letter, she translated this at- tractive rule into action. The noblest elements of the Irish character mingled in her kind-heartedness and large-mind- edness. To her, as a typical representative of holy Ireland, might be applied the words of the Gaelic Poet, David Broderick: she gave prelude and promise, and she was like a raindrop of grace in the blaze of the world's evil.

How stood the country now? The clouds which came down on Irish life, after General Patrick Sarsfield sailed away to France, almose a century before, were at last dis- solving. In the year 1782, Ireland got back its own Par- liament, mainly through the exertions of a great Protestant Patriot, Henry Grattan. England surrendered its claim to make laws for Ireland. From 1698 to 1783 this contest had gone on between the two countries, and Ireland now victoriously started on its career as a nation and not as a settlement. For eighteen years Ireland was to have its own Parliament, until, in 1800, Pitt abolished it by sinister bribery and corruption. After that, Ireland did not have a native Parliament till the year 1922.

In the political developments of the year 1782, Catholics had little showing. Whatever mercies or privileges they enjoyed were the result of patriotic fairplay on the part of individual Protestants, such as Henry Grattan. Had there been a number of men in politics as good as Grattan, the story of the Catholics would have been a happier one. However, Grattan must have had high hopes for the future of the old land as he greetingly proclaimed her perpetuity: "Ireland is now a nation; in that character I hail her, and bowing in her august presence, I say *Esto Perpetua*".

The American Colonies had redressed their grievances by their own remedy of speedy separation from Old World ties. The Irishman, Edmund Burke, was the first great statesman of Europe who penetratingly saw a great and glorious future for the United States of America. Distinguished Irishmen in America had already founded "The Society of the Friendly Sons of Saint Patrick," and into this famous Society George Washington was unanimously adopted as a member. Its first President was one of Washington's Generals, Stephen Moylan, brother of Mother Nagle's dearest friend, Bishop Moylan.

The world in general was waking to new ideas of Freedom, and to a more enticing Social Order, as Mother Nagle was about to go to her Everlasting Rest.

Saint Thomas Aquinas suggests that Man is a horizon between two worlds. Within that horizon lay hidden many hopes and aspirations for a better world in the eighties of the eighteenth century. Mother Nagle had done more than her part to dispel the shadows from the human horizon, and let shine, here, some of the radiance from God's better world. An old world of privilege was fading with its vain bubbles, cobwebs, shadows, smoke. There was to be a better chance for all. The poor at least could be allowed to think and be taught.

One final survey of Mother Nagle's crowded career will suffice to show why she was almost prematurely worn out.

As a young woman she suffered from hemorrhage of the lungs. By nature, her constitution was delicate. Teaching was overstrainingly hard work for her. In rain, and frost, and cold, she suffered agonies in doing her manifold errands of mercy. She met with opposition on all sides. She was overtaxed in mind and physique by the teeming trials that blocked her way. Having expended herself unsparingly, the critical collapse of her health came suddenly.

By the New Year, 1784, her fond flock saw her strength rapidly failing, though she strove to remain cheerful and enlivened, despite her excessive fatigues. She, who was once as a rose for her perfect beauty, was now worn, wrinkled, and wan. She, who once graced with lightest step the ball-room of the Royal Court of France, was now crippled in the cause of her children at home. But was not "death in Erin" one of the gifts for which the Irish traditionally prayed to God? Through the streets of Cork, from one of her schools to the next, struggled the once-lovely Rose of Desmond on those last wintry days. In her deep humility she set little value on what her radiant presence meant to all around her; fourteen years previously she had remarked: "I am afraid you will all be tired of me, I may live to be so old." No, they would never grow tired of her, but she was now wanted elsewhere in a happier world. They were heart-broken at the thought of losing her.

April, the month whose very name signifies opening, and budding, and blossoming, marked the close of Mother Nagle's life. April skies were over Ireland, and the sunshine of Spring upon her fields. An April day was the appointed date for Mother Nagle's everlasting farewell to the Sisters, and the children, and the land that she loved. The month that heralds birth to all God's green array, on lea or hill, saw the soul of her, who was one of His tenderest flowers, blossom into an unfading life of Heavenly Rest. The sweet sounds and the gentle airs of the Irish April were a fitting swansong for the adieu of one of Ireland's most graceful daughters.

In a more peaceful and propitious age, some great painter like Sir John Lavery might perhaps have commemorated on canvas the death-bed scene of the beautiful lady, Mother Nagle, who had left glittering prospects at Court in order to become a guardian angel to endless throngs of needy children. A touch of the painter's brush might here prove more adequate than the attempt of a writer's pen.

But who can fully capture, on canvas or printed page, the heaven-sent magic of the Munster atmosphere in which she died?

I have unfading memories of an evening in Munster, at the advent of Maytime, when the surrounding world of Nature presented as bewitching a panorama as eye could see. A light fall of snow belatedly blessed the brows of the purple mountains, and gradually the holy haze of a silver moon whitened the earth into an altar of delight. Oncoming May blossoms, greening buds, filmy snowflakes and friendly moonlight combined to create an enrapturing symphony that remains forever a blessed recollection.

As we try to picture, on the film of imagination, the death-bed scene of Mother Nagle, we dream of a Munster day in Spring. Her Sisters were gathered around about her and were bending over her in fond farewell. For them, her life of heroic virtue was not terminating here. Its influence was to live on in the Congregation which she had founded.

Communicated to her spiritual daughters were the effects of her virtues, and influential upon their future sanctification was the deep filial memory of her virtuous life and of her devout death. Well too did her Sisters realise that the enticing virtues of their dying Foundress were to have a holy and lasting effect upon the fortunes and development of the new Congregation and of its work in future years.

Though dead herself, as far as mortal eyes were concerned, Mother Nagle's spirit and sanctity were to remain a hallowed incentive and were to be perpetuated by her daughters, who were so firmly resolved to follow in the salutary footsteps of the Foundress. The lovely and tender vision of a sainted daughter of God rendering up her soul to Him, the presence of her young Community in a reverential circle around her — thus simple seems the death-bed scene of Mother Nagle. But it left its memorable mark on the future flowering of her Congregation, as Time itself reveals.

To such a beloved spouse of the Eternal Bridegroom, Death was shorn of its forbidding and colder trappings: to her it was but the kiss of God. In her last moments on earth, the Blessed Sacrament was her Peace, as it had been the Peace of her forefathers for hundreds of years before. The beautiful old Irish hymn, the *Sancti Venite*, expressed this devotion:

> Draw near, all ye who are holy,
> Receive the Body of Christ,
> Drinking His Sacred Blood
> By which you were redeemed.
> Saved by the Body
> Of Christ and His Blood,
> Now nourished by the same,
> Let us all sing praises to God.
> By this very Sacrament
> Of Christ's Body and Blood,
> All are saved
> From the jaws of hell.

Such was the olden spirit of her race, and in a similar spirit was Mother Nagle going to join her God.

She was fortified by the Sacrament of His Love, and her farewell words were centred round that same Love of the Redeemer, Who loved us so dearly that He became rose-red with the Blood of our Redemption. Having called her infant Community around her, she gave them in few and simple words her final message. Little of the treasures of earth did she have to bequeath to them, for she had already devoted her fortunes freely to the causes that were dear to her heart, and to theirs. She gave into their charge the poor of Christ who are always with us. To the poor she had paid her loving homage when she entertained them, and waited upon them, on that Christmas Day, six years before. When she opened her first Convent the poor came first: she bade her Sisters to let it be so, unto the very last, for the poor were her prize beyond all treasures. Let her Sisters expend themselves unto their last breath for the poor.

Many beautiful things are recorded concerning the passing of God's holy ones. In Mother Nagle's case, appropriate Scriptural phrases occur to our mind in depicting her heavenly transit. In the twentieth chapter of the *Acts of the Apostles* there is the verse: "And now behold, I know that all you among whom I have gone preaching the kingdom of God shall see my face no more." Her life, offenceless, innocent and charitable, from first to last, may be summarised in verses 16 and 17, of Chapter 24, of the *Acts*: "And herein do I endeavour to have always a good conscience without offence towards God and towards men. Now after many years I came to bring alms to my nation, and offerings and vows." Truthfully she could declare that, to God, and to her people, she had given everything she possessed.

But it is to the master of inspired utterance, Saint John, to whom we turn when we seek the source of her last spiritual behest to her daughters. From prayer and penance came the most delicate refinement of Mother Nagle's spirit. It was in such a spirit that Saint John wrote his Gospel of Love. Saint Jerome mentions that the brethren asked John to write: the Evangelist agreed, if they would enter upon a common fast and a common prayer. And so they did. When this was over, Saint John broke forth, about God and the Word, into the most lofty outpourings of the soul that have ever thrilled the heart of man.

His lays of Light and Love found remembrance on the lips of the parting Foundress. She wished her Sisters to love God, love the poor, and love one another. From the

Gospel according to Saint John, there occur to mind those words in Chapter 17: "And I have made known Thy name to them, and will make it known; that the love wherewith Thou hast loved me may be in them, and I in them." Filial words of Christ, from the same Chapter, may help to express the farewell of the woman who had wholly served Him: "I have glorified Thee on the earth; I have finished the work which Thou gavest me to do." Unitedly she followed Him.

To her Sisters on earth, Mother Nagle's last instructions were a perfect epitome of the new commandment of Love, which Saint John recorded of Christ: as He loved all, so let all love one another. Why, it may be asked, this protracted accentuation on the word Love? Because the Sisters had to work in a world which was obviously infected and festering with hate: against hate and ignorance they were to match their lives of love and gentility, as the Foundress herself had done, and so triumph over the blight of bitterness and ungodliness.

Biographers and Historians long to trace the very last words of the famous. Happily, the records declare for our edification that Mother Nagle's last words were these: "Love one another as you have hitherto done." Her words were a tribute to the affection that united the Community, and an encouragement to continue in that harmony begotten of Divine Love, which alone can make Community life, or any life, possible and liveable. These words of her leave-taking express the guiding spirit of her Sisters in every clime. Her entire life was a Psalm of Love. In the spirit of Love is her memory perpetuated. This blessed spirit does not change, does not die. In it she still lives.

Appositely does the beautiful *Preface* to the Mass of Requiem suggest the meaning of our transition from this life, in a world of impermanence, to the Life that awaits us in the world of the Permanent: *Tuis enim fidelibus, Domine, vita mutatur non tollitur.* As for Thy faithful souls, O Lord, Thou hast not taken away life from them, Thou hast only changed it. Transplanted from this valley of the shadows, to the Light of Glory, was the gentle soul that the world knew as Nano Nagle: thence does her influence still live on in the light of Love, the Love that continues to be reciprocated between herself and her Sisters. That was her efficacious prayer.

And since Saint John's Gospel of Love formed the basis of her last goodbye, there is one more image that we may borrow from the pen of the sainted Seer. It occurs in his last chapter, when he is describing the appearance of Christ Who has already triumphed over sin and death: "When morn was come, Jesus stood on the shore." It is a memorable picture for painter, poet, or dramatist. The word "shore" occurs so frequently in our earthly imagery. "Soon may we reach the shore." So do we sing, as we envisage the harbour which is Heaven. Correspondingly, we talk of "Life's tempestuous sea." We ask the Mother, who is the Morning Star, to guide us safe to port, over the howling waves of Life's sea. We talk of Life's frail barque being storm-tost. Haunting us is the image of a peaceful shore and a calm sea, when we pray: "Save us, O Lord, or we perish." At rest, on the shore of Eternity, with Christ, after years of storm, may the holy Foundress be pictured.

It was at morning's dawn, in Paris, that God granted His first great revelation to Nano Nagle. From then on, she remained close to His Heart at every moment — quick to recognize the Lord, as was John on that far-off morning when He stood on the shore. So, instantly, can Love identify Love. It was morning in April, in Ireland, the twenty-sixth of that month, when Christ's Angels came to take His heroine home for ever. It was in the year 1784, and in the fifty-sixth year of her age. Eternal Morn it was for her, Birth anew in Heaven, and Reception at the Throne of her King. Leaving her Sisters her fondest blessing, she set forth to dwell with Christ for ever, safe at last on the Eternal Shore, where, as Saint John says, "there shall be no night, and they shall need no candles, nor light of the sun; for the Lord God gives them Light, and they shall reign for ever and ever."

CHAPTER 16

IN MEMORIAM: BY DUE RITES, RESPECTS, AND HONOURS, THE DEPARTED FOUNDRESS IS EXTOLLED

Under the date of April 30, 1784, the *Annals* of her Convent record that the remains of Nano Nagle were interred in the cemetery belonging to the Ursulines, and enclosed in a large tomb which stood in its centre. Two Communities, the Ursuline Sisters and her own, conjointly mourned her departure.

But we do not think of Mother Nagle's mortal resting-place as merely a tomb or a grave. Rather is it a shrine and a place of pilgrimage. Thither do reverential souls repair, for it is a sacred spot that holds the hallowed relics of a noble virgin, whom her people wish to see raised to the Altars of the Church.

The old hymn, entitled "The Blessed City of Jerusalem," can nicely express the people's honour for the Bride called the Church, and for the sainted Brides of Christ who dwell therein:

> "A crown of pearls is on thy brow,
>   Thy gates are opened wide;
> The ages bow before thy throne,
>   And hail thee as the bride,
> That moves mankind to deathless love
>   Of Christ the Crucified."

As bright an ornament as may be traced in the modern history of the Catholic Church is the woman whose revered relics repose within the walls of the Convent which she built, as a rebuke to enforced ignorance and Penal benightedness, in the dreariest hour of her country's annals.

Her venerators had recourse to the Old Testament for an inscribed phrase to honour the Foundress, who expired with one of the noblest sayings in the New Testament on her lips — after she had received the Blessed Eucharist and become, as Saint Cyril of Alexandria would say, a "blood relation of Christ." To *The Book of Numbers* they went, Chapter 23, and they put the inscription therefrom in Latin: "Moriatur anima mea . . . "

In order to sense the full import of the reference, we quote the Scriptural verse indicated above: "Who can count the dust of Jacob and know the number of the stock of Israel? *Let my soul die the death of the just,* and my last end be like to them." The Lord put these good words into the mouth of Balaam, who had been asked by Balac, the King of the Moabites, to go and curse Israel. But, instead, Balaam was obliged to bless Israel, under the inspiration of God.

As the Lord blessed Israel, so surely did He bless and spare Mother Nagle's harassed kindred. Who today can number the stock of the Irish throughout the world? It would be an interesting effort in calculation. The unjust and alien laws which sought to revile and defile Mother Nagle's people, and to curse them and degrade them by the bane of ignorance, fell foul of the plotted purpose, within a century after her death. Transplanted by God's beneficent purpose to scattered lands afar, the Irish bore with them the blessings, the joys, and the peace of the Faith. Holding pride of place in this divinely predestined dispersal, Mother Nagle's own Sisters promptly followed in the wake of their race, to bestow the blessings of Christian Education, wherein their Foundress was the pioneer at home.

In Cork, on a slab of stone, they engraved some of those virtues of the Foundress, whose name was already written in the hearts of the multitudes that loved her. This is the tribute:

> *"Here lie, waiting, 'tis hoped, a glorious resurrection, the remains of Miss Honora Nagle, daughter of Garrett Nagle, Esquire, of Ballygriffin, and venerable Foundress*

of this monastery of Saint Ursula, and of
the Institute of the Charitable Instruction:
whose life and fortune were always devoted
to the service of God and of the poor: whose
piety, humility, and self-denial made a most
salutary impression on an admiring public;
and whose charity and zeal were most singu-
larly and successfully exercised for more
than thirty years in the instruction of multi-
tudes of poor children, rearing them true
servants of God, and useful members of
society. She departed this life, envied by
many, regretted by all, on the 26th day of
April, 1784, aged 56 years. Requiescat
in Pace.
  MORIATUR ANIMA MEA.
      Numbers, XXIII, 10."

Her biographer, Archdeacon Hutch, observed that she merited a monument in Cork's leading thoroughfare, where already stands a statue to her illustrious cousin, Father Theobald Mathew. He enthusiastically added that her "public services have been far greater than those of Father Mathew." She merits many a monument, in towns at home and abroad. But statuary, at best, is a faint and frail memorial for the sainted servant of the Lord, whose benevolent influence animates her people in new lands and in old. Her loving memory is securely locked in the casket of many a heart that has followed her. In two hemispheres, the added work of her Sisters must be witnessed as her universal, her desired, and her visible shrine. The winds of Time have by now breathed her name and her fame to every corner of the rounded earth.

Mercifully, for the sake of the narrative, there was saved in the Presentation archives, from the unsettlement and wreckage wrought by Penal fury, a tender tribute to the memory of Mother Nagle from the pen of a devoted friend. The name of Mother Mary Angela Fitzsimons is already familiar to the reader, for she was the first to volunteer for Nano Nagle's new Ursuline Community, in the year 1767. From Cork, on May 21, 1784, Mother Fitzsimons wrote the following letter to Miss Mullaly in Dublin — almost a month after the demise of the Foundress: —

"I flatter myself, my dear friend is sufficiently persuaded of the gratification your dear and edifying letters are always to me, yet am content to be deprived of that favourite pleasure as often as I wish, when I consider the multiplicity of your occupations, and how painful it is to apply to writing, perhaps *with* or after violent headaches, which I often experience, and have been the excuse which prevented me giving you sooner the account you desired of our dear, respectable, and much-neglected N. Nagle, whose strength has been visibly declining those twelve months, particularly this last and severe winter.

Her limbs were so feeble she was obliged to use a stick in walking, and has been seen to stop frequently in the streets to get a little strength to proceed in her long and painful walks; that you know the extent of, better than I, as you have seen them. They were indeed so many steps on the road to eternal life.

She added to her usual austerities that of fasting every Wednesday and Friday, on bread and water, since she left our convent, and lived in her own house. She enjoined secrecy of this matter during her life to all her religious sisters. She took the discipline four times each week during the *Miserere;* she made instructions three hours each day during Lent, fasting, and passed eleven hours last Holy Thursday night before the Blessed Sacrament, kneeling all that time.

Her fervour increased so much towards the

end of her course that I believe she lost all sense of bodily pain or suffering. She told me last Easter Monday (when I enquired how she was after the Holy Week) that she never remembered to have been so strong as the last Easter Saturday, and that though she had read the Passion of our Lord three times at different schools the Monday and Tuesday before, she did not perceive the least fatigue; 'and you know it is pretty long,' she said.

She had repeated, neglected colds during the winter, yet walked abroad when anyone else would have been in their bed.

On a very wet day she went as usual to all her schools, and was penetrated with rain, as of late she walked so slow.

The next day, which was a Wednesday, she was taken ill (with a hemorrhage of the lungs) at a lady's house where she breakfasted, who told me that she requested her to go no farther that day, but to return home. Nano Nagle answered: *What a coward you are!* I have a mind to go to the schools, and walk it off as I am used to do.' But a weakness ensued and the dear woman walked home for the last time.

However, she did not complain to her Sisters, nor even to the doctor who went to visit one of them, till, in the evening, they perceived her to change colour and perspire. We did not hear one word of it till next morning, by chance.

I heard that she was not out that morning, and inferred that she must have been very ill, and immediately proposed sending for the doctor. But first we sent for Sister Mary Augustine Fuohy, who confirmed all our apprehensions, and prayed us to send for the doctor, as she had positively forbid them to send for him. He ordered her immediately to be let blood; next day to be blistered; and the day following another bleeding, which was again repeated — but all without success.

An inflammation had been long formed in her lungs; a violent cough, great oppression, and total weakness, were the symptoms; but she never once complained, not even of the blister, and had hopes of recovering, till about twenty-four hours before her death. On seeing her blood quite corrupted and inflamed, she knew it was impossible; however, she sent money (as offerings and alms) to three of her favorite children, and desired them to pray for her recovery, if it was for the glory of God, that she might have more time to prepare for eternity.

The doctors would not permit her to receive the Last Sacraments till about seven hours before she died, lest the application and her extraordinary devotion would exhaust her too much, as they had still hopes that God would spare her longer to the poor and the distressed, to whom she was a tender mother.

She expired on Monday, 26th April, the sixth day of her illness, in the fifty-sixth year of her age, as much regretted on earth as she was welcomed in Heaven, where I hope she is now interceding for us, that we may follow her great example.

I refer you to Sister F. for an account of her burial. (Sister Augustine Fuohy, apparently.) She ordered herself to be buried in the poor ground which is near this . . . , and desired that all her Sisters should be interred there also; but we would not consent that her venerable remains should be in such a place, exposed to be disturbed by the multitudes that are hourly brought there! and in order to comply with her orders of being interred with her Sisters, we have con-

sented to permit all those who will die in the
house she instituted to be interred in our burial
place, where she lies.

To prevent this being taken notice of by the
parish minister, *et cetera*, we have made a door
which opens into her garden, and is never to be
opened but for this purpose, as Nano Nagle
gave positive orders to her Sisters never to have
any connexion with this community, for very
prudent reasons, to prevent what happened when
you were here . . .

You will be pleased Miss Nagle has left a very
sufficient maintenance for five Sisters — two
thousand pounds (about ten thousand dollars),
and two thousand pounds more at the death of
her brother Joseph, if he dies without issue; all
on condition that they comply with, and observe
the rules she has left them, and to be under the
inspection of her sister (Mrs.) Ffrench and family, to whom she has left two thousand pounds
more.

I hope I have complied with my dear friend's
request as well as my memory allows . . .

Adieu, dearly beloved friend. Pray for me,
and believe me,

Ever yours most sincerely,

Sister M. A. F.

(Sister Mary Angela Fitzsimons)"

By her noble birth, Miss Nagle might have enjoyed the
ultimate privileges, and pageantry, and pomp of ancestral
heraldry, but it will be seen that, in her humility, she
wished to be buried in the common burial ground of the
city, among the poor whom she loved, and whom the Law
fiercely and harshly called paupers. The graceful lady,
connected by blood with the proudest titled families in the
land, was so enamoured by God's poor that she even
yearned to lay her bones among them in the humble part

of God's Acre, the part that classical sculpture does not deign to deck. She, who inherited those large financial fortunes, which she devoted to the social and educational improvement of the unfortunate, wished to sleep her last sleep with the fortuneless ones of God. It was but one more of the many endearing examples she set to all who are crazed in the quest of the world's flickering baubles: herself she reckoned as naught, and her God was her all.

The *Annals* of her house relate that the dying Mother Nagle gave up her charge of Superioress into the hands of Sister Angela Collins, who was one of the first Presentation helpers that rallied to her side, seven years previously. The Foundress recommended Sister Angela to be vigilant, to be kind to those whom she committed to her care, and to be sure that the good work, so recently initiated, should be continued and perfected. Mother Nagle remarked that she herself was not worthy to witness the progress of the Society, which she had begun in unpromising days, when neither Church nor School was legal.

Not long before Mother Nagle's passing, a slight decree of relief came for Catholic teachers. Quaint in its concessions to "Popery", the fiat of George the Third was called "An Act to allow persons professing the Papish Religion to teach School in this Kingdom, and for regulating the Education of Papists." There were more unshrouded days ahead for the Second Superioress, Sister Angela Collins, and for the first native teaching Community that blessed Ireland since the Reformation. An account will follow in another section of the narrative.

Across the sea, in England, Miss Nagle's cousin, Burke, was flouting the furies and vanities of men. "What shadows we are; and what shadows we pursue," said the sublime philosopher, as he gazed on the antics of the human hive, both great and small. He, too, would bid the players, that make up the Passing Show, to raise their heedless eyes to God, Who guides and guards and rules, while Pomp passes and men's meannesses shrivel into the

pit of Oblivion. To the Lord, Who is feted by every breeze
and tree, we join our honour in Milton's lines:

> "His praise, ye Winds, that from four quarters blow
>   Breathe soft, or loud; and wave your tops, ye Pines
> With every plant, in sign of worship wave."

Burke had declared to swollen and empty men, who
could not see their way to exercise God's Charity towards
His creatures, that the only final landed security for every
mortal is the grave. When he passed his boyhood days at
Nano Nagle's home, he had many moments for meditating
on the fleeting flowers of the early Irish Spring. The snow-
drop or the primrose may be an example. The memories
and images of a flower peep through his correspondence
with the high-souled Grattan, who had won a Parliament
for Ireland, and hope for the Catholics. Burke wrote of
his own hopes for Ireland at this stage of the story:

> "This poor, vapid primrose, that comes out on
> the sunny side of an old mouldering bank, ready
> to tumble into the ditch, has all its value from its
> season. It appears in the rear of winter, amidst
> the blighting winds of calumny and persecution.
> By and bye it will be forgot; I hope and trust
> it will be forgot amidst the luxury of colours and
> of odours which your poor Country, warmed into
> gratitude, will shower upon your head, from all
> the pomp and profusion of a genial May. God
> send it."

Burke's own ardent hopes for an Ireland that would
know the white and full and free luxuriance of Maytime,
may be best realised from his expression of dependence
on our Bounteous Creator: "But God is all sufficient; and
that we exist and exist with any degree of hope at all, is
a proof of it." Some of the temper of the time reflects
itself in Burke's heavenly determination to keep on waging,

in East and West, "under the standard of the Captain of our Salvation, a war without quarter upon all cruelty, and oppression, wherever they appear, in whatever shape, and in whatever descriptions of men."

Ireland seemed only a faint geographical suggestion to some of the obscurantist politicians who attempted to rule her in the eighteenth century. All his life Burke believed in the Destiny of Ireland and he served her fondly from afar. Serving and believing in that Divine Destiny at home, there was no more prophetic woman in eighteenth century Ireland than his kinswoman, Nano Nagle. She was far removed from the blaze of public life, and, violet-like in her modesty, she trod what seemed to the worldly-minded a very obscure path. But, so sure was her vision, that her humble path eventually wound its way to the Mountain of Transfiguration: she led her nation to the Light that is not on land or sea.

In a *Life* of Ireland's beloved Saint Columba, written by Manus O'Donnell, Lord of Donegal, almost four hundred years ago, there is a poetic picture of Saint Patrick, who will judge the people of Eire on the Day of Doom. Therein we are assured that it will be a happy day for the reverent, the prayerful, and the alms-givers, when they meet the eye of their advocate, judge, and Patron, Patrick, at that august hour: happy will it be for all those who shall have followed the ways of Patrick and the other saints of Eire. So runs the exquisite picture painted by the transcendent Irish imagination.

Only on that "Day of the Mountain," as the Irish call it, will it be fully possible to estimate the merits of the white flower of their race, the sainted soul, the giver of gifts, Nano Nagle.

CHAPTER 17

A RECAPITULATION OF MOTHER NAGLE'S
SAINTLY CHARACTER

Of all the Greek words we use, one of the most familiar is the noun *Character*. It is a difficult word to define. We know what we have in mind when we use it, but it is a problem to express a full and satisfactory definition of it. Our dictionaries tell us that it means a distinctive mark; it can mean a person's mental or moral nature; it may indicate a person's moral strength, backbone, or good reputation, or it may be a description of a person's qualities. We employ many adjectives in this connection: we talk of a character as being noble, sterling, grand, fine, strong, exemplary, and so on. The word is sometimes used for a person, as when we say that somebody is a public character. From its Greek origin, the word character denotes an engraved mark or stamp. We learn, for instance, of certain Sacraments that leave upon the Soul a spiritual mark or character, that can never be effaced.

Mother Nagle's saintly character captivates us the moment we begin to study her life. Her distinguishing mark is heroic holiness. This holiness manifested itself specially in her practice of charity. Engraven in her heart was an outstanding love of Christ's poor. On her part it was no momentary sentiment, no ephemeral emotion. The grace of God evoked every power of her soul and body in the service of the poor. She loved them with her whole heart and soul. In them she instantly beheld the image of the Crucified Man of Sorrows. Her avowed aim was to make their lives happier on earth, by teaching them, feeding them, and clothing them. The faithful manner in which she devoted her whole life to doing corporal works of mercy, among the poor, would alone win the utmost praise of her character as a practical humanitarian, and as a social reformer. But, to her worthy aim in the temporal order of good works, she exquisitely and far-reachingly added the still more exalted aim of teaching her people the ways of spiritual happiness, so that they might achieve the Life Everlasting for which they were destined.

It was natural that the character of Mother Nagle should have attracted the profound power of Father Tom Burke's pulpit oratory. Father Thomas Nicholas Burke was one of the greatest Dominican Preachers of all time. He was born in Galway, in 1830, a year after O'Connell won Catholic Emancipation, and forty-six years after Mother Nagle had gone from this earth. His tributes to O'Connell and to Mother Nagle are masterpieces of abiding eloquence. He lived long enough to preach at the hundredth anniversary of the founding of Mother Nagle's Presentation Sisters.

There was much in Mother Nagle's character to attract Father Burke, who, as a boy, was deeply affected by the heart-rending scenes among the poor in famine days. It is said that those sights and scenes impressed him so memorably that they had a good deal to do with his decision to enter religion. Deeply impressed was he also by the memory of the noble woman, who had walked her beneficent ways among the poor, and who had made history in the evil years before his birth.

Father Burke's sensitive intellect was keenly alive to the sublimity and sorrow of his nation. God gifted him with the fullest possibilities of carrying out the Dominican mottoes: *Laudare, Benedicere, et Praedicare.* His work of praising, blessing, and preaching, carried him far afield. Bishop Leahy took him as his theologian to the Vatican Council. Throughout America, vast audiences thronged to hear Father Burke's enrapturing oratory. In New York he gave versatile discourses, wherein he levelled the artillery of his rhetoric against bad history, against alleged history which had been maligning his faith and his people; Froude's fantasies he refuted in particular, with a wit and a wisdom that captivated the huge audiences, and inspired them, highly and holily, with a respect for the

Catholic creed, and for the Irish Nation that remained loyal to the Truths of the Church, "in spite of dungeon, fire, and sword."

Who was more fitted to do justice to the character of Mother Nagle, the ardent lover of the neglected babes, than the eloquent Dominican, Father Burke, who preached his last sermon in the Jesuit Church, in Dublin, in aid of starving children in Donegal? To the inexhaustible fount of the Old Testament he repaired for an appropriate text. He found exactly what he wanted in *The Book of Judges*. Comparing Mother Nagle of Ireland to Deborah of Israel, his text suggests his historical parallel:

> "The Lord chose new wars, and He Himself overthrew the gates of the enemies: a shield and a spear was not seen among forty thousand of Israel. The valiant men ceased, and rested in Israel; until Deborah arose, a mother arose in Israel . . . Arise, arise, O Deborah, arise and utter a canticle."

Of Mother Nagle and her work Father Burke said: —

> "A Deborah appeared before the eyes of our people, and her name is in our minds and upon our lips today. It was Nano Nagle.
>
> In the days of Ireland's worst national calamities, colleges and schools were found everywhere throughout the land; the traditions of Ireland's learning which in the early ages of Christianity made her the light of the world — an Island of Saints — that tradition remained and was carried on, gloriously, until a new war was proclaimed, and this was when the Penal Laws prohibited, under penalties of confiscation, exile, and ruin, the most sacred work of education.
>
> The ferocious and brutal laws of King William the Third, and Queen Anne, the object

of which was to make it penal, under penalty
of banishment, fine, confiscation, or imprisonment, for a Catholic in Ireland, man, woman, or
child, to teach or be taught, were set in motion.

She (Mother Nagle) is strictly and historically truly the mother of Irish Catholic education. She is the Deborah who turned the tide, the
woman who took up the lance that had fallen
amongst forty thousand in Israel. She is the
woman whom God chose, and whom He raised
up to be the mother of that Catholic Irish Education which has preserved our Faith, preserved
the glory of the purity and morality of our Irish
womanhood, which has sent us forth to the ends
of the earth to be apostles to nations, which has
achieved the greatest victory of Ireland's Faith
and apostleship over all the powers of darkness.
Such was this woman."

Mother Nagle was constrained to do her heroically
charitable work in the face of unjust laws. In his panegyric, Father Burke pointed out that the Catholic Church
always teaches obedience to law, but "when a law comes
to stand between a people and the Altar of God, that law
binds no man, cannot bind, because it wants the first ele-
ment of law, the principle of Eternal Justice."

It may be well to reflect on Deborah and her character,
in order to appreciate the full force of Father Burke's
comparison of Mother Nagle with the heroine of Zion.
Deborah was both a prophetess and judge. God gave her
very clear prophetic gifts. The tribes of Israel were de-
plorably divided in her time. In their disunity lay their
weakness, which made them an easy prey to united foes.
Deborah used her God-given oracular powers to weld her
disorganized people into effective unity, and great became
her holy authority over them.

She was a real and true judge in our legal meaning of
the term. As she sat under a palm tree she dispensed

justice, and litigants came freely to have their cases tried before her. She cured her nation of disorders within, and led her people to meet the enemy without: the Canaanites were the enemy that harassed Israel. Small indeed was the martial equipment of Israel, but God was with His people in the person of Deborah, and success was assured.

Barac was leading Israel, and Deborah was in the battle. She told him the right moment to attack in the Battle of Thabor. God miraculously sent a rainstorm, wherein the chariots of the enemy became stuck with mud. Thus did the small host of Israel providentially scatter the numerically superior forces of the enemy. Deborah led her people to victory — which only her inspired vision could have foreseen. All others had despaired.

In thanksgiving, Deborah uttered one of the most beautiful songs in the Bible. She made her people gratefully and unanimously aware of the One True God, Who watched and ruled lovingly over them all. Her lyrical love of her Lord lingers forever in the stirring lines of the Fifth Chapter of the Book of Judges: —

> "Hear, O ye kings, give ear, ye princes; It is I, it is I, that will sing to the Lord, I will sing to the Lord the God of Israel. My heart loveth the princes of Israel. O you that of your own goodwill offered yourself to danger, bless the Lord. The remnants of the people are saved, the Lord hath fought among the valiant ones. So let all thy enemies perish, O Lord: but let them that love thee shine, as the sun shineth in His rising."

It will be readily recognized why Father Burke compared the heroine of Ireland with the heroine of Israel. In Israel there was no man with enough heavenly trust to rescue the remnant of a broken nation. God raised up Deborah to do the deed. In Ireland there was no man sufficiently inspired to do the deed which the Lord desired.

God raised up Nano Nagle to rescue the Faith of a broken nation.

Indeed one may quote in regard to Mother Nagle's character, from the closing lines of *The Song to David*, by Christopher Smart, a great and frenzied genius in English Literature, who died in the year 1771, about the time that Mother Nagle was launching the first educational community in Ireland. "Glorious is the song when God's the theme": that was the burden of Smart's poetic ecstasy, as he addressed David and Christ, Who is called the Son of David. The poem is immortal:—

> *Glorious — more glorious is the crown,*
> *Of Him that brought salvation down,*
> *By meekness called thy Son;*
> *Thou at stupendous truth believed,*
> *And now the matchless deed's achieved,*
> *Determined, dared, and done."*

Mother Nagle's deed was matchless in the history of her nation. Her character and her achievement may be compressed into those three words: determined, dared, and done. Through the spectral mists of almost two centuries the figure of the heroic foundress still appears as clearly as the bright sun at noon.

What did her contemporaries say of her? Here is an utterance from one of her learned admirers, quoted under date of April 26, 1784, from the *Annals* of her own Convent. "Miss Nagle," says this distinguished man, "was a person gifted with a mind which appeared almost divinely inspired to foresee and remove every obstacle to a great work; a mind beneficent by nature — gentle, from habit; generous, from disposition; and exemplary, from the workings of divine grace. A mind, in fine, formed at the school of the Cross, and there convinced by Jesus Christ, Who is meek and humble of heart, that His yoke is sweet and His burden light, and that those who hope in Him shall not be confounded. Her manners gained and engaged the heart; her authority commanded respect, without seeking its rights; her piety showed good example, while it strove to hide itself; her prudence excluded every excess; no labour could abate or release her zeal; nor could any difficulty shake her resolution; she was ever equally submissive, and willing to receive as to communicate advice or instruction."

Mother Nagle's charity was of such an extended character that it embraced all God's creatures: no thought of creed, or class, or country, narrowed its scope. The charity that flowed from her, who was an angel of true tolerance and broad vision, was only bounded by this rounded Universe. She meant it to extend afar. Her spiritual daughters have seen to that. Her motto was Pauline: *omnia omnibus.* She was all things to all: her sole consideration was to win all to God. Quoting Shakespeare in her behalf, her early biographer says that "she had a tear for pity, and a hand open as day for melting charity."

The financial fortunes of Nano Nagle could have verily gifted her with a life of ease and luxury. Like many fortunate people, she could have given generously to charity and could still have maintained a stately home, and servants, and coaches, and the numerous appointments and amenities of domestic felicity. Or she could have continued to enjoy her court life, "along the cool sequestered vale," charitably emerging into slumland, from time to time, and winning those plaudits that are fulsomely accorded to the wealthy, when they make social and philanthropic visits among the poor. All sorts of worldly possibilities for leisure and enjoyment lay open to the young lady who was the adored *belle* of the gayest Court that history has ever known. Blessed by privileges of aristocratic birth, and by gifts of intelligence, beauty and wealth, Miss Nagle could have won social fame and popularity in the highest circles in any land. Her godly character preferred the service of her own poor in her own country. When her social hopes were brightest, she turned her back on every material prospect, in order to help her piteous people when their hopes were darkest. This weighty step needed a character that abounded in moral excellence. Grace called Christ's heroine apart, and the poor won a friend whose strong character led her to serve them unto death.

What were Mother Nagle's other outstanding characteristics? Judicious common sense guided her life: a strong will and a practical wisdom were hers. The short-sighted world might regard her as a visionary, because she fled from a glittering circle to bury herself in seeming drudgery among the neglected poor. But her practical planning is easily evident from a study of her work, which has stood the test of time.

Great was her staying power, and great was her tenacity of purpose. Some there are who can do things in the white heat of success, victory, and glory, but, when serious obstacles arise, these temperamental souls wilt, crumple, collapse, and quit. Mother Nagle's powers of perseverance are all the time evident in the apparently overwhelming difficulties which she overcame. Her friends, her family, and her foes, had to be conciliated: the lukewarm and the hostile had to be studied and placated. There were times when everything appeared to be going against her. Her biographer adds that "the very Bishop of the Diocese, to whom she ought principally to have looked for support, did not favour her views." But, all the way, God upheld her and her cause, and He rewarded her heavenly perserverance with unimagined success in the growth of her schools.

Very effectively did Archdeacon Hutch illustrate her characteristics by passages from some of the Romantic Poets. She answers to Wordsworth's ideal:

> *"The reason firm, the temperate will;*
> *Endurance, foresight, strength, and skill.*
> *A perfect woman, nobly planned,*
> *To warn, to comfort, and command.*

Her amiable character is imaged in the lines of Samuel Rogers:

"She was as good as she was fair,
None — none on earth above her!
As pure in thought as angels are,
To know her was to love her."

Manifestly, to name Mother Nagle is to praise her. Words occur to us from Pope's translation of the *Iliad*: "Wise to resolve, and patient to perform, gentle of speech, beneficent of mind." That description fits the character of our heroine. She blended activity and contemplation in a perfect balance, so that the one never hindered the other. After strenuous hours of teaching, she took care to spend other concentrated hours in communing quietly with her Maker. At five in the morning she was on her knees for prayer, and when the busy bustle of the scholastic day was over, she made her prolonged evening devotions.

Though her aching limbs caused her endless agony in her latter years, she never once complained: to kneel meant acute pain, but she kept on kneeling in prayer. On the night of each Holy Thursday, she knelt before the Blessed Sacrament till morning. Each year she made her spiritual retreat of eight to ten days: so perfectly was she under the influence of self-abnegation that she joyfully bore the physical pain it cost her to follow the devotions. Only after her death were these facts fully apparent.

The *Annals* of her Convent afford us a glance at her character: "Mother Nagle's private austerities were so uncommonly severe that they were in fact more likely to excite astonishment than imitation. Her zeal was most unremitting and most ardent. She often assured the Sisters who laboured with her in religion, that she never enjoyed any more sensible pleasure in her life, than that which she experienced on seeing great crowds of children assemble round her to receive instruction. It was under this virtue of zeal she sank."

Emerson observed that "a great soul will be strong to live as well as to think." To illustrate the strength of Mother Nagle's character, we mention one phase of the battle that she won. In her day, the Protestant Primate of Ireland wrote to the Protestant Bishop of London: "The great number of Papists in this Kingdom (of Ireland) and the obstinacy with which they adhere to their own religion, occasions our trying what may be done with their children to bring them over to our Church."

On one side, therefore, there were the official, wealthy, and powerful Protestants, who tried to steal away the native children from the Catholic Faith. On the other side, there was the solitary figure of Mother Nagle, as she battled single-handed to keep the children of her nation safe within the household of the Faith. The entrenched and ruling Protestantism of the day could offer many material temptations to wean the young from the Old Faith. It is one of the many tributes to Mother Nagle's determined character that she held fast against this sinister campaign, opposing it by her courageous work of shepherding, and teaching, and feeding, and clothing the little ones, in order to keep them Catholic. Her triumph, over such an evil design as proselytism, is the best testimony to her unyielding character.

As we have already seen, Mother Nagle's spotless character had to do battle against calumny. Though she was universally appreciated, her fair name did not escape the venom of this corrosive and rodent vice. The dear good angel was called almost everything that perverted tongues could pelt at her. They ridiculed her as an impostor and a hypocrite.

Because she spent her own money freely in supporting her schools, it was suggested that she was merely indulging in the extravagance of vanity. In the same breath it was contradictorily insinuated that she conducted her schools solely for personal profit. One is reminded of the double-barrelled attacks that viperish calumniators made on the character of her Lord and Master, Christ: if the

Saviour supped with sinners, He was accused of being a wine-bibber and a friend of evil-doers; if he came neither eating nor drinking, like John the Baptist, He was accused of having a devil. Calumny enters the double-edged knife stage when its victims are accused at one and the same moment of opposite charges.

The records of her own Convent again supply the facts on her heroic character, which always brought her unruffled through indignities:—

"It was her solid and practical humility that caused her to rejoice when God permitted her to be publicly insulted and reviled as an impostor. She certainly was an imposter on one occasion, a holy impostor! For the poverty and wretchedness of her appearance so far imposed on a stranger as to cause him to offer her a few pence as an alms, which she humbly and, no doubt, most joyfully accepted for the love of Him, for whose sake she really classed herself, as to the sufferings of poverty, with the most destitute mendicants. She was accused of having squandered her money in building houses to acquire for herself a good name, and of deceiving the world by her throng of beggars' brats. Her schools were even said to be seminaries of wickedness and vice. These, and many other insults, she silently and patiently bore; nor would her humility have ever permitted her to disclose them, did she not feel it a duty to communicate them, that she might thus prepare the Religious of her community for the same humiliating treatment."

Defamers went to the depths of devildom in order to heap their malicious misrepresentations on the noble character of a gentlewoman, whose frail life was forspent in tireless charity to the poor. Slurs were cast upon her fair name, because, in her embracing mercies, she moved boldly among the outcast and tabooed Magdalens of human society, and she reclaimed to virtue those whom nobody else attempted to reform.

But Mother Nagle's character was a faithful mirror of Christ's meekness: when she was reviled she did not turn back to revile, but rather went straight ahead with her holy work. The insults of noxious obstructors did not dismay her, nor did she waste a second of her precious time in answering any of their arrogant falsehoods. The gifts and fruits of the Holy Ghost bore her unspotted through the blackest atmosphere in the earthly arena. Many essays might be written on the moral teaching of Shakespeare, but emphatically appropriate are his words in the present instance:—

"*Be thou as chaste as ice, as pure as snow, thou shalt not escape calumny.*"

During the thirty hard-working years wherein she served the poor, Mother Nagle especially edified those around her by her prevailing regularity. She did not deviate from duty, or waste a moment in worldly distractions. Prayer, Action, and Sacrifice, formed her daily trinity of offerings to the Eternal Three in One. The fire of suffering was as welcome to her as it was to Saint Francis, when he said: "Brother Fire, God made you beautiful and strong and useful; I pray you be courteous with me."

Though the lives of Mother Nagle and her companions were austere, and rigorous to the utmost extreme, yet they were always happy, always glad and gay, and joyful in their labours. She led them in this heavenly cheerfulness, and cheerfully they followed.

Moodiness, moroseness, or melancholy gloom never cast their sullen shadows over her happy presence, either in public or in the community. Joy and hope were her watchwords: to be at once holy, and cheerful, and uncomplaining, was her ideal. It is a cherished and inspiring tradition among her Sisters that the hours of recreation never passed so pleasantly as when Mother Nagle's radiant presence enlivened the community, in happy relaxation, after a day of exactions and toil. To be dreary, dismal,

lugubrious, and atrabilious, may suggest being sancti-
monious. But Mother Nagle's bright and winning characteristics of sanctity stand for all time as correctives against
assuming funereal features, or sour and sulky faces, that
would seem to turn the freshness of each day's exciting
task into a stale, grim, and exasperating routine. She was
a happy saint.

No doubt the Foundress made it a point to introduce
some of the joyful spirit of the Liturgy of the Church
into daily life. No matter how harrowing the hour, she
found time for an encouraging *Gaudete,* or a *Jubilate,*
or a *Laetare*: rejoice, exult, and be happy in the Lord.
From Daily Mass, of course, may be learned the joy of
Sursum Corda. Certainly, by her example Mother Nagle
taught all to lift up their hearts in happiness to God, and to
show that the Church Militant can borrow some of the joy
of the Church Triumphant, that grieves not or sorrows.
No wonder that she was beloved and reverenced and vener-
ater by her Community, as she led them along, through
difficult days, in holiness, happiness, calm and content.

Since Mother Nagle was compared to Deborah of Israel
it was also fitting that a comparison be made between her
and the illustrious Patroness of Ireland, Saint Brigid.
Though Brigid died in the sixth century, and Mother Nagle
in the eighteenth century, there are many similarities in
their lives. Saint Brigid was the first Irish Nun. Mother
Nagle was the first Irish Nun to found a new native Community, since the great tradition of Brigid was broken at
the Reformation. Both Brigid and Nano Nagle were of
noble ancestry. Both declined the lives of privileged ease
and honour that were readily available to them in the
world.

Under a large oak tree Brigid built her first Convent at
Kildare — Kildare, which means the Church of the Oak.
The Oak Tree is a suitable and sturdy symbol of the
Presentation Sisters. Brigid's little oratory so flourished
that Kildare grew into a Cathedral City. She founded two
institutions, one for men, one for women. She founded

schools of art, metal work and illumination, which later won the praise of Giraldus Cambrensis — Gerald Barry, of Wales. As a Patroness of students, Brigid became nationally and internationally famous. She was hailed as Queen of the South and the Mary of the Gael, and she bequeathed to Ireland a city and a school that were both justly honoured all over Europe.

In less opportune days Mother Nagle established schools for boys and girls in the Irish southland. Her Sisters were quickly established in the old town of Kildare, and, just as quickly, the Kildare Community sent subjects to found schools in Australia. As in Brigid's case, Mother Nagle's work attained world-wide fame. They were both educational pioneers: Brigid in a Golden Age, Mother Nagle in an age of nightmare. When public celebration was accorded, in Ireland, to Mother Nagle's memory, at the Centennial Commemoration, in 1871, it was well said that no other woman had had her name so widely interwoven with the Irish Race, since the days of Brigid, as the venerated Nano Nagle.

Breviaries on the Continent of Europe commemorate Saint Brigid of Ireland. Her name is included in a Litany in the famous and ancient *Stowe Missal*. Relics of her found their way to Lisbon and Cologne. The Manuscript of an Eighth-Century life of her is preserved in a Dominican Friary in Bavaria.

Europe knew the fruitful work of Brigid. The whole modern world enjoys the fruitful work of Mother Nagle, from England to India, from Australia to America: all have been blessed by the work that started so modestly in Ireland, in 1775.

But it is a similarity of character that strikes us most, in studying the lives of those two illustrious Irishwomen. From an old seventh-century Life of Brigid we glean her character:

> *Saint Brigid was not given to sleep,*
> *Nor was she intermittent about God's Love;*
> *Not merely that she did not buy, she did*
>   *not seek for*
> *The wealth of this world below."*

From an ancient Latin hymn, in honour of Brigid, we learn more of her fame: "In our Island of Ireland, Christ was made known to man by the very great miracles which He performed through the happy virgin — Brigid — of celestial life, famous for her merits throughout the whole world."

She was a friend of Saint Patrick, as is shown in *The Book of Armagh,* which is over a thousand years old:— "Between Saint Patrick and Saint Brigid, the columns (or pillars) of the Irish, there was so great a friendship of Charity that they had but one heart and one mind; through him and through her Christ performed many miracles."

Brigid propagated the Faith of Saint Patrick. Mother Nagle propagated the Faith of both: the Light of Faith was almost extinguished when God raised her up to fan the flickering flame into a brightness whose glow re-enlightened a nation that lay hidden in the shadows. "That you may remain Christians and also Romans"—such was the prayer of Saint Patrick. That her ancient Christian nation might keep the Faith of the Holy Roman Church intact, Mother Nagle dared all for the Vicar of Christ. The words of a poet may be applied to her:—

> "*I stood amid the Lights that never die,*
> *The only stars the dawning passes by,*
> *Beneath the whisper of that central dome,*
> *That holds and hides the mystic heart of Rome."*

The strength of her heavenly character led Mother Nagle to follow in the footsteps of Saint Brigid and Saint Patrick. Great was her victory. She securely stands amid the Lights that do not die. There are stars that the Dawn does not dissolve, and the Morning Star is One, Mary the

Mother. The Lights that illumine the Altar of Faith give imperishable rays of cheer and hope. There, among those Lights, it was that Mother Nagle took her stand. In "the mystic heart of Rome" she found her rest.

Sentire cum Ecclesia: that is a sacred motto. Mother Nagle's pure heart beat in unison with "the mystic heart of Rome," the centre of Christian Unity. She successfully thwarted the wicked schemes that would wrench her people from such an Apostolic Unity. She gave her whole life to defend such an abiding Unity among her children. Many a faithful name may be whispered beneath the central dome of Saint Peter's: no name can be found more loyal to the Throne of the Fisherman than that of Mother Nagle. For the Faith that Saint Patrick brought, from Rome, she gave her saintly life.

There is an Approved Prayer for the Beatification of the holy Foundress; fifty Days Indulgence is granted to all who recite the Prayer, daily, for the Cause of Mother Nagle:—

> "O most amiable and adorable Heart of Jesus, we prostrate ourselves before Thee in all humility and pour forth our supplications on behalf of Thy servant, Nano Nagle, who during her life had such a tender devotion towards Thee. Cast a favourable look on her virtues and works and, if it be for the glory of God and the sanctification of souls, hear us, we beseech Thee, that soon she may be raised to the Altars of Thy Holy Church. Amen."

Such is naturally the prayer of all the children of her race, all the children of her benefaction, throughout the world. They pray that Nano Nagle, the Sainted Pioneer of Catholic Education among her people in the modern world, may take her honoured place beside her prototype, Saint Brigid, the Patroness of Education in Ireland's Golden Age. God speed the day.

CHAPTER 18

EXPLAINING SOME HISTORICAL POINTS IN THE LIFE AND TIMES OF MOTHER NAGLE

HOW did some Catholics continue to possess their lands in spite of the Penal Laws? The question occurs in the study of Mother Nagle's work. A few facts concerning the Nagle family may help to answer the query, in part.

We know that Catholics were prohibited from purchasing property, and that the whole estate of an Irish Catholic could be given to his son, if that son became a Protestant.

Mother Nagle's first cousin, Garret Burke, elder brother of Edmund Burke, died unmarried, in 1765. Both brothers were Protestant. Garret left to Edmund his interest in an estate called Clogher, in County Cork. This estate had been acquired by Garret Burke on a lease of 999 years, in order to protect the interests of the Nagles, to whose family his mother belonged. It was not till the year 1778 that Catholics were allowed to lease land for 999 years. Hence, the Protestant Garret Burke had been obliging his Catholic relatives by leasing the property for them. The Nagles, as Catholics, were penally prohibited from holding the land for any term more than 31 years. Even if the Nagles did obtain any lease, they were liable to lose the property if some mercenary member of the family became a Protestant. Under the Penal Code any family member could demand the whole property by turning Protestant.

It is to the eternal credit of so many of the Protestants that they did everything possible to help their Catholic relatives, friends and neighbours, to retain personal properties. Official Protestantism was resolved to maximize the Penal Laws: individual Protestants helped to minimize the Code, for the benefit of their Catholic fellow-countrymen, by setting up seeming Protestant owners who would actually hold the properties for the real Catholic proprietors. It was all a humane and friendly connivance to outwit the imbruting Penal system, and it was the only way in which kindly Protestants could safeguard their Catholic friends against constant loss of lands. This was what Garret Burke did for his Catholic relatives, the Nagles.

When Garret died, his brother, Edmund Burke, took his place in holding the property on trust for the Nagles. It was a serviceable family arrangement, and, in the present instance, it worked well for a number of years. Edmund was deeply interested in his mother's family, to many of whom he had done services. In 1766 he was in Ireland, and he made himself thoroughly familiar with his responsibilities in holding the Clogher property for the Nagles.

But, in 1777, the very thing happened that the Penal legislators wished. One member of the family, Robert Nagle, became a Protestant, and he tried to win the whole property for himself. He failed. Edmund Burke, as trustee, honourably refused to have anything to do with such a mean claimant, who wanted to put the rest of the family out in the cold.

Is there a convenient historical example of how fully the Penal Laws could be enforced? Yes: a specimen of their ferocity is shown in a famous Irish poem called "A Dirge on the Death of Art O'Leary." It was written by his wife, Eileen of the Raven Locks. This dark-haired poetess was a daughter of Daniel O'Connell of Derrynane, County of Kerry, grandfather of "The Liberator" — Daniel O'Connell, who won Catholic Emancipation.

Art O'Leary was a noble Irish gentleman who had been an officer in the Hungarian service. He came back to Ireland, having extensive property in County Cork. Handsome, warmhearted, and distinguished, he was very popular because of his gracious qualities. In fact, he became so widely beloved that a neighbour grew jealous of him. This was Mr. Morris, whose horse had been beaten in a race by Art O'Leary's proud mare.

Mr. Morris spitefully proceeded to take advantage of the Penal Laws, which, as we have already mentioned, did not permit a Catholic to own a horse valued at more than five pounds. So he demanded the mare from Captain O'Leary for this sum. The proud O'Leary refused, adding that he "would surrender his mare only with his life."

A magistrate speedily proclaimed O'Leary an outlaw. Soldiers hid in wait for him as he was coming home at night, and they shot him dead. That was in May, 1773. Mother Nagle was then a woman of 45, herself facing the full fury of the unjust Penal Laws, by proceeding with her educational work in the same County of Cork. Art O'Leary's wife only learnt of the tragedy when the beautiful mare returned riderless. Then did the dark Eileen O'Leary burst into a piercing poem on her young husband's murder — he was only 26. It was many years before his body was even allowed to be buried in consecrated ground. O'Leary's grave is to be seen in the nave of Kilcrea Abbey, in County Cork. His wife's intensely affectionate and fine poem gives a touching sketch of the local scene in eighteenth-century Ireland.

To show the happier side of things, as an example of the reciprocal goodwill and generosity that sometimes existed between Protestants and Catholics, an extract from Edmund Burke's correspondence may be introduced. The letter was written in 1792, by Edmund to his son Richard, who was then in Ireland. Because of his father's honoured name, the young man had been appointed to act as Agent to the Irish Catholics, who were already struggling for Catholic Emancipation — a cause most dear to Burke. From old family ties the Nagles were specially remembered:

"When you go towards the Blackwater, (in County Cork) if we have got any friends alive, and not quite ruined there, hinder them from showing you any honours in the way which, in old times, was not unusual with them, but which since are passed away, for in the present age and reign of newspapers they would be very mischievous. I have long been uneasy in my mind when I consider the early obligations, strong as debts, stronger than some debts, to some of my own family now advanced in life and fallen, I believe, into great penury. Mrs. Crotty is daughter of Patrick Nagle to whom (the father) I cannot tell you all I owe. She has had me a child in her arms, and must be now, I dare say, 74 years old, at least. I wish her much to have some relief, so do I to Kitty Courtnay."

Edmund had just received a legacy of two thousand pounds from Sir Joshua Reynolds, and he told Richard to give a twentieth part of it to the two women mentioned above — "you know how much I love them; God knows how little we can spare it."

Mother Nagle's teaching Community was twenty years old when the famed College of Maynooth was established in 1795. Here again her cousin Burke enters into the history of Catholic Education. So much does Burke enter into the Catholic story that it is said he died a Catholic; that he was received into the Church of his fathers by his great friend, Bishop Hussey.

Burke's motto was, "do to others as others would do to you." He believed that the Catholics should take whatsoever good offer they could conscientiously get. The British Government was interested in a Catholic College at Maynooth. So was Burke. He suggested to Doctor Hussey to make the most of the Government proposals for a Catholic College. But let the Catholics be true to themselves. For Burke was suspicious lest Catholic Education be made subservient to a Protestant State.

To Doctor Hussey, who was a leading light in the establishment of Maynooth College, Burke wrote warmly and warningly about the Government:

"Be well assured that they never did, and that they never will consent to give one shilling of money for any other purpose than to do you mischief. If you consent to put your clerical education under their direction or control, then you will have sold your religion for their money." Burke continued to caution Doctor Hussey that a Protestant Government must not have undue interference: "I am sure that the constant meddling of the (Catholic)

Bishops and Clergy with the Castle (seat of British Government in Ireland) and, of the Castle with them, will set them ill with their own body."

Doctor Hussey was a historic figure in the development of Catholic Education in Ireland. He was quick to bring Mother Nagle's Presentation Nuns to teach in the ancient city of Waterford. He was a generous friend and patron of the ardent educational reformer, Edmund Ignatius Rice, who founded the Christian Brothers of Ireland. Bishop Hussey also founded Saint John's College in his own See of Waterford, which to this day sends forth priests unto many lands abroad.

Some of Bishop Hussey's courageous pronouncements on our Holy Faith attracted the wrathful attention of reactionary bigots. He inspirited drooping souls by pointing out the heroic perseverance of Ireland in the Apostolic Church. He declared that less persecution had blighted the Faith in other countries. More and more persecution had only served to strengthen the Irish Faith. The Bishop felt proud that his people had kept aglow the spark which Patrick lighted. He declared that "they were as unrivalled in the history of the Church, as isolated an exception to the prevaricating versatility of man, as the geographical situation of the Irish Island itself is to the rest of the world."

So the cultivated Doctor Hussey, Catholic Bishop of Waterford, was violently attacked by the sceptred forces of fashionable Protestantism. Burke was prompt to champion and praise him: sympathetically he wrote to the Bishop in defense of the very poor — to whom Mother Nagle was an angel of rescue:
"My dear friend,

How could they expect that you, a Catholic Bishop, should not prefer your religion to all others? How could they expect, that if you, as a Catholic Pastor, did not strongly assert the advantages and pre-eminence of your religion, yet as a good citizen you would endeavour to keep the people attached to the only religion which they can possibly have?

How dare they assert that it is not the religion of the country, in which more than 100 to 1 in your Diocese are of your Communion?

If they should say that this is the religion of the common people, it is only to speak more in its favour. It is for them that all religion, and eminently the Christian religion, is meant for a guide, for a control, and for a consolation. These are principles you have always held.

To be sure, Christ himself has given as a conclusive proof, in his answer to John the Baptist, of His Divine mission, that the Gospel was preached to the poor."

We have seen that the Catholic poor were eager to be taught. They promptly flocked to Mother Nagle's schools. This was a traditional feeling, inherent in the race through endless ages. Wakefield, an English writer, shortly after 1800, recorded that "the people of Ireland are I may almost say universally educated; I do not know any part of Ireland so wild that its inhabitants are not anxious, nay eagerly anxious, for the education of their children."

Lord Palmerston wrote of his Irish-speaking tenants, in the County of Sligo, in 1808: "The thirst for education is so great that there are now three or four schools upon the estate. The people join in engaging some itinerant master; they run him up a miserable mud hut on the roadside; and the boys pay him half a crown, or some five shillings a quarter. They are taught reading, writing, and arithmetic, and what from the appearance of the establishment, no one could imagine — Latin and even Greek."

Protestant children also went to these Hedge Schools, and the wandering Catholic schoolmasters never interfered with their religion. In fact such schools helped to create friendly relations between Catholics and Protestants. On the other hand, the temptation of apostasy was held out to Catholics by the official Protestant institutions called

"The Charter Schools." These were financed by the Protestant Parliament of Ireland and the Imperial Parliament of Great Britain. They were founded for "the conversion of the lower orders of the inhabitants of Ireland from the errors of Popery." But some of the Catholic Philomaths, who persevered with their academies by the hedgerow, lived long enough to see Catholic Education victorious.

Another historical feature needs to be stressed in limning the background of Mother Nagle's Ireland. Though Catholic Culture was eclipsed in the homeland throughout the sixteenth, seventeenth, and eighteenth centuries, native scholars from Ireland then won highest distinction in the great seats of Culture on the Continent of Europe. Mother Nagle's native County of Cork gave a Rector to the celebrated University of Louvain in the seventeenth century. The counties of Kerry, Monaghan, and Tipperary also gave Rectors to that same proud European University in that same seventeenth century. Penal darkness thwarted the Irish genius at home, but abroad in Europe it shone with fourfold brilliance. In Irish and Latin studies the names of Fleming, Ward, White, and Colgan, are for ever dear to scholars. They, in dark days, maintained the learned connection of Ireland with Europe, a connection which dated back to the sixth century.

The English Statesman, Sir Robert Peel, was well aware of the popular love for education in Ireland, when, in 1816, he admitted "as a fact within my knowledge, that the greatest eagerness and desire prevails among the lower orders of Ireland for the benefits of instruction."

Though the people deeply desired learning, there was little opportunity for developing either the theory or practice of Education in Eighteenth Century Ireland, as far as the Catholic majority was concerned. In other countries, there were great names connected with educational reform and educational philosophy in that century. There was Pestalozzi, the Swiss Educational Reformer. There was the German Educator, Froebel, the father of the Kindergarten system. The German Philosopher, Herbart, also arose in the eighteenth century. Into the early years of it, Locke, the English Philosopher lived on.

Catholic Ireland was struggling for survival and had but little time for the academic subtleties of sensism or sensationalism, apperception or psychodynamics. But the hedge schoolmasters did their work well, in the academic hovel or by the academic hedgerow. Such were the schools for boys. The girls were gathered together, beneath a roof, by the pioneering heroine of our story, Mother Nagle. She, who had a habitual sense of the Presence of God, made this the basis of the sound and practical education which she gave to the children. Success crowned her efforts. Her schools multiplied. Her work goes on gloriously to this day. She was the true and great Educational Reformer of her age in Ireland.

Burke wrote that "England and Ireland may flourish together; the world is large enough for us both; let it be our care not to make ourselves too little for it." By the greatness of Mother Nagle's vision, the work of popular Catholic Education, which she began in Ireland, has been beneficially extended throughout the English-speaking world.

To illustrate how the Ireland of Mother Nagle was bereft of the flower of its youth, we may mention that in one century France absorbed half a million Irish troops. There was an Irish Brigade in the service of France, over twenty thousand strong. An old Irish Ballad, entitled "John O'Dwyer of the Glen," tells us the sad story that followed the fall of Limerick in 1691, when the brilliant General Sarsfield sailed away from Ireland to die serving France. The Ballad was translated by the eminent Irish novelist, Canon Sheehan, as follows:

> And to Sarsfield underneath whose flag
> We'll cast once more a chance.
> For the morning's dawn will wing us
> Across the seas and bring us
> To take our stand and wield a brand

Among the Sons of France.
And though we part in sorrow,
Still Sean O'Duibhir, a cara,
Our prayer is *God Save Ireland*
And pour blessings on her name.

The young men of Ireland were scattered everywhere, serving every people but their helpless own. In Spain, King Philip gave the Irish their proud Latin motto: *"In omnes terras exivit sonitus eorum."* In France, King Louis gave them their equally proud Latin motto: *"Semper et ubique fidelis."*

Yes: they were everywhere famous and faithful. But, exiled from their homeland by unjust laws, all they could do was to bless her from afar. The brave men went forth. A brave maiden returned to fight alone for the educational salvation of Ireland. Nano Nagle it was. Blesssings pour for ever on her triumphant name.

CHAPTER 19

FROM THE BLESSED VIRGIN MARY THE PRESENTATION SISTERS TAKE THEIR TITLE

NATURALLY every community, nay, every member of the Catholic Church, has a special devotion to the Mother of God, whom we ask to pray for us "now and at the hour of our death." The spiritual daughters of Nano Nagle have their particular devotion to the Presentation of the Blessed Virgin Mary in the Temple. Under the title of Mary's Presentation do they work and pray.

Mary, who in the Gospels is, eight times, called the Mother of Jesus, was, like her Divine Son, presented in the Temple. Her parents Joachim and Anna presented her there, and the Church officially celebrates this Feast. It has been observed throughout the Western Church since the Sixteenth Century, and in the Eastern Church "for twice as long on the same date." The date is November 21.

In the Byzantine Rite "the Entrance of the All Holy Mother of God into the Temple of Jerusalem" is kept as a Feast of five days. On what occasion Our Lady's presentation in the Temple took place "is uncertain," says the *Catholic Dictionary*. So the Church celebrates the Feast, but does not specify at what age Mary was presented, when she made her vow of virginity. In 1585, Pope Sixtus the Fifth extended this Feast to the whole Church.

It was particularly in keeping with the traditional spirit of the Catholic Church in Ireland that Mother Nagle's distinctly Irish teaching community should be associated with especial devotion to the Mother of God, whom Pope Pius the Eleventh in our own day called "Queen of Ireland." There is an old Irish Litany of Our Lady which dates back to the eighth century. The distinguished English Jesuit Scholar and fearless critic, whom the present writer remembers with grateful affection, Father Herbert Thurston, was an enthusiast for that venerable Irish Litany of Mary.

He said that it "yields in nothing to the Litany of Our
Lady of Loretto" — which seems to have come into use
commonly in the Sixteenth Century.

In the Irish Litany, Mary was the recipient of the most
beautiful titles, fondly bestowed by a spiritual people,
twelve hundred years ago. She was called *Mistress of the
Heavens; Mother of the Heavenly and Earthly Church;
Recreation of Life; Mistress of the Tribes; Mother of the
Orphans; Nurse of the Infants; Queen of Life; Ladder of
Heaven.*

England too, which was known as "Our Lady's Dowry,"
had its widespread devotion to Mary. Cynewulf in Anglo-
Saxon days wrote of her:

"Hail thou glory of the middle-world!
Thou purest woman throughout all the earth
Of those that were from immemorial time,
How rightly art thou named by all endowed
With gifts of speech! All mortals throughout earth
Declare full blithe of heart that thou art Bride
Of Him that ruleth the empyreal sphere."

It was Chesterton who wrote of Our Lady: "She grows
young as the world grows old." We Catholics are sometimes considered old-fashioned by the changing world
around us. But it is the world itself that grows old. Our
Lady to us is ever young. With her we take our stand
through the rosaries of the years.

All ages proclaim devotion to Mary. Saint Ephraem,
the Syrian, in far-off days, sang his hymn to her: "The
Babe that I carry carries me, and He hath lowered His
wings and taken and placed me between His pinions and
mounted into the air, and a promise has been given me
that height and depth shall be my Son's."

Saint John, the Evangelist, envisioned Mary in the
Apocalypse as "a woman clothed with the Sun and the
Moon under her feet, and on her head a crown of twelve
stars." Again she is described:

"I am the root and flock of David, the bright and morning Star."

In the first Chapter of the *Acts*, we are told of the Apostles, after the Ascension of Christ, that "all these were persevering with one mind in prayer with the women, and Mary the Mother of Jesus, and with his brethren."

Saint Ambrose says of Mary: "In Heaven she leads the choirs of virgin souls; with her the consecrated virgins will one day be numbered."

In their special devotion, therefore, to the name of Mary, which is said to mean "The Perfect" or "The Beautiful One," Mother Nagle's Sisters are at one with the Church in a deeply-rooted devotion, which keeps blossoming in every Christian century.

One of America's most beloved poets, Father Abram Ryan, the singer of the Southern cause, was inspired to write one of his rare lyrics for the "Feast of The Presentation of Mary in The Temple."

"The priests stood waiting in the holy place,
Impatient of delay
(Isaiah had been read),
When sudden up the aisle there came a face
Like a lost sun's ray;
And the child was led
By Joachim and Anna. Rays of grace
Shone all about the child;
Simeon looked on, and bowed his aged head —
Looked on the child and smiled.

Low were the words of Joachim. He spake
In a tremulous way,
As if he were afraid,
Or as if his heart were just about to break,
And knew not what to say;
And low he bowed his head —
While Anna wept the while — he, sobbing, said:
"Priests of the holy temple, will you take
Into your care, our child?"
And Simeon, listening, prayed, and strangely smiled.

And twelve years after, up the very aisle
Where Simeon had smiled
Upon her fair, pure face,
She came again, with a Mother's smile,
And in her arms a Child,
The very God of Grace.

And Simeon took the Infant from her breast,
And, in glad tones and strong,
He sang his glorious song
Of faith, and hope, and everlasting rest.

Painters as well as poets have depicted the Presentation of Our Lady. She is delineated as a little child going up the steps of the Temple, there to be dedicated to the service of God.

Protestant writers have often addressed themselves to the Mother of God. The restless Lord Byron, at eventide, when the Angelus Bell peals for Mary's name, burst forth with "Ave Maria! 'Tis the hour of Prayer!"

And George Eliot also invoked our Mother Mary:

> Heart of Mary, bless the way,
> Keep us all by night and day.
> Heart of Mary, morning star,
> Ward off danger, near or far.
> Heart of Mary, by thy sorrow,
> Keep us upright through the morrow,
> Heart of Mary, by thy grace,
> Give us with the saints a place.

Rudyard Kipling had a prayer to the Mother of all living:

> Oh Mary, pierced with sorrow,
>   Remember, reach and save
> The soul that goes tomorrow
>   Before the God that gave!
> As each was born of woman,
>   For each in utter need,
> True comrade and brave foeman,
>   Madonna, intercede!

An admirer of Mother Nagle's Sisters appropriately observed that "the Queen of Virgins was the first true Presentation Nun." Joachim and Anna brought their little daughter Mary to be placed in The Temple of Jerusalem, under the care of the Holy Women. One of these women we historically meet in the Gospel according to Saint Luke. She was the venerable prophetess Anna. In the precincts of the Temple the devoted women passed their days serving the Lord, and assisting with the education of those children committed to their charge. There is a tradition that Mary was about three years old when she was presented in The Temple, and that she lived there for about ten years. Devout writers interpret the intervening seven years as Mary's school days, which were a time of preparation for the wonderful work of her life.

We have no definite details of how Mary's days were occupied during those holy years of initiation. We only have the certitude that the Lord of Love was perfecting the beautiful soul of Mary by the generous activity of His Grace, making bright that soul which we call "Full of Grace," and which was the chosen dwelling-place of the Most High. In the miraculous dispensation of Providence, every human soul is specially created to be the dwelling-place of God. The soul of the Immaculate Mary, after the soul of her beloved Jesus, was to be the most surpassingly beautiful of all souls. Her own exquisite Song, the *Magnificat*, tells us all the glorious things that God did for her.

Mary's days in the Temple have therefore been described as a noviceship, with the indwelling of God working its wondrous miracles upon her soul. Thus, following the chosen example of Mary, do the Sisters of the Presentation consecrate themselves to the service of God. They spend all the days of their lives in serving the Eternal Teacher: for Him they study and teach, and they invoke her, who is "Sedes Sapientiae", as the model for themselves and their pupils. Inspired in all their work by love of Christ and Mary, they win the affections of their pupils for the Holy Family. No earthly reward do the Sisters envision for their meritorious services, none but the heavenly guerdon of an unbroken Eternity in the solacing Vision of God, after life's busy years are over, and their task in guarding and protecting youth has been shiningly well done.

Spiritual writers have naturally been attracted by the striking conversion of Nano Nagle, and by her complete surrender to her Maker and to His service, through His Divine Grace. Here again occurs the mention of God's Holy Temple. The beautiful Miss Nagle was returning from an all-night dance at the smartest Royal Court of France, when the Temple of God caught her eye in the dawn. Fervent and hard-working worshippers were entering that Temple to join in receiving the benefits of the Holy Sacrifice of the Mass. The heroine of this story was quick to respond to the lesson which she learned from the steps of God's Temple.

In the spiritual order, we are assured that, when there is complete co-operation between God and His creature, then there is the blessed peace of Sanctity. Such apparently was the entry of God into the temple of Nano Nagle's soul. And, as Mary surrendered herself entirely to God's Eternal Will, so did Nano Nagle victoriously and unreservedly correspond with His Grace, and commit herself to His service without ever turning back.

Round about her, Mother Nagle attracted a true spiritual family, her Sisters, whom she inspired with the same ardour of complete self-surrender to the service of God, which must ever mean for them a sequence of good days and bad days in a life of sacrifice. Through such a spirit of Grace the soul of the true Presentation Sister is a temple of God. To help in making the souls of her pupils the everlasting dwelling-places of God is her life's aim. Within her own soul the Lord dwells by His Grace; He is with her in the classroom, with her in recreation, and with her in study. Attention to the temple of God is her watchword. Following the spirit of her Foundress, her prayer is to abide uninterruptedly in the Presence of God. In the classroom she is a true representative of her Patroness Mary.

The Presentation Sister is a true and thorough teacher. The educational needs of her pupils are many and varied. Particularly in the scholastic crescendo and competition of modern life are there endless studies and examinations to demand exacting care, and skill, and patience. It is the holy resolve of the Presentation Sister to present her pupils to that actual yet mysterious thing we call "Life", so soundly trained in mind and body and soul, that they will be a credit to God and country, loving the Grace of God above all things at all times. Mother Nagle's Sisters love the souls of their pupils first and foremost, and then the educational progress, happiness and human welfare of these same pupils who are committed in thousands to their care. Unto many lands have their pupils perpetuated those valuable lessons, from generation unto generation.

The perpetual presentation of souls to God, through the grace of sanctity and through sound Christian education — that is the work of Mother Nagle's Sisters in the name of the Presentation of the Blessed Virgin Mary.

Particularly of Mother Nagle's deeply-needed Congregation of teaching Sisters may be said what Dante recorded of the Religious Orders, which he compared to suns: "How many souls warmed by their beams have blossomed into beauty, which otherwise were dwarfed and stunted as in a wintry clime."

Only in sable perspective can the Catholic Ireland of Mother Nagle's youth be portrayed. With the dawn of the nineteenth century her Sisters had given to that sable scene something of the brightness of the House of Gold, and something of the white cheer of the Tower of Ivory. The Comfortress of the afflicted was at hand to light their way. It was their Patroness, Saint Mary of the Presentation.

CHAPTER 20

MOTHER NAGLE'S WORK EXTENDS FAR AND WIDE

PROVIDENCE manifested its prompt hand in extending Mother Nagle's work. Though the beloved Foundress had gone to the Heaven of her reward, after her thirty years of superhuman toil, still her spirit enlivened and inspired her Sisters. They vigilantly continued to carry out the spiritual and corporal works of mercy, enlightening those that sat in darkness, visiting the sick, distributing food and clothing to the needy, solacing the afflicted, guiding the wayward to virtue, and generously rendering endless acts of educational and social service to the people of Cork. But those sorely-needed services were soon to be extended to places further afield than the parent house.

The Light of Mother Nagle's work could not be hidden under a bushel. Its beams cast their beneficence afar, bringing Hope to many another town and village in Ireland, and, a little later, to new towns in new worlds, where the scattered children of the Gael fondly welcomed the Sisters' vivifying Apostolate, which was initiated for universal service by the heroine of the Motherland.

Conscious of the worth and benefit of the new Society, Bishops in adjoining dioceses were immediately eager to seek the services of the Sisters in helping to raise the needy from the slough of despond. We have already mentioned that Mother Nagle's admiring friend, Bishop Moylan, of Kerry, was hoping for a branch foundation in his diocese during the lifetime of the Foundress. It was only in 1786, two years after her demise, that the project could be started, when Mother Curtayne and Mother Lane entered the Motherhouse in Cork as first subjects for Kerry.

They returned to Killarney in 1793, where their way

was the way of the Cross; and it was only after many vicissitudes that they emerged through the Cross unto the light of success. Shortly after their arrival, their Convent was taken from them through some technical flaw in the lease. But friends were providentially at hand to help. Lord Kenmare, of the old Catholic family of Browne, whose ancestral seat was in Killarney, generously joined with the leading townsfolk to ensure the Sisters a dwelling.

Within a decade the new Community triumphed over all obstacles, and they entered their permanent Convent in 1803. In the course of a few generations the Presentation Sisters became a flourishing Community in Beauty's Home, doing priceless work in the educational training of hundreds of young girls, and teaching them the practical arts of crochet, point lace, and embroidery, so as to guarantee a future livelihood.

Modesty and self-effacement are easily observable marks of the Presentation Nuns. They are downright hard workers in serving the Lord and His Children, and they envisage no fame in mortal eyes. Happily the present writer has had first-hand experience in personally knowing the Sisters in the Old World and in the New, and has had the pleasure of witnessing the wonderful work they do in their finely equipped Schools at home and abroad. After twenty years of constant lecturing in Colleges, Academies, and Schools, throughout a good part of the English-speaking world, I am often asked by educational groups to "compare notes."

Suffice it to declare here, that in my humble opinion, the Presentation Sisters are first among equals for their thoroughness, efficiency and results. The names of many places will follow in this narrative, to indicate the extension of Mother Nagle's work. In Tralee, Waterford, Listowel, Castleisland, Rathmore, Lixnaw, Millstreet, Tuam, Athenry, Killarney, to name but some of the towns and villages wherein the work of the heroic Foundress flourishes; in New York — at Newburgh and in Staten

Island; in Dubuque and the Dakotas; in California — both at San Francisco and Los Angeles; in Rhode Island, and at Fitchburg, in Massachusettes; from Ireland to the Golden Gate — in places great and small, it has been my privilege to study the work of the Presentation Sisters. I have met them as College students. Wherever I have met them, they carry with them that zeal, and charity, and lady-like graciousness, which adorned the happy character of their noble Foundress.

An Irish Protestant Bishop — Berkeley — is famed for saying that "westward the course of Empire takes its way." And Berkeley, the seat of the great University of California, bears his name. In the upbuilding of another Empire, that Spiritual Empire of God, which is the life work of the Irish Race, the Sisters of Mother Nagle are to be met with in Berkeley too, preparing young ladies for their future avocations by imparting to them a traditionally sound Christian Education.

Dublin society once knew Nano Nagle as a young lady of fashion, with aristocratic connections. It next knew of her as an eminent Foundress, whose worthy work had many benefits to offer to the needy and submerged section of humanity within the national Capital. Mention has already been made of the shining name of Miss Maria Teresa Mullaly, who knew of Miss Nagle when the latter still dwelt in the upper ranks of secular society. Though the artificial society of the day might regard these two young ladies as being poles apart socially, yet were they closely united in spiritual affinity towards the service of God's poor.

Miss Mullaly was the daughter of a hard-working Dublin tradesman. She herself became a busy dressmaker, and, by her industrious devotion, she set aside her savings for the education of necessitous Catholic children. We marvel at her financial courage in buying the site and in completing schools thereon for the poor. From the start her approach was systematic and determined. She first rented a small house in Mary's Lane, and, with the assistance of Miss Anne Corballis, and Miss Judith Clinch, she there instructed large numbers of poor children at all available hours, on Sundays, Holydays, and on possible weekdays. The work grew so rapidly that Miss Mullaly finally decided to seek funds for building a Convent, whereby teachers would be ensured for perpetuating those educational facilities that were so sorely needed in Dublin.

Of course there were educational institutions in the Capital, but they were for the Protestant minority. Catholics might only frequent them at the price of apostasy.

Among the clergy who encouraged Miss Mullaly in imparting permanency to her apostolate, a Jesuit, Father Mulcaile, was outstanding in his aid. The laity corresponded in their interest and generosity, and it was fortunate that Mother Nagle and her Community in Cork were able to promise their co-operation.

The Dublin foundation, at George's Hill, was completed in 1789. Suitable subjects presented themselves for training at the Motherhouse in Cork, and, by 1794, they entered into the Vineyard of the Lord in Dublin. Among the lists of the early candidates we find the names of the Misses Doyle, Doran, Biggar, and Clinch. Though Miss Mullaly has been appropriately called "the Nano Nagle of the Metropolis" she did not enter the Religious Life, nor did she consider herself worthy to dwell under the same roof as the Nuns. Humbly she watched the success of her foundation from her abode in an orphanage which she had built nearby. Only the scrupulous Ledger of the Recording Angel can tell all the good things that Miss Mullaly did for the needy Catholic children of Dublin. Among human documents that testify to her services, there is a contemporary letter from Bishop Moylan of Cork, dated 26th of June, 1794, and addressed to her personally:—

Dear Madam,

I received your favour of the 7th, and beg leave to assure you of every good wish of my heart for the success of your new establishment, and that I shall be always happy to contribute everything in my power to forward an object of so much importance to religion.

The two Sisters, who have been lately professed for it, seem blessed with the spirit of the Institute, and will, I trust in the Lord, answer your expectations; it were indeed to be wished that they had a little more experience. But the enlightened direction of our worthy friend, Father Mulcaile, together with your good advice and example, will, under God, supply whatever might be deficient. Whenever you may deem it expedient, they will be prepared to set off and attend your call. I would, however, recommend their remaining here until after the annual Retreat in the beginning of August.

Be assured it would be the highest satisfaction to me to send with them an experienced Sister. I know how advantageous it would be at the commencement of this charitable establishment. But, circumstanced as our house here is at present, I don't see it possible.

Mother Tobin, by what the Sisters assure, and, indeed, I feel convinced of it, cannot be spared from the office she now fills; besides, the weakness of her constitution would render her by no means suited to so arduous a task. Were the strength of her body equal to the vigour of her mind, and to the virtuous quality of her heart, no one would be better fitted for the undertaking.

Mother Lane, now at Killarney, is the person I had in view to send with the two Sisters. She was to have returned this month; but, as Miss Conway, who was received for the foundation in Killarney, and was to replace her, thought proper to quit the Institute before the time of her profession, it will be impossible to remove Mother Lane until we can send another subject in her place. This we cannot do until next Summer, as the person now preparing for it will not be professed until then. This is a disappointment we did not foresee. But God's Will be done!

I shall abridge, according to your wishes, the time of

postulation and probation of the two you purpose sending to Cork, and by the time they will have finished their course here, we shall be able to send Mother Lane with them, or sometime before, if it be deemed necessary.

You may depend on every exertion in my power to promote your pious views in regard to your infant establishment — it is the work of God, and He will in His own time consolidate and perfect it.

I shall soon send an account to Rome of the progress of the Institute, and will profit of the occasion to supplicate for what you have so much at heart, and to call for the Indulgences you wish for on the Feasts of Saint Francis Xavier and Saint Teresa.

I request you will present my respects to my most honoured confrere and friend, Doctor Troy (Archbishop of Dublin), and my affectionate salutes to Father Mulcaile. I beg you will both remember me before the Lord; and believe me to be, with every good wish for your happiness,

Dear Madam, your affectionate in Christ,

And most humble servant,

‡F. Moylan

Through the zeal and generosity of a lowly hard-working woman, the Presentation Sisters were therefore established in Dublin. To the last, she watched over their temporal welfare. Cheerful and devout, she regularly joined in converse and recreation with the Community she cherished. Her presence symbolised edification, and her wholesome advisory motto was: "My child, make your election sure." Like Saint Francis, she was so humble that she elected not to go up higher.

On a Spring day in 1803, God took His good servant Teresa Mullaly unto Himself. It was a year of political ferment in Dublin, when the romantic young patriot, Robert Emmet, transfused his memory into the national scriptures by dying for Ireland after an ill-fated rebellion. The political heroes and heroines of Ireland have never remained unsung — the dead who died for Ireland. But there were also those who lived for Ireland, lived for her educationally, and socially, and morally, and religiously, far from the flare of the political crucible. Such was Miss Mullaly. In her obscure and humble abode, surrounded by Sisters that bewailed her loss, the Foundress of the Presentation Sisters in Dublin gave up her pure soul to God after a useful life devoted to civic as well as religious service. She certainly was a heroine of the Lord among her people, whom she loved right well.

From their places beside the Throne of the Timeless, Mother Nagle and Miss Mullaly could look lovingly down on the continuously increasing good works that proceeded from the Dublin foundation at George's Hill. Hundreds and hundreds of useful citizens have been taught within its portals, through the long and busy years of its existence. And who can tell how many vocations it has sent to the harvest fields of the Redeemer, at home and beyond the seas?

The storied City of Waterford sadly needed the services of the Presentation Sisters, when, at the close of the eighteenth century, the famous Bishop Hussey prepared to introduce them into his diocese. Protestant Schools prevailed in Waterford at the period, and, when Catholic children had recourse to them, they were not happy in their experiences, owing to the acute sectarian feeling of the penal times. It fell to Mother Nagle's Sisters to restore Catholic Education to the native populace within the ancient See of St. Carthage, once so famous for learned Schools.

Amongst high-minded Protestants, Bishop Hussey was respected, and he knew that the Sisters, who had been already so successful in Cork, would quickly conquer any local prejudices by their edifying charity. Candidates were instantly forthcoming for the new foundation. They returned from their training at the parent house, in Cork, to start their new Convent in Waterford, in the fateful year of 1798, probably the most harrowing year in all of Ireland's troubled story.

Miss Eleanor Power, Miss Jane Power, and Miss

Molony, were the three pioneers who composed the Waterford Community. On their way home from Cork they met a band of infamous mercenary soldiers called Hessians, who, by their savage cruelty, were the terror of the people in the rebellion of 1798. However, the Nuns reached Waterford safely, where they opened their first school on November 6th, 1798 — the Feast of all the Saints of Ireland. It was in a temporary building attached to the old house of the Jesuit Fathers, who were then enduring the heavy cross of their Suppression. As it was a Jesuit who bade Mother Nagle to go home to Ireland and start her great work, so it was a Jesuit who gave to her spiritual daughters a place to start their work in Waterford. Father John Barron it was: he remained to do duty as a secular priest after the Society was suppressed.

In 1799, the foundation of a permanent Convent was made by Bishop Hussey and the future Bishop Power. The Nuns had of course to get a "license" from the Protestant Bishop of Waterford, in order to carry on their Catholic Schools. The document gives a picture of the position of Catholics in the penal days, and the original has been preserved by the Presentation Sisters. It bears the Seal of the Consistorial Court of the Protestant Diocese, and is addressed, under her secular name, to Miss Eleanor Power — Mother de Sales, the Superioress. In it, the Protestant Bishop's Court also names the three responsible Catholic sponsors of the Superioress.

The permit reads as follows:—

"Richard, by Divine permission, Lord Bishop of Waterford and Lismore, to our well-beloved in Christ, Miss Eleanor Power, greeting.

Whereas, you are presented to us by the Reverend W. Keating, the Reverend John Power, and Peter St. Leger, merchant, all of the City of Waterford, as a fit and proper person to teach females and keep a boarding school for the education of females in the City of Waterford aforesaid.

We, therefore, confiding as well in the integrity of your

morals and honesty of your life and conversation, as in your skill and ability in instructing or causing females to be instructed, do by the tenor of these presents give and grant unto you, the said Eleanor Power, in whose fidelity we confide, full power and authority to keep a boarding school, and perform the office of schoolmistress, to teach and instruct, or cause to be well and sufficiently taught and instructed, such females of the Roman Catholic profession of said city, as now are, or shall hereafter be, committed to your care, strictly enjoining and earnestly recommending it to you to pay the greatest attention, as well to the morals of such children, as to teaching them the fear of God and keeping His commandments.

And we do by these presents inhibit all other person or persons from teaching within the said city without our license of faculty first to them for that purpose granted, in pain of the law and contempt thereof.

In testimony whereof, we have caused the seal of our Consistorial Court of Waterford and Lismore to be hereunto affixed, this 16th day of December, in the year of Our Lord one thousand seven hundred and ninety-nine.

George Fleury, Registrar.
R. Dobbyn, Vicar-General."

The Sisters had opened their Schools a year before the date of the license. It has been suggested that bigoted persons were planning to prosecute them, and that the license was obtained to safeguard the Sisters against the endless penal mulctings which ill-disposed persons might at any moment invoke against them.

The Waterford Convent prospered. The Sisters began in an obscure house in a narrow lane. But a day came when the great Gothic architect, Welby Pugin, designed an artistic home for the Congregation that had triumphed over superhuman obstacles; thousands of happy children in the course of years have received their education in these dignified surroundings.

The first Superioress of the Waterford Community of

the Presentation Sisters, Mother de Sales Power, was a friend of Edmund Ignatius Rice, the wealthy Waterford merchant, who generously helped the Nuns from the first day of their endeavours among the needy schoolgirls. So impressed was he by the excellent work of the young Community that he speedily decided to inaugurate a similar movement for poor boys, who had no opportunity of being educated.

The Presentation Sisters are therefore credited with inspiring Mr. Rice to found the celebrated Congregation of the Irish Christian Brothers. Their services were timely, and, like the Presentation Sisters, they too have widely extended the sphere of their meritorious labours to fields far beyond their Motherland. Edmund Rice governed the new Congregation till the year 1838: his first schools were opened in 1804. Thus were his useful years and his great wealth spent in the popular Catholic Education of boys. And the Christian Brothers are happy to recognize the helping hand of Mother Nagle from her home in Heaven, and of her Congregation on earth, in inspiring their holy and privileged Founder to establish a work which blesses the world to this day.

So swiftly did the work of Mother Nagle's Sisters grow, in Cork, that another Convent was soon needed in this city that saw the birth of the Congregation. Mrs. Connell O'Connell, a widow of means, rented a house in the northern part of Cork City, and this served the Sisters as a simple dwelling. Subjects were readily found to volunteer for the new foundation, and, under the worthy pioneering Superiorship of Mother Mary Patrick Fitzgerald, the new Convent started on its useful way in the year 1799. Hard work, tenuous finances, privations, austerities, and mortification — these were the lot of the new Community as it struggled towards success. A leading Cork physician of the time, Doctor John Barry, was so astonished and edified at the sufferings of the four Sisters, who guided the destinies of the new house, that he said, "if there were but four persons in the world destined to inherit the Kingdom of Heaven, these would be the four Nuns of the North Presentation Convent."

Again we may study the history of the period through the medium of the "License", which had to be obtained from the Protestant Bishop of Cork, by the Sisters, before they could safely start their Catholic School. In this document the Protestant Bishop greets Miss Margaret Fitzgerald — Mother Mary Patrick, the Superioress:—

"Thomas, by Divine permission, Lord Bishop of Cork and Ross, to our beloved Margaret Fitzgerald, greeting.

Whereas you are recommended to us as a proper person to be licensed to keep a poor school in the parish of Saint Mary's, Shandon, in our diocese of Cork.

We, therefore, by these presents, give you full power and authority to teach and instruct children in the English tongue, writing and arithmetic, and other lawful and honest documents allowed and approved of by the laws and statutes of this Kingdom, within the said parish, and we appoint you a schoolmistress within the said parish during our will and pleasure, with all wages, stipends, salary, and other profits and emoluments to the office of schoolmistress belonging and appertaining; you having first taken the oath required by the law as Roman Catholic in this behalf to be taken and subscribed. All which by law you ought to subscribe.

In testimony whereof we have caused our episcopal seal to be hereunto affixed.

Dated the 14th day of November, in the year of our Lord one thousand seven hundred and ninety-nine.

Thomas Gregg.
Thomas, Cork and Ross."

Hundreds of helpless and neglected little children came under the redeeming care of these Sisters: space was sadly needed, and pupils crowded the lower storey and the upper storey of the unpretentious building which was improvised as a Convent. Efforts had to be made to keep the definitely religious nature of the institution a secret, lest bigoted forces might be inflamed. Even then there were hints that the sheriff had secured a writ to eject the Nuns.

However, Providence continued to guide them to unbroken success, and, in 1803, four years after they opened their Convent, these Sisters felt emboldened to wear the full religious dress distinctive of a Presentation Nun, being the first Community to wear it so. Bigotry is the hateful hobby of the homunculus, and it soon vanished when men of public spirit and civic nobility recognized the presence of a good work in their midst. Thus did the generous minds of the city prevail in the case of the Nuns, who advanced unmolested.

Within a few years after they founded their Convent, the Presentation Sisters were joined by a prominent convert from Protestantism — Miss Elizabeth Jackson. Through their own hard work, and through the responsive co-operation of zealous citizens, the time came when the Sisters were able to establish themselves in a commodious property, appropriate to the needs of their hundreds of pupils. So great was their influence that a priest said it would not be good for the Nuns to know the extent of their valuable work.

The story of one foundation appears to be the story of all others — a story of trial, sacrifice, heroic charity, and blessed success. Within the size and scope of this book it would not be possible for me to give a detailed account of the many foundations. It would take hundreds of pages to present an adequate story of all the Presentation Convents.

In 1797, Miss Isabella McLoughlin and Miss Catherine Meighan, went from their native city of Kilkenny to undergo their religious training at the parent house in Cork, so that they might open a branch house of the Congregation in the ancient city of Saint Canice. These two

Sisters began their School in Kilkenny, in 1800, and from the Kilkenny Convent there came the filiations in Carlow, Galway, Thurles, Wexford, Maryborough, Castlecomer, Mooncoin, Enniscorthy, Portarlington, and in part, San Francisco. The Lord gave a tenfold increase to one house in a brief span of years.

Well aware of their worth, Canon Byrne brought the Presentation Sisters to Terenure, Dublin, in 1866; and, in common with the name of so many other foundations, this Convent will be mentioned again in the story of the extension overseas.

In 1809, Mother Joseph Curtayne and Sister Mary John Sheehy came from Killarney to open the Presentation Convent in Tralee. Doctor Shea Lalor, of Killarney, had seen the fine work done by the Sisters in that town, and so he allocated the finances to found a house in Kerry's capital. This monetary provision does not mean that the pioneering Sisters escaped the Via Dolorosa. Far otherwise. Only after indescribable sufferings did the Tralee Community behold lighter skies.

Exigency taxed them to the utmost in their efforts to cater to the hundreds of needy children committed to their loving care. But God's growth finally blessed them with adequate buildings. With deep affection, the present writer cherishes the memory of many happy visits to the beautiful modern Presentation Convent in Tralee; it has schools so efficient and impressive that they can hold their own in comparison with those of any land.

It was a relative of Mother Nagle, William Pembroke Mulchinock, who gave to the world that popular song, "The Rose of Tralee." The green mountains and the beautiful vale of Tralee have found wide mention through its verses. Within that vale, amid so attractive a natural setting, the Presentation Sisters today have a central house for training subjects from the several foundations of the Congregation in the Diocese of Kerry. Significantly, the house of Noviceship bears the name of Oakpark. Remembering that the oak is the symbol of the Presentation Congregation, we may well say that the tiny tree first planted by the Presentation Sisters, under circumstances of almost personal martyrdom, in Tralee, has grown to be a great oak, with strength and endurance in root and branch.

In 1809, the Sisters came to Dungarvan, where, by prayer, sanctity and surpassing zeal in the service of Christian Education, they added yet another shining chapter to the inspiring story of their Congregation.

From the early years of the Nineteenth Century, Presentation Communities continued to multiply. To name them would be like geographically naming most of the towns and villages of Ireland. From Dublin they went north to Drogheda; from Waterford to Carrick-on-Suir, where the Sisters bravely severed connection with the Board of National Education, which forbade religious emblems in the school during hours of secular instruction.

From Dungarvan, a Community branched to Clonmel. From Clonmel the Sisters sent a Community to Manchester, in England, where the present writer has seen excellent evidences of their fine work, and where he also has had the happiness of visiting a Sister of the renowned poet Francis Thompson — Mother Mary Austin, a Presentation Nun.

Father Bartholomew Burke, of Galway, was God's good agent in bringing the Presentation Sisters to Connaught's capital. He collected substantial funds for the purpose, but did not live to see the day of the Sister's arrival. From Kilkenny they came in 1815, the eventful year in which Europe began to breathe more freely as Napoleon bade everlasting farewell to all his greatness.

Bishop Ffrench, of Galway, wrote that he prayed Heaven "to inspire these pious Sisters to remain among us, in order, mercifully, to instruct the poor but much neglected female children of the town of Galway," and that he thought it his "bounden duty to cherish, console, advise, and assist these truly charitable Sisters in their pious but arduous work, as also to use every possible exertion in establishing the house, increasing the funds, and thereby mutiplying the Community with valuable and effective postulants." The Bishop told the Superioress of the Kilkenny Convent that "it has been for a considerable time the anxious desire of the inhabitants of the town of Galway to establish a House of the Order of the Presentation for the religious instruction of our poor female children." Mother Nagle's work was described by Bishop Ffrench as "that truly merciful institution."

Mother McLoughlin, of the Presentation Sisters in Kilkenny, in accepting Bishop Ffrench's invitation to found a House in Galway, wrote to him that she viewed it as "a flattering prospect of promoting the great end of our holy Institute — the instruction of poor female children." Bishop Marum, of Ossory, gave permission for Sisters Mary De Chantal McLoughlin, Mary Gertrude Breen, and Mary A. Martin, to proceed to Galway to found "a new Convent of this excellent Institute for the instruction of poor female children, and consequently for the promotion of the best interests of religion and society."

The people of Galway welcomed the Sisters with the greatest joy. Significantly enough, they took over premises that had been used as a Charter School, so that an institution, which had been used in attempts to wean children from the Faith, was now utilized to instruct them therein. Almost a thousand pupils were attending the Sisters' School within a short time. In an Industrial Department they executed orders for lace and shawls. From unpromising premises, that were almost ruins, the Sisters established a suitable and commodious Convent, which proved a Godsend physically, mentally, and spiritually, to thousands of neglected children.

Within twenty years, in 1835, the Galway Nuns sent a Community to Archbishop MacHale's See of Tuam; and, in 1861, they sent another Community to Oranmore in the same County.

From Dublin the Sisters came to Rahan, in the Diocese of Meath, in 1817. In that year also the Convent at Thurles was founded by Mother Power, from Clonmel, in the same County of Tipperary, and by Mother Cormack from Kilkenny. In turn Mother Cormack founded a House at Cashel, in 1830. Thurles also sent Communities to Fethard and Ballingarry.

Mother Nagle's work was branching North, South, East and West; and Divine Destiny brought a group of her spiritual daughters to open a Convent very near the place where she was born, and where her lordly ancestors formerly owned extensive lands. This was the foundation at Doneraile in the County of Cork, which was begun, in 1815, mainly owing to the generosity of a devout widow, Mrs. Mary Flynn, who became a Nun and founded this House. The many Protestant gentry, who lived around Doneraile, vied with one another in helping the Sisters, whose Schools became an immediate success.

A remarkable novice of the Doneraile Convent was Angelina Gould, who became Mother Mary Magdalen. She was born in Lisbon, in Portugal, in 1792, whither her parents had gone to escape the prevailing laws against Catholics. There they acquired great commercial success and wealth, and they marked their daughter for a marriage of rank and fortune. She was educated at the historic Benedictine Convent of New Hall, in England, and thereafter took her place in fashionable Society in Lisbon, as her parents wished. But all the time she was resolved to devote her inheritance and her talents to the service of God, after the manner of the beautiful heiress Mother Nagle.

Her father opposed her to the last in her decision to become a Nun. When he died, she was able to obtain permission to enter Religion — from her mother, who had been hitherto opposed to such a resolve. Miss Gould wished to join a Contemplative Order in Portugal, but an English priest, who was Rector of the English College in Lisbon, at that time, directed her to devote her vast fortune and her holy services to the welfare of the Irish people at home.

Cheerfully the young heiress acquiesced, but we can picture her parting pangs as she left her beloved mother and set sail for Ireland in 1826. At the Presentation Convent in Doneraile she exchanged her rich raiment for a simple religious habit. Rising at five every morning, the young novice, who had been waited upon by so many servants in her society days, now became the prayerful and hard-working servant of needy children. So well did she succeed that her holy example became a tradition in her Convent.

Before Miss Gould was professed she handed over her immense fortune to trustees, for the founding of Convents in the diocese of Cloyne and Ross. That fortune was over sixty thousand pounds — about three hundred thousand dollars. Through it, the Presentation Sisters, and the Sisters of Mercy were enabled to found Houses whereby endless numbers of girls received the blessings of education. Untold have been the benefits that have flowed from the fortune so nobly sacrificed by a lovely heroine of God, who proved herself a treasure beyond telling in the Community where she served and edified all.

From Doneraile came Presentation Communities to Youghal and Mitchelstown. Kilkenny sent a foundation to Wexford, in 1818, the first Convent founded in the Diocese of Ferns since the Reformation. From Wexford the Sisters branched to Enniscorthy in 1826.

Within a little over forty years after Mother Nagle's death, there were eighteen Presentation Houses. The Book of Life alone can tell of the privations that led to their triumphs, and of the fruits that followed their sacrifices. Imbued in every case with the salutary spirit of the Foundress, the Sisters added new laurels to the story of modern Irish Education.

CHAPTER 21

THE SALUTARY WORK CONTINUES TO GROW IN GOODLY PLACES

G ROWTH repeatedly marks the spirit of the Gospel. Closely attuned to the spirit of the Gospel was Mother Nagle's work, and grow it did for all to see. Its heavenly growth was destined to check the stagnation and torpor that had been recently inflicted on the intellect of an ancient Race, that had so readily responded to the Gospel fourteen hundred years previously.

By the middle of the Nineteenth Century the Presentation Sisters to a renewed degree had the triple task of caring for the Irish children spiritually, intellectually and physically. The black disaster of the year 1847 had cast the blight of famine all over the hapless land. In such a terrifying crisis the Sisters were not found wanting. They rose to the true stature of the noble lady who founded the Congregation, and they cheerfully faced disease and death themselves in order to save the lives of the starving people.

The present part of the narrative lies within the pale of those evil years near the mid Nineteenth Century, years which are a pall of ebon and unforgettable tragedy in the history and diaspora of the Irish Race.

In the year 1824 the famous Bishop Doyle introduced the Presentation Sisters to Maryborough, the ancient Irish town which was given the name of Queen *Mary* Tudor of England, in the Sixteenth Century.

When Bishop Doyle espoused the cause of Mother Nagle's Sisters they found in him a true champion of Christian Education. He was a keen scholar and a vigorous ecclesiastical statesman. As the friend and follower of O'Connell he occupies a storied page in Ireland's annals. The young Bishop became so rapidly famous that his initials alone automatically served to identify him. Every

student of Irish History is confronted with a major character in the person of J. K. L.   And though James, Bishop
of Kildare and Leighlin, died all too young, his busy span
proved that one crowded hour of a glorious life is worth
an age without a name.   A sorrowing nation wrote the
letters J. K. L. unfadingly on the national escutcheon, for
he had served his people well.

Naturally, Bishop Doyle yearned for the blessing of
an educated flock.   In this wise he expressed himself on
the subject of Education: — "Next to the blessing of redemption, and the graces consequent upon it, there is no
gift bestowed by God equal in value to a good education;
other advantages are enjoyed by the body; this belongs
entirely to the spirit; whatever is great, or good, or glorious in the works of men, is the work of educated minds."

Bishop Doyle wished for a sane and balanced education based on Gospel principles.   Like Socrates, he realized that evils might arise from an imperfect or distorted
education.   He wished for the greatest possible diffusion
of useful knowledge, but he insisted that "this mighty
moral engine" of education should be guarded, checked,
controlled, and wisely regulated against those "who would
avail themselves of the public feeling in favour of education, for the purpose of engrafting upon it their own wild
theories in religion."   Let error and passion be not introduced but eradicated, and let habits of piety and virtue
be inculcated; since the mind of man, in its unimproved
state, is more under the influence of passions than of
reason, let its training be characterised by the implanting
of the principles of true religion.

The progressive Doctor Doyle was satisfied that his
beloved principles of orthodox education were shared and
practised by the Presentation Sisters, and he was eager for
the wide diffusion of their work.

With penetrating clarity the Bishop also summed up the
Sisters' Rule of Life, whereby their teaching was to
fructify.   "God calls us," said J. K. L., "and He gives us
graces equal to our calling and vocation.   He, from the

abundance of His mercy, bestows particular graces on religious houses and institutes; but, to continue them, something on our own part is strictly required — a most faithful and fervent correspondence with all His graces; unremitting attention to duty; no relaxation of the rule but what sickness requires; to seek the glory of God alone in everything, purely, entirely and perseveringly; to be as victims ever immolated to His greater honour and glory — aiming at this alone, seeking this alone; to be fervent in the morning in consecrating all to His glory, and renewing this consecration often during the day."

On the question of desirable subjects for a Community, the Bishop continued: "Never retain one in whom the spirit of the world cannot be subdued. Let no consideration whatever induce you to profess such a one. Mark my words, and if I would have any of them written in your house, or handed down to posterity, they would be: *Do all for the glory of God; keep strictly to the rule; and never profess any one in whom the spirit of the world cannot be subdued.* We sometimes meet with those who seem to soar to Heaven by prayer, and by pride fall suddenly like stars from the firmament; the least deviation from the rule often occasions these fatal falls."

Under harrowing conditions the Nuns worked in Maryborough, five of them dying early like martyrs to an overpoweringly difficult duty. A prominent Protestant physician was one of the first to help them — Doctor Jacob, who knew their innate worth and prized them accordingly. He appealed for help to his friends, both Protestant and Catholic, and, by 1844, adequate schools were opened — to bless the Sisters and pupils, who had been hitherto battling against odds in a dismal sort of cellar. It was one more example of *per Crucem ad lucem,* in the Presentation epic.

In 1823, the Sisters came to Maynooth and began their sacrificial work in a wretched hut by the Dublin road. Benefactions came to them from the neighbours. The scholars and Professors of Maynooth College esteemed their work and donated to them. By 1826, the neighbouring Duke of Leinster laid the foundation stone of the new Schools for the Sisters: he was a lifelong and generous friend to them and to their pupils, proving himself worthy of the family spirit of Lord Edward Fitzgerald who had only recently sacrificed his life for Ireland.

In 1825, the Presentation Convent in Mullingar was founded by Mother Xavier Doyle, Sister Mary Clare Healy, and Maria Nugent — a postulant. New subjects entered here in large numbers, and, after thirty years, these Sisters were extending their meritorious labours to India's spreading vineyard.

The daughters of Nano Nagle knew no surcease or standstill, as the extension continued apace. Appropriately they relighted the educational fires of Saint Brigid in Kildare, in the year 1830, hard by the ancient mouldering fane of the National Patroness. Irish Catholics had been emancipated the previous year. Within a short time the Sisters were catering to pupils of all classes and their perseverance was rewarded by the erection of additional and serviceable buildings.

To Ireland's colliery district of Castlecomer, in the County of Kilkenny, the Presentation Sisters came in 1829. The children of the miners were in especial need of them. Here, Father Aylward gave the Nuns a small and neat Convent, and their worthy work was an instant success.

Readers of the delightful poet, Gerald Griffin, remember how peacefully he blended the merits of Protestant and Catholic in Bandon town. Bandon, located in one of the most beautiful parts of County Cork, was long noted as a centre of Protestant feeling akin to the Orange intensity of Derry in the North. Party feelings and religious bigotry ran blendedly rife in "merry Bandon town."

But a young lady named Catherine O'Neill pertinaciously braved this uninviting atmosphere to found a Presentation Convent there, in the significant year of Catholic Emancipation. Miss O'Neill's mother had opposed her entry into religion. Finally she agreed to her daughter's proposal, but humorously added that if Catherine must be a Nun, then let her found a Convent in Bandon! The Irish love the challenge of the seemingly impossible, especially when the honour of God is at stake, so, Catherine O'Neill, the only daughter of a widowed mother, welcomed the challenge and successfully established the Presentation Sisters in Orange Bandon. A site for the Convent and the Schools was obtained from the Duke of Devonshire, and Miss O'Neill devoted her own entire fortune to the happy project, as well as enlisting the support of her friends therein. Hundreds of pupils soon filled the schools — ample proof of their need and popularity.

To the town of Dingle, in the West of Kerry, the Presentation Sisters next extended the work of God. Bishop Egan had bequeathed the finances for this purpose; hence Mother Agnes Lonergan and Mother Teresa Fitzharris arrived in Dingle in 1829, where they were publicly welcomed by the people of this sturdy Gaelic outpost, who immediately began to contribute subscriptions towards the cost of erecting schools.

The people dwelling on the holy ground of Dingle, where Saint Brendan once trod, had not known the full public ceremonial of High Mass, Exposition, and Benediction of the Blessed Sacrament, since the eve of the Reformation. The year 1829 was a time of particular triumph in Kerry, whose own O'Connell had proudly defended the Mass before the might of the British House of Commons, and who had come home to the people of Kerry as the victor of Emancipation.

On the Feast of the Presentation of the Blessed Virgin Mary, November 21, 1829, Dingle liturgically rejoiced in the full and solemn ceremonial of the Holy Roman Church.

The Altar was a blaze of lights, and hearts beat high with praise for the Eucharistic King. The children of Dingle fishermen, who had remained loyal to the Throne of The Fisherman, were at last openly able to honour their God in the Real Presence. Their joy on this occasion was comparable to the relief of storm-tossed mariners who are greeted by a peaceful Dawn after a long night of battling with the tempestuous ocean. So perceptible was the Peace of the Lord, and, so edifying was the simple piety of the people, that local prejudices began to melt away: neigbouring Protestants were so impressed that they extended every kindness and attention to the Nuns in launching the new Foundation.

More pupils flocked to the Dingle Convent than could at first be taken care of. So successful were the Sisters that within a decade they were able to send a new Community, headed by Mother Joseph Mahony, to Cahirciveen, in the O'Connell country. In the dread lean years of 1846 and 1847, the Nuns in Dingle timely and tenderly turned their Schools into hospitals, where they nurtured and consoled the stricken population. Administering angels assuredly were they.

The illustrious Bishop Dupanloup, of Orleans, in France, observed that there was enough food produced in Ireland at this time to nourish sixteen million mortals; "somebody consumed it," the Bishop added, "but is was not the Irish."

In the midst of such a catastrophe as the Famine, the Presentation Sisters opened an Industrial School in Dingle, whereby hundreds of girls became self-supporting through knitting and lace-making. Protestant Bible Societies were locally active at the height of the distress, promising food to any proselytes lured over from Catholicism. Stemming this dangerous drive against the souls of the flock were the Presentation Nuns, who saved so many from loss of life and loss of faith. When the shadows fled, the Sisters were able to open elegant and commodious Schools in 1872.

In 1830, a Presentation House was opened in the pretty village of Mooncoin, six miles West of Waterford. In a short time over three hundred pupils, ranging from four to eighteen, were being instructed; and the parishioners, most of whom had never seen a Nun before, were soon reaping the benefits of Mother Nagle's work. The first Superioress, Mother Cormack, died a martyr to duty within three years. Her successor was Mother Magdalen Gore, a convert to Catholicism, who conquered the prejudices of her Protestant relatives by her sweet charity, so that her own mother, and also her brother, Doctor Gore, became generous helpers of the daughter's Convent. For seventeen years, one large parlour served as schoolroom and chapel, but then came a bright day when Providence provided the sorely-pressed Sisters with spacious and well-ventilated school buildings.

In a little over fifty years the work of Mother Nagle had spread to twelve dioceses of Ireland, and it numbered twenty-seven Houses. With duplicated enlivenment the branches of the Order continued to grow in the following fifty years.

The Presentation Convent, which was founded at Cashel in 1830, was born in sacrifice and grew in suffering. But the faith of the Sisters in their work was solid as the very Rock of Cashel itself, and, though the Convent seemed doomed to failure, it had a happy rebirth when the distinguished Prelate, Archbishop Leahy, took over the Metropolitan See of Munster. He sent Mother Joseph Ryan to reorganize the fortunes of the Cashel Foundation in 1857. A Convent and School buildings of architectural dignity arose where Franciscans once trod, and the surrounding grounds were tastefully laid out. An Industrial School was opened, and the entire work won the praise of British Government Inspectors for the health, happiness and efficiency of both teachers and pupils. The Archbishop, and the Vicar-General, Dean Cantwell, together with a faithful following of Clergy and Laity, loyally supported the Presentation Nuns at Cashel, who made their foundation one of the most flourishing in Ireland, and who continued to do untold good through all the years of stress.

The pretty town of Youghal, in the County of Cork, is popularly associated with Sir Walter Raleigh, who is said to have puffed the first pipe-smoke in Ireland. Mother Nagle's relative, Edmund Spenser, here held converse with Raleigh in Elizabethan days. And to sea-sprayed Youghal in Victorian days came the Presentation Nuns. It was the first Presentation Convent to be financed from the three hundred thousand dollar fortune of Mother Magdalen Gould, the wealthy Irish heiress, who left Lisbon society to teach and serve her own people.

Mother Gould herself was chosen to make the Youghal foundation, in 1834. It proved to be her shrine and her grave. Amongst her first subjects was the sister of Gerald Griffin, the poet and the Christian Brother. Within three years the Sisters had six hundred pupils. During the Famine years Mother Gould's charity rose to the most heroic degree. Like Mother Nagle, she extended her love to the utterly outcast of God's creatures, and for those, whom hardhearted society regards as flotsam and jetsam, she founded a Magdalen Refuge which she supported unaided, and wherein she reclaimed the seemingly unreclaimable to the Lord, whose Pity marks not only the fall of the human, but even the sparrow's fall. Incidentally, the Youghal Convent became so noted for fine lace that it supplied its prize designs to the Vatican and to the Royal Court of England.

To the trustees of Mother Gould's fund a young priest applied in order to bring the Presentation Sisters to Midleton, in County Cork. This was the invalided Father Stephen Coppinger, whose perseverance was unbroken when the Trustees, unflatteringly for Midleton, thought the place too insignificant for a Convent, since there were larger towns awaiting the benefit of the bequest. The good priest kept on asking, on the principle of "seek and you shall find." Finally the trustees allocated about eight thousand dollars so that he might establish his beloved Nuns in Midleton, and he and his family contributed another four thousand dollars to the project.

Father Coppinger then got a grant of three acres of land from Lord Midleton for the site, and, in 1834, Mother Francis de Sales O'Flaherty, Mother Charles O'Sullivan, and Mother Vincent Cantillon, came from the North Presentation Convent, in Cork, to open the newly-erected Convent. A tremendous influx of pupils awaited their services. Within eighteen years the Nuns were able to construct new and adequate Schools at their own expense, a clear proof that Father Coppinger's hopes were justified. The missionary zeal of the Midleton Convent so flourished that, within twenty years after the date of the foundation, it was able to send a new Community to the happy soil of San Francisco, where the story of its efflorescence awaits another chapter.

As the May blossoms were whitening during Mary's Month in Galway in the year 1835, the Presentation Sisters were brought to Tuam by the homeric hero of Christian Education, Archbishop MacHale, popularly known as a Lion of the True Fold, and ecclesiastically identified by His Grace himself to the withstanding forces of Government as "John of Tuam." The Tuam pioneers were Mother de Sales Coppinger, Mother Ignatius Blake, and Mother Louis Tighe. They opened their Schools immediately, and three hundred pupils were enrolled. Scarcely had they set their worthy work under way, when the shattering spectre of famine stalked over this Western seaboard. It was lucky for the population that the Nuns were at hand in what the Irish phrase mildly calls "The Bad Times." Instead of formal education the Sisters then had to substitute Social Service, and unreservedly did they spend themselves in feeding and clothing the needy: for this purpose a large quantity of food and clothes reached them from the generous people of Boston and Charleston in 1847.

To the beautiful town of Lismore, Bishop Abraham of Waterford accompanied a little group of Presentation pioneers in 1836. The Duke of Devonshire gave them, rent free, a grant of two acres of land; and a suitable Convent was soon built. Skilful workers among the Cistercian Monks at famed Mount Melleray came and helped to complete the interior. This was the return of a courtesy, for, when the Cistercians came from France to find a refuge in Kerry, in 1830, their most helpful friend was Mother Teresa Kelly, of the Presentation Convent in Killarney.

The Sisters in Cork sent a Community from the Motherhouse to open a Convent in Limerick, in 1836. The Foundress was Miss Maria Catherine King, a young lady of social position and a convert from Protestantism. She was heiress to considerable property, and decided to devote her means to the education of the poor children in Limerick. Like Mother Nagle, Miss King realised that her own work could only achieve continuity through the services of a Religious Community. Accordingly she arranged for a Presentation House in Limerick. Mother Joseph Harnett, Mother Stanislaus Drinan, and Mother Francis Cantillon were the Nuns who opened the new Foundation, whose story was one of prosperity from the very start, and whose members were soon joined by Miss King herself as a Religious.

A tribute was given to the Presentation Sisters by the Protestant Bishop of Limerick, Doctor Higgin, who inspected their school: this was his verdict: —"I have this day visited this school and have great pleasure in recording my complete approbation; the order, attention, cleanliness, and proficiency of the children reflect the highest credit on its manager and superintendent; and it cannot fail to impart the greatest advantage to the community at large."

It was a proud day for the Presentation Nuns of Limerick, when, in 1937, they celebrated the centennial commemoration of their Convent's establishment. Through their fine Schools have passed thousands of Irish girls, who are a credit to God and the homeland of Mother Nagle.

At Milltown, in Kerry, a Presentation Convent was established in 1838, and, after dire storm and stress, the blessings of success ensued.

To Bagenalstown in County Carlow the Presentation Nuns sent a Community in 1838, and there they were asked to attend to the education of the children of all classes. This Foundation in turn sent a Community in 1854 to Mountmellick, in Queen's County — now called Leix. In Mountmellick the present writer has witnessed the fine work done by the Sisters in secondary education: here they have taken over premises formerly used as a Quaker School. In the year 1854 the Sisters opened a Convent in Portarlington, in King's County — now called Offaly.

It was not far from Fermoy, at her picturesque home on the River Blackwater, that Mother Nagle first dreamed her dreams of founding Catholic Schools for needy children. We have already seen how her dreams kept coming true. Within a little over fifty years after her demise, the Presentation Nuns came to Fermoy, a prettily located town, formerly much garrisoned by military. Aptly did Longfellow's lines suit the scene: —

Were half the power that fills the world with terror;
Were half the wealth bestowed on camps and courts,
Given to redeem the human mind from error,
There were no needs for arsenals or fort.

The name Fermoy is said to mean "the sacred plain", and certainly the happy spirit which the Presentation Sisters brought to hundreds of children in Fermoy was in keeping with the *genius loci*, within a region where Mother Nagle's ancestor, Sir Richard Roche, founded a Cistercian Monastery in the Thirteenth Century under the attractive title — "Our Lady of the Camp of God." As energetic daughters of the Church Militant the children of Nano Nagle served the poor of Jesus Christ spiritually, educationally and sociologically, and within a short time they sent some of their members to do the same for exiled Gaels in distant Tasmania.

To Clane, in County Kildare, the Presentation Sisters came in 1839, and here they were warmly befriended by the Jesuit Fathers of the noted College of Clongowes Wood, nearby.

Bishop Egan, of Kerry, brought the Sisters to Millstreet, in Cork, in 1840. Cahirciveen, in Kerry, welcomed a Presentation Community in 1840, where the immortal Daniel O'Connell esteemed them highly. His appreciation was practical too, for he granted them the ground for their Convent, rent free for ever, and he also gave them five thousand dollars towards erecting their new buildings. Almost another three thousand dollars came to them through a bequest of General O'Connell, uncle of the Liberator.

The old Geraldine town of Listowel, in Kerry, was blessed by a Foundation in 1844. This was due to the vigorous and venerated Pastor of the town, Father Darby Mahony, whose fear of God was great, and whose fear of man was nil, for he led his faithful flock against the Goliath of coercive landlordism, like an ecclesiastical field-marshal. He was firmly resolved that his people should be educated, and was equally intent that his new Presentation Schools should eclipse all others. The good

Pastor even decided on borrowing the services of the most experienced Superioress in the Diocese for the prosecution of his high aims: this was Mother Teresa Kelly, of the Milltown Convent, whom we have already mentioned as the friend of the French Cistercian exiles in Kerry. Bishop Egan wished her to continue in Milltown and Father Mahony wanted her in Listowel. The latter wrote to the Milltown Community: "This morning, at six o'clock, I offered the Atoning Blood to the Eternal Father, asking Him to give me your Reverend Mother; I know long, and you know now, her unalterable sweetness, her burning charity; Prayer is all-powerful; unworthy though I am, our good Lord may grant this blessing to me and to my people. — Darby Mahony." Who could resist that?

Though Darby signifies Jeremiah, it was not Jeremiad but jubilation that occupied Father Mahony's mind, for he won his point; and Mother Kelly, one of the many uncanonised saints of the Presentation Congregation, served Listowel unto her death. The celebrated Bishop Moriarty, of Kerry, preached her panegyric; he declared that only God's Day would reveal all the good she had done in the service of so many.

The Listowel Sisters figured in a five-year controversy with Queen Victoria's Commissioners of National Education over the Sign of our Redemption — a large Cross in front of the Convent. The authorities requested its removal — in terms varying from spidery blandishments to ungodly ultimatum. The Sisters "kept on never minding," and the Cross of the crisis remained where it was. *Stat Crux, dum volvitur orbis.* The Commissioners have gone. The Presentation Sisters and the Cross of Christ remain.

In 1846, Archdeacon O'Leary brought a Community of Presentation Sisters from Limerick to Castleisland, in County Kerry. It was a difficult time to start a new Foundation. Famine and pestilence were invading the land. The available finances were as inadequate as the accommodation. But, with the staying-power of the Saints, the Sisters braved every sequence of sorrows until a day of joy finally shone out of the mists. Today the Castleisland Convent flourishes like the Cedar on Lebanon, and the present writer can pay personal tribute to the fine education imparted by the Sisters to crowds of rosy-cheeked children in this happier age of Eire.

The Presentation Convent in Stradbally, Queen's County, was founded in 1852. Difficult days first transpired, and the Convent was refounded, in 1860, by Mother Augustine Ganly — a convert from Protestantism, who was received into the Church by her friend, the great J. K. L. — Doctor Doyle, Bishop of Kildare. Miss Ganly grew up in a strongly Protestant family, and her early views were very antagonistic to Catholicism; but, *mirabilis Deus in sanctis suis*, she became a convert and a Presentation Nun, and led a new Foundation to enduring success and universal service.

Mitchelstown, in County Cork, was next blessed by the Presentation Sisters, in 1853. Hedge Schools still existed in the mountain regions round about. Dean Morgan O'Brien was the priest responsible for the new Foundation and he wanted a system of Education which was truly patriotic and Catholic. His distrust of alien teaching may be measured from the fact that, while he himself was yet a child, his own father was hanged as an Irish rebel from the old clock gate of Youghal, during the agonies of the 1798 uprising.

An able and remarkable Superioress was appointed to lead the new Mitchelstown Convent to success; this was Mother Aloysius Tuite. Her father had been a governor in the West Indies, and he belonged to one of the ancient Irish Catholic families exiled by Cromwell. During the war between France and England, Miss Tuite braved the seas to go home to Ireland where she was educated under the care of her relative, the Countess McCarthy; she attended the School conducted by Mother Nagle's beloved Ursuline Community in Cork. Such are the mysterious dispensations enjoined by the Lord of Destiny in respect to the scattering and gathering of the Irish Race, that this young Irish lady from the West Indies, petted in society and tended by slaves, came home to Ireland and became herself a slave in the service of poor children, as a humble, charitable Presentation Nun.

The Presentation Convent in Clondalkin was founded in 1857, and that at Lucan, in 1867.

The zealous Dean Cantwell brought the Sisters to Fethard, County Tipperary, in 1861, where, within a month they had three hundred pupils, such was the Irish hunger for education. Dean Cantwell, and the flourishing Community, had the happiness of seeing splendid schools serving hundreds of children within eleven years after the Foundation was started.

The Convent at Lucan, County Dublin, was founded under striking circumstances. A young Irish Officer, a member of the Protestant Gentry, became a convert to the Catholic Church, in 1857: he was Captain Robert La Touche Colthurst of the Vesey-Colthurst family. During his visits to the family mansion at Lucan he noted that schools were badly needed for the poor children. From his extensive means he resolved to found a Convent and Schools where the Presentation Nuns could carry out the work that was dear to his heart. Though Captain Colthurst donated ten thousand dollars towards starting the project he did not live to see his dream realised, for he died in London at the early age of 34, his last request being that his body should be taken home to Ireland and there interred in the village churchyard attached to the Catholic Church at Lucan, and that only a plain black cross should mark his place of rest; his earnest wish was that he "might not be forgotten in the prayers of the poor."

The wishes of the devout young man were carried out by his brother, Colonel David Colthurst, an officer in the British Army, who also became a convert to Catholicism, and who took prompt steps for the erection of Schools and Convent. Thus, through two fervent converts, did Mother Nagle's Sisters begin their welcome activities in the peaceful retreat of Lucan.

In 1871, the Presentation Sisters came to Ballingarry, County Tipperary. In the same year a House was founded at Granard under the Superiorship of Mother M. John Hughes — a name which will re-occur in the narrative. In 1873 a Convent was founded at Baltinglass in County Wicklow, by Mother Magdalen Hussey.

At another time it is the intention of the present writer to add an up-to-date list of Presentation Foundations in Ireland and overseas.

The name and fame of Mother Nagle's Sisters continued to arise on the wings of the Four Winds of Erin; and their deeds made music to God, as they carried out the loving precepts commanded by the Son of Man in the perfect Sermon preached from a mountain slope on a far-off day. From Irish lips there floated to the Lord of Love the praises of His handmaiden, Nano Nagle, who had wrought a great work for Him, and for His chosen people in Ireland. The praise of that work rose through the white fleece and azure of the pure Irish skies like the incense of a perfect prayer reaching the Throne of the Eternal.

Viewed from the standard of either chronology or merit, it will be seen that Mother Nagle's Sisters occupy a premier place in the history of modern Irish Education.

CHAPTER 22

BEYOND THE WESTERN WAVE THE PRESENTA-
TION SISTERS EXTEND THEIR APOSTOLATE:
NEWFOUNDLAND WELCOMES THEM FROM
IRELAND

THE first Presentation Nuns to tread westward in the
trans-Atlantic path of Saint Brendan the Navigator,
one of whose heavenly tasks it is to keep a Patronal eye
on the people of Galway and Kerry, were a Community
from Connaught's Capital, who set out for Newfoundland
in the year 1833.

Some years ago, when it was my pleasant duty to introduce to University audiences in England, the distinguished
Catholic Statesman, Lord Morris of Newfoundland, he
always replied that he came from Newfoundland via Ireland. This distinguished leader in the Government of
Newfoundland then went on to show the large part played
by the Irish in the history of that Island. Entering effectively into its ecclesiastical and educational history came
the Presentation Sisters from the ancient city of Galway.

Newfoundland was discovered by the Explorer Cabot,
in 1497. During the sixteenth century the English and
French made rival settlements there. The French ceded
the Island to the British in 1713. It is about one and a
third times the size of Ireland, and its surface is diversi-
fied by hills, lakes, rivers, and extensive pine forests.

The four Nuns from Ireland, who arrived at St. John's,
Newfoundland, on September 21, 1833, were Mother
Bernard Kirwan, Mother Xavier Moloney, Mother Xavier
Lynch, and Mother Magdalen O'Shaughnessy. There was
as yet no Convent ready to receive them, but luckily there
was room for them at the Inn which was called "The Rising Sun," a hopeful title in a land where the Catholic
Church was just then energetically emerging from days
of shadow and jeopardy into solidarity and vigour.

The Sisters cheerfully began their work from the Inn, at which they were glad to find momentary accommodation. They humbly rejoiced in the fact that their housing was better than that of the Holy Family, who could find no such room at a great moment of Christian History. An Inn can have a very historic significance. Mr. Chesterton once assured me that the greatest event in his life took place in an Inn, for it was there he was received into the Catholic Church, when he began life anew as a militant Convert at forty-eight.

The Sisters lost no time in starting their work. They rented what seemed to be most unscholastic-looking premises, which they successfully converted into a School. It shows that they were not dismayed by difficulties. Like their busy Foundress, they realised that the only way to begin a thing is to begin it immediately. The motto of "Action This Day" can be most profitable. It is no use letting the Day of Judgment overtake us while we are still waiting for the right "atmosphere" in which to begin a good work.

The historical summary therefore is that, immediately upon their arrival, the Presentation Sisters filially commenced their much-needed work in Newfoundland, and with popular support they quickly succeeded. An adequate residence was soon prepared for them on a picturesque site; of this, Bishop Fleming wrote: — "Its position is magnificent, commanding a view of the City, the harbour, the ocean, and a vast extent of the country round." The new school could accommodate over a thousand children, and the people of Newfoundland eagerly sought the exceptional educational facilities afforded by the Sisters. Within a decade, some thousands of children passed through their hands, proving themselves a credit to their teachers.

Bishop O'Donnell was appointed to be the first Vicar-Apostolic of Newfoundland, in 1794. He was succeeded by Bishop Lambert and Bishop Scallan; and then came Bishop Fleming who intensified the progress of the Catholic Church during his reign of twenty years. Born in County Tipperary, in 1792, Bishop Fleming succeeded to the See of Newfoundland at an early age. He was a Franciscan, and had already served as a young priest on the Island, where he was familiar with needs and conditions.

Bishop Fleming zealously increased the number of priests in Newfoundland. But he needed the holy women to teach in his diocese, so he went to Ireland in 1833, and brought back with him from Galway his treasured Presentation Community. Of them the Bishop wrote: "The same voice that summons these ladies to rescue hundreds of souls will awake many a heart in their favour." His prophecy has been well fulfilled, for today the people of Newfoundland hold the name of the Presentation Sisters in benediction.

To Bishop O'Donnell, of Galway, Bishop Fleming wrote, in 1846, praising the fine work already accomplished by the new Presentation Community within thirteen years after their arrival: he described them as "the most useful, the most zealous and efficient co-operators in the holy work of imparting a knowledge of the Most High to my people." So greatly did Bishop Fleming appreciate the Presentation Sisters that he appealed for further volunteers from Ireland. Two more Nuns from Galway responded.

By 1846, the Presentation Sisters in Newfoundland were enjoying the bright noon of success. Though the skies were dark with the shadow of pestilence in Ireland, the prospects in Newfoundland were promising and numerous. Hundreds of happy pupils and splendid new buildings: such was the favoured lot of the Irish Nuns at Saint John's. But even here the work of the Sisters was to pass through a Fiery Cross, and their beautiful buildings were to melt into a rainbow of ash and flame. A fire in the City of Saint John's, one fatal night in the year 1846, swept the Presentation structure into the Atlantic mist. The Bishop, and the clergy, and the people, were as heartbroken as the universally beloved Sisters: for the tragedy touched the hearts of all. Protestants and Catholics vied

with one another in offering their houses to the stricken
Community, who promptly proved themselves capable of
making the melancholy ruin a stepping-stone to renewed
and wider activities.

Everybody joined in hastening the day of rebuilding,
for the Sisters were publicly esteemed as profitable
servants of the Lord and His people. Within about four
years the fire was but a memory and the new structure
became a consoling and finished reality. From that new
hour of hope the work of the Presentation Congregation
has gone on prospering anew in root and branch. New
Houses and new Schools rose up apace all over the Island,
and, in each case, it has been for the Sisters a triumphal
entry.

It is well over a century since those exiles from the
Galway Convent braved "crashing wind and lashing sea"
to aid in the propagation of the Faith in Newfoundland.
Their thriving story is a bright epic of success. Cheering
rays have shone forth from "The Rising Sun", where those
unfaltering missionaries first embarked on the work of
Christian Education. Today the name of the Presentation Congregation is written as indestructibly in the
scholastic history of Newfoundland as is the name of
Mother Nagle in the story of Ierne's Isle, from which they
first consolingly came.

CHAPTER 23

FIRST FOUNDATION IN THE UNITED STATES: FROM IRELAND THE PRESENTATION SISTERS ARRIVE IN SAN FRANCISCO

THE swallows must have been making one of their first flights to Capistrano about the time that Mother Nagle's Sisters were consolidating their work of charity in a small house in Ireland, almost seventeen decades ago. Little did the followers of the Foundress realise that, in seventy years after her death, there was to be a Foundation made by the Presentation Sisters in the expansive and glorious land which we know as California.

It was equable and salutary that they should begin in the attractive City of San Francisco. The venerable Diocese of San Francisco rests its patronage under two of the most popular Saints in human history, Saint Francis and Saint Patrick. Deeply twined in the story of Ireland are the names of Saint Francis and Saint Patrick. Likewise, in California, are their names imprinted upon grateful annals.

The abiding impress of the Irish in California convincingly belongs to American History. Early into the development of that Golden State entered a heroic group of Presentation Nuns from Ireland.

These missionary children of Saint Patrick selected a most auspicious year to begin their educational work by the shores of the Pacific. It was in the year 1854, when the dogma of the Immaculate Conception was promulgated to the world. Dedicated to the Immaculate Conception are these United States. An Irish Franciscan had irrefragably championed this doctrine at the University of Paris in the Middle Ages — John Duns Scotus — who summed it up in his memorable phrase, *ergo Mater Dei omnino Immaculata est.* As an English poet, Father Gerard Hopkins, expressed it — Duns Scotus set all France aflame in devotion to "Mary without spot." Significantly, in our own day, the most popular picture given by California to the world is "The Song of Bernadette," wherein, with outstretched arms, Mary is represented, proclaiming to the people her purity and sinlessness — "I am the Immaculate Conception."

Mention has already been made of the young priest who established the Presentation Convent in Midleton, County Cork. It was the work of his frail brief life, and having helped to achieve its success, he rendered up his spirit to the God Who gave it; his mortal remains being laid to rest within the Convent Chapel. From this Convent in Midleton came the Community to San Francisco in 1854 — they left Ireland on a Beloved Feast Day of Our Lady, September 8.

The Nuns were Mother Joseph Cronin, Mother Francis Xavier Daly, Mother Augustine Keane, and Sister Clare Duggan; they were joined by Sister Teresa Comerford who volunteered from the Kilkenny Convent.

The exiles were warmly welcomed in San Francisco by the clergy, and by layfolk of all creeds. Like Mother Nagle they began in the humblest surroundings. At North Beach the Sisters opened their first School on December 1, 1854, a few weeks after their arrival. Through the trials and sufferings that ensued they emerged to complete success. Appreciative friends came to their aid and helped them to erect a splendid Convent and Schools on Lombard and Powell Streets, in 1855. It was the usual happy story of Presentation Foundations: pupils quickly came in increasing numbers.

In 1904, it was found necessary to erect a four-story building for the younger classes, and progress continued undisturbed until the fire and earthquake of 1906; the Sisters all the while were bringing a first-class education within the gratuitous reach of all, and there were fourteen hundred pupils in daily attendance when the catastrophe came.

A new Convent was constructed on Taylor and Ellis

Streets in 1869: here five hundred pupils attended.

A Convent and a School were opened at Berkeley in May 1878. Patiently and perseveringly the Sisters extended their work till a day of accelerated progress dawned. Impressive buildings rewardingly grace their grounds today. Elementary and Secondary Schools are well attended. Here also there is an excellent Boarding School for girls, appropriately located in a City internationally renowned for Education.

Archbishop Riordan, an Ecclesiastical Statesman of apostolic repute, petitioned Rome, in 1888, to have the Presentation Houses amalgamated — within his Diocese: previously each house formed an independent unit. The request was granted, and took effect on June 8, 1889, with Mother M. Josephine Hagerty as Superior General. This happy step led to further rapid progress — *e pluribus unum:* today the work of the Presentation Congregation in California is deep-rooted and thriving.

The April skies seemed filled with peace in Easter Week, 1906, as the Presentation pupils in San Francisco were planning to return to school on the date set therefor — Wednesday, April 18. But, the Providence which manifests Itself in calm, now proclaimed Its awesome mystery through the medium of the storm: at 5:13, on the morning of April 18, the City of San Francisco was gripped in the throes of a mighty earthquake which continued through fifty-five seconds. It demolished many buildings and killed many people.

A worse tragedy befell the city when people began to light fires: they had not fully realised the devastation wrought by the quake. The innocent home fires made many homeless, for they began a blaze which burnt the greater part of the city in the ensuing days of renewed disaster. The Fire Department could not cope with the fatal conflagration as the water mains were already burst by the quake.

Into the smoke and ashes passed the two beautiful Presentation Convents, with their Schools, their libraries, their valuable works of art, their all. Through the trial of human ordeal at their first arrival and next through trial by fire, the Sisters passed undismayed: they repaired to their Convent in Berkeley and there heroically opened a Relief Station to help the harbourless. They also attended Refugee Camps and there taught the children. Meanwhile a new and beautiful city of San Francisco arose Phoenix-like from the universal flames.

The time of reconstruction was not long, and in 1908, the Mother House was ready, at 281 Masonic Avenue, San Francisco. To this is attached the Novitiate, and there is a splendid and successful Secondary School for Girls, with an enrollment of five hundred students.

Saint Mary's Presentation Convent in Gilroy was an independent House founded from Fitchburg, Massachusetts, by Mother Agnes Barry in 1890. It was amalgamated to the San Francisco Community in 1917. Here the Sisters have a primary and grammar school, and also an excellent Boarding School for girls.

The following Convents and Parochial Schools have been entrusted to the Sisters of the Presentation, besides those already mentioned: first of all in San Francisco there are: — Saint Agnes Convent, Ashbury Street, opened in 1907; Saint Teresa's Convent, Pennsylvania Avenue, opened in 1912; Saint Francis Convent, Mason Street, opened in 1913; Saint Anne's School, opened in 1920, and the Convent thereof — at 1330 Fourteenth Avenue — opened in 1924; the Cathedral Presentation School, Eddy Street, opened in 1924; the Salesian Parochial School of Saints Peter and Paul, for boys only, has been in charge of the Presentation Sisters since 1930; Epiphany Convent, Vienna Street, opened in 1938.

At San Jose there is Saint Patrick's Convent which was opened in 1925, and in Oakland there is Saint Columba's School, opened in the same year. In Sierra Madre, Saint Rita's Convent was opened in 1936.

Religious Instruction of Public School Children is

attended to by the Presentation Sisters in all of the afore-mentioned Schools.

We have already mentioned how the Presentation Nuns were helped in their extension in County Tipperary by Dean Cantwell. Significantly, Archbishop Cantwell, the distinguished Metropolitan of Los Angeles, has introduced the Presentation Sisters into his large and expanding Diocese. His Grace, who has done such magnificent work in extending the scope and influence of the Catholic Church in Southern California, has gladly welcomed Mother Nagle's Sisters to play their part in that work. In Los Angeles they have a Convent and Parochial School — Our Lady of Lourdes, East Fourth Street, opened in 1919; and another — Our Lady of Loretto, opened in 1921. At the splendid High School for Catholic Girls in Los Angeles, opened by Archbishop Cantwell in 1923, five Presentation Sisters, in their worthy tradition, conduct the History Department.

California was admitted to the Union as the Eighteenth State, on September 9, 1850. Within four years after that, the Presentation Sisters from Ireland entered beneficently into its educational history. In this Golden State, which is almost five times the size of Ireland, the Sisters have made their helpful presence felt from North to South. Their past and present are here a manifest matter for just pride, and their future is as bright as the clear blue skies under which they advance.

CHAPTER 24

ON THE ATLANTIC SEABOARD OF THE UNITED STATES THE PRESENTATION SISTERS EXTEND THEIR CONGREGATION: CONVENTS AND SCHOOLS IN NEW YORK, MASSACHU-SETTS AND RHODE ISLAND

THE purple wealth of heather on the Irish Hills was aglow with the oncoming of Autumn, in the year 1874, when a devoted group of Presentation Missionaries left Dublin for the Empire City of New York. There they arrived significantly on the natal Feast of their Patroness, the Madonna, on September 8, 1874.

The group was composed of Sisters from the Convents of Terenure, Clondalkin, and Tuam. From Terenure came Mothers Joseph Hickey, Xavier Jones, and Teresa Reynolds. From Clondalkin were Sisters Magdalen Keating and Angela Griott. From Tuam was Mother Aloysius Talbot. And in the following year Sister Stanislaus Cummins from the Castleisland Convent joined them in New York.

They visited the tomb of Nano Nagle before they departed, and begged her to intercede for their success beyond the seas. Their prayers were assuredly heard, for they prospered in New York from the very start.

Father Arthur Donnelly, Pastor of Saint Michael's Church, West 34 Street, New York, was the promoter of the new Foundation. He constructed magnificent Schools capable of accommodating hundreds of children, and also built a suitable Convent for the Sisters. Six hundred children, who had previously been attending the Public Schools, presented themselves at Saint Michael's. Excellent work, spiritually and educationally, has been accomplished by the Sisters here. They also have a very spacious and successful Secondary School for Boys and Girls. This School has given an exceptionally large number of its students to the Priesthood. In Staten Island the writer has had the pleasure of meeting the Presentation Sisters from Green Ridge and New Dorp, who today help to carry on the great work envisioned by Mother Nagle. It is not possible here to list in detail the extension of that work in New York, except to observe that a number of Parishes are now blessed by its benefits.

Picturesquely located at Newburgh, overlooking the Hudson, is the flourishing Motherhouse of the New York City Presentation Nuns. Here too the present writer has experienced the gracious hospitality of the Sisters, and has had a first-hand opportunity of realizing how the work of the Foundress has fructified so effectively within the Empire State, through the seven decades of its existence therein.

To Watervliet, New York, came Mother Paul Cahill with four Sisters from the Presentation Convent in Fermoy, County Cork, in 1881, their duty being to take charge of the Orphan Asylum — dedicated to Saint Colman of Ireland. It was the purpose of Bishop McNierney, of Albany, to keep children of the same family together, and accordingly Saint Colman's Home was opened on June 6, 1882. Brothers and sisters are not separated until boys reach the age of ten years. They are then transferred to the De La Salle Brothers. The girls remain until they are sixteen.

Saint Michael's Home for Children was opened at Green Ridge in Staten Island in 1884. It was a filiation from Saint Michael's in New York, and Mother Teresa Reynolds was the first Superior. This Foundation has its own Novitiate, and, as already mentioned, it has extended its useful services to a number of Houses on the Island.

In 1886, Saint Michael's sent out a Community from New York to Massachusetts. The group was composed of Mother Magdalen Keating, Sister Francis, Sister Rose, and Sister Bernard. Their duty was to take charge of the Schools of Saint Bernard's Parish in Fitchburg. In Fitchburg today is the new and impressive Motherhouse of the

Presentation Sisters, ample proof of the growth and success of Mother Nagle's work in historic New England. It has been my privilege to witness some of the admirable work of these Sisters at Fitchburg, and also at Central Falls in Rhode Island. One felt proud of these enterprising and efficient teachers who uphold the high standards of a venerable Congregation that has manifested its happy influence on modern Education, far and wide. A high tribute to the Sisters today are their eight Schools in Massachusetts and two Schools in Rhode Island; thorough and thriving in both places has been their work, which is now approaching a further Jubilee of its existence.

CHAPTER 25

FURTHER FOUNDATIONS IN THE UNITED STATES: FROM IRELAND THE PRESENTATION SISTERS COME TO THE MIDDLE WEST

FORTUNATELY I have had the pleasure of visiting the town of Dubuque many times within the past decade, and therefore I have been able to gather some first-hand evidence of its importance as a Catholic centre in the vast wonderland of the Middle West, which was visited by Marquette and Joliet, as far back as 1673. In this region today Nature's zephyrs blow over rich agricultural fields; and smart railroad "Zephyrs" glide like a silver gleam by the glistening waters of the Mississippi.

Mother Nagle's Sisters had been thirteen years established in Ireland by the time the French were attempting a first settlement near the site of Dubuque — about 1788. The State of Iowa formed part of the Louisiana Purchase of 1803, and of Missouri Territory; the Indian lands were ceded in 1832. This, the twenty-ninth State, was admitted to the Union in 1846.

Into Iowa, which is about one and three quarter times the size of Ireland, came the spiritual daughters of Nano Nagle, from the Homeland where their Congregation had been founded almost one hundred years before. Dubuque, the oldest place in the State, was their destination. Little more than forty years of its town history had passed, when, as a member of the Dubuque Community recently expressed it for me, with poetic delicacy, "the Sisters of the Presentation of the Blessed Virgin Mary slipped quietly into the town's everyday life."

It was on the evening of November 13, 1874, that these holy pioneers arrived in Dubuque: they had come from their beautiful Convent in Mooncoin, picturesquely located in an Irish countryside, where blue mountains blend with white clouds, and the River Suir ripples past a plain of rich green grass.

Bishop Hennessy, of Dubuque, visited Ireland on his way home from Rome, in 1870; this able Prelate, whose honoured name is treasured in ecclesiastical annals, was desirous of having Presentation Sisters to teach in his Diocese. True to the tradition of Mother Nagle, who declared her readiness to go anywhere if she could save souls, a group of volunteers offered their services. Among the distinguished relatives of Mother Nagle, we have already mentioned the family name of Hennessy — which had influential connections in France and Ireland. They say the name originated from Aengus, the Irish god of Love in pre-Patrician days.

The leader of Bishop Hennessy's volunteers was Mother Vincent Hennessy. Since all the Irish are said to be related, we attempt no further genealogy. Ready to accompany Mother Vincent were three young women — the Misses Kate Reide, Alice Howley and Ellen A'Hearn. All plans worked well for the Dubuque foundation. The old Visitation Convent on West Third Street became the first Dubuque home of the Presentation Sisters. There, for about two months, the Irish Missionaries received hospitality from the lovable followers of the gentle Saint Francis de Sales. The New Year bells of 1875 rang in their home that was to be, and the Sisters settled in the newly built Rectory at Key West, which was handed over to them for use as a Convent.

By the time Saint Brigid of Ireland had, from Heaven, uttered her festal benediction for February, 1875, these children of Saint Brigid's modern counterpart were already teaching in Key West. Their classes began in two rooms which now serve as Chapel and parlour. Twenty children were enrolled, and the numbers happily increased — so that new premises were soon sought.

For his community, Bishop Hennessy secured the district school from the public school officials, and there the

Sisters began in April. By September they had eighty pupils.

The first religious ceremonies of the Presentation Nuns in Iowa took place at the Catholic Church in Key West, when, on August 16, 1875, the three postulants from Ireland received the habit and veil from Bishop Hennessy. Miss Reide became Sister Mary Patricia; Miss Howley, Sister Mary Josephine; and Miss A'Hearn, Sister Mary Evangelista. On September 8, 1876, these three Sisters made their vows, thus becoming the first Presentation Sisters professed in this country, east of San Francisco.

During the winter of 1879 the Sisters were established in their new Motherhouse on West Hill, and the First Mass was celebrated there on December 14, 1879, by Father John Reilley of the Cathedral. On the Feast of the Purification, in 1880, a priest came with Cope, Monstrance, and Thurible, from the Cathedral, so that the Sisters might share the joys of Benediction: Father Garrett Nagle this was, a distant relative of the illustrious Foundress.

Brief, alas, was the stay of Mother Vincent Hennessy at the new Motherhouse. Pneumonia stole her from the sorrowing young Community on February 19, 1880, ere the new House was yet dedicated. Summer brought the day of dedication, and the Bishop appropriately found a name: he turned to the Sisters before he blessed the building and said: "We'll call it Saint Vincent's, in honour of Mother Vincent."

Young indeed were the members of this bereaved Community: to earthly eyes, its unbroken existence might seem jeopardised by the loss of its wise and sainted foundress. But the Bishop had confidence in the cherished little group and he took every step to ensure that the work so blessedly begun should be happily perpetuated. Mother Patricia Reide was placed in charge, with Mother Aloysius as her assistant. This arrangement brought the Community out of the shadows of anxiety into God's clear daylight, and within fifteen years the new Foundation was firmly established.

The present Motherhouse of the Presentation Sisters is Mount Loretto, which was built during the Superiorship of Mother Benedict Murphy, and dedicated by Bishop Garrigan, of Sioux City, on August 15, 1909. On November 4, that year, Mass and Benediction were celebrated for the first time in the new Motherhouse by Father Patrick Leahy, first Chaplain of the Convent.

The number of members, who have entered the Iowa Community, is now approaching three hundred. The Sisters are in charge of eighteen regular schools, and a varying number of vacation schools.

Since their arrival in 1874, the Presentation Nuns have therefore extended their activities to many parts of Iowa. They have Schools at Lawler, Waukon, Elkader, Danbury, Farley, Clare, Whittemore, Dougherty, Mason City, Ryan, Monona, Humboldt, Algona; Winner — in South Dakota, Monticello — in Minnesota.

The Sisters who came from Munster's vale to the Mississippi's shores, so many years ago, can now look down from the Beatific Home of their reward upon a rich Presentation harvest.

CHAPTER 26

DUBLIN SENDS A GROUP OF PRESENTATION SISTERS TO THE NORTH-WEST: THEIR FAR-REACHING MISSION IN THE DAKOTAS AND MONTANA

GUIDED by the spirit of Nano Nagle, the Presentation Sisters came from Ireland direct to the vast Dakota Territory, in September, 1880.

This Territory formed part of the Louisiana Purchase of 1803, and was organized in 1861. Bishop Martin Marty was appointed Vicar-Apostolic of Dakota in 1879: he was a distinguished Missionary and a worthy Son of Saint Benedict; and his name is an honoured one among the line of Bishops of Sioux Falls.

On his way from Rome, in 1880, Bishop Marty visited the Presentation Convent at George's Hill, in Dublin. Volunteers were obviously needed to open a school in the new Diocese of Dakota — over four times the size of Ireland. The Bishop was not disappointed: five Sisters answered his call, and, in September, 1880, they arrived at Charles Mix County, to embark on a heroic enterprise that required the apostolic endurance of Saint Patrick and Mother Nagle combined.

Like Mother Nagle, the Sisters began in a very humble way. Their new home was built of lime and sod, and it had to serve the triune purpose of School, Church and Convent. About thirty pupils presented themselves. These were of mixed Indian and French races, speaking both languages. The French-speaking Irish aristocrat, Nano Nagle, who turned her back on the unreal life of the Royal Court at Paris, must have looked lovingly down from Heaven on this new offshoot of her work, as her Sisters grappled with problems that nobody among the green fields of Ireland could have envisaged.

God is the Father of all things: praise Him. So says the

poet, whom we join in adoration, whether things be sweet or sour, shining or beclouded. Through fire and earthquake the Presentation Sisters in California calmly passed to new successes. Through the historic blizzard, which greeted the Sisters in the course of their already severe work, the Dakota Community endured unspeakable privations: it was their first winter too, and the snow, during that winter of 1880, lasted from Thanksgiving to Easter. But they did not lose hold of their task, and the Bishop found them a home in Fargo, in what is now North Dakota.

In their new home the Sisters continued to prosper. The name of Mother John Hughes has already been mentioned in the Irish part of the narrative. From Dublin she had led the heroic little group to Dakota. From Fargo, in 1886, she was asked to open a School in Aberdeen. Mother Hughes, Mother Aloysius Chriswell, and Sister Joseph Butler performed this happy task: for two years they lived in the Pastor's residence, and the Church was used for classes during the daytime. In October, 1888, their new Convent was ready.

The Dakota Territory was divided in 1889: on November 2, that year, North Dakota was admitted to the Union as the twenty-sixth State to enter after the adoption of the Federal Constitution, and on the same day South Dakota was admitted as the twenty-seventh State in order of admission. Fargo now remained the Motherhouse for the Presentation Sisters in North Dakota, and Aberdeen for South Dakota.

In North Dakota the Sisters have a splendid large Academy, a Home for orphan children, seven Parochial Schools and recently they have opened two fine hospitals.

How did the children of Nano Nagle, who incidentally so loved to tend the sick, come to have Hospitals? Again the God of the inscrutable visitation provides the answer. In 1899, the Aberdeen territory was swept by an epidemic of black diphtheria, and, at the request of the Bishop, part of the Convent was transmuted into a temporary Hospital. With the characteristic charity of their Foundress,

the Sisters here served the sick and also attended to them
in their homes until the epidemic ended. But Providence
did not permit the nursing talents of the Sisters to end
here. On account of the unsettled state of the country at
the time, the Bishop secured the necessary permission for
them to erect and conduct a Hospital.

Today the Aberdeen Presentation Sisters conduct four
fine Hospitals; three are in South Dakota, and one in
Montana. They have one Children's Home, one Junior
College, eleven Parochial Schools, in South Dakota, and
two Religious Vacation Schools in Minnesota.

This is one more happy Chapter of due triumph in
Presentation annals. Here the Irish Sisters outdid the
hail and tempest, and built their Houses on an imperishable foundation. She who is honoured under the lovely
title of Our Lady of the Snow blessed their bravery on
the uplands of the great North-West.

Deservedly hallowed is the memory of the undaunted
Mother John Hughes, under whose valiant leadership the
extension thrived in root, and bud, and branch.

CHAPTER 27

PRESENTATION SISTERS SET OUT FROM IRELAND TO START THEIR NEW SPIRITUAL VINE-YARDS IN AUSTRALIA AND INDIA

THE IRISH Race may take a justifiable pride in the noble part they have played in the upbuilding of a vigorous Church in Australia. The emerald gem of the Eastern World assuredly is that Church. It was only natural that Mother Nagle's Sisters should have been invited, welcomed, and established beneath the Southern Cross at an early date.

From Fermoy, a Community was established in distant Tasmania in 1866, and a number of Houses have by now eventuated through the grace of this happy migration.

In 1874 the Limerick Convent sent a Community to Melbourne. Here again it is a story of advancement and extension.

Also in 1874, a group of Sisters went from Kildare to found the new Convent at Wagga-Wagga, in the Diocese of Goulburn. At the time of the Golden Jubilee of this Foundation in 1924, Bishop Dwyer wrote of the Presentation Sisters: "Those religious women have bravely carried with wonderful success, the banner of religious education, and spread the light of Divine and human truth to illuminate the minds and uplift the souls of the womenfolk, not only of Wagga, but of a great portion of the Commonwealth of Australia." A good many Presentation Houses have been founded from the original Convent at Wagga, which won the high admiration of Michael Davitt when he visited Australia.

At another time, when communications are more normal, it is hoped to add complete details on the progress of Mother Nagle's Sisters in Australia. Meanwhile their work may be summarized here by saying that there are some fifty Convents of the Presentation Congregation in the great

Commonwealth, and that it would take many pages of appreciation to convey an idea of their fruitful deeds, wrought during the seventy years of their toil beneath those bounteous Southern skies.

"India's coral strand" may sound a romantic line in poetry, but it meant realistic labour for the four brave Sisters of the Presentation, who first unfurled the banner of Nana Nagle there, over seventy years ago.

From the Presentation Communities at Rahan and Maynooth these courageous exiles set forth in 1841 — *peregrinari pro Christo*. Through hazardous seas they skirted the Cape of Good Hope in a sailing ship, and after five months they arrived safely in Madras.

In Dakota the children of Nano Nagle conquered the blizzard, and in India they triumphed over the heat. We leave to the imagination what the Sisters must have suffered in India before the era of modern sanitation, refrigeration, and general scientific advancement. Suffer they did, in plenty.

In Madras the new Community opened a School for Indian and Eurasian pupils, and also a School for the children of the military. Nor did they forget to provide a building for the orphans.

A grant from the British Government in India helped the Sisters to establish one of the finest Schools in the country. It was a change from the days when Nano Nagle and her Community lived as educational outlaws in the penal eyes of a British Government in Ireland. And as proof that the Irish Sisters could brave the Indian heat we offer the case of Mother Ignatius Moore who went forth as a volunteer from the Presentation Convent in Mullingar and lived for sixty-seven fruitful years in Madras, where her great name is venerated in due benediction unto this day.

From Madras the useful work of the Sisters expanded rapidly, and their services ranged to Orphanages, to High Schools, and to the establishment of a Training College for Teachers — which has sent out over a thousand trained

Catholics to help to staff the Schools in all parts of India.

Christians and Hindus, the poor and the prosperous, all alike benefit from the thorough educational and social services of the Presentation Sisters, who have made many converts for the Church among those teeming millions of the tropics. The tiny hands of children, who at first brought garlands to Siva, the Destroyer, have been taught to deck the Shrine of the Gentle Mother of God, and to join in prayer to Christ.

The Presentation Sisters of India have a Training School and Novitiate in England, whereby subjects are assured for the new foundations constantly needed in the vast mission field of their choice. It is significant that the Presentation Sisters in Galway sent three members to found a Community at Pickering, Yorkshire, England, on Saint Patrick's Day, 1919, and that this young foundation amalgamated with their Sisters of England and India, in 1933.

The children of Nano Nagle in India share with their Sisters in the Dakotas the distinctive honour of doing excellent Hospital work. In her own day in Cork, Nano Nagle charitably established a dispensary. Today her Sisters re-enact her tender charity in nursing the sick, and they have won repute and renown among all creeds and classes for their heroic devotion in this arduous calling.

In the development of the work of the Presentation Sisters in India it is interesting to note the record of Mother Xavier Murphy, their Superior-General. The Holy Father manifested to her his interest in the wonderful work done by the Sisters in India. The Government honoured her for so many useful public services.

Again it betokens a happier age when we read that the name of an Irish Nun, Mother Xavier Murphy, appeared on the list of Royal New Year Birthday Honours in 1935: His Majesty, the King of England, the late King George the Fifth, awarded her the Kaiser-I-Hind Gold Medal in recognition of her lifelong good deeds to the people of India. Much of the first part of this book was occupied with the story of how Mother Nagle was hampered in her Catholic Educational work by the impeding enactments of the earlier King Georges. We bless God for a more fortunate age when a native Catholic Government in Ireland grants the fullest facilities to Protestant Schools for the five per cent minority professing the Protestant Faith. We also bless God for the fortunate fact of a new Religious Freedom wherein the services of an Irish Nun have won just recognition from a recent King George — especially as this Nun has proved herself to be the modern counterpart of Nano Nagle in India.

Merely to show that Mother Nagle's family name is intertwined with many a historic cause we may here mention that one of her immediate relatives, a young officer, Lieutenant Arthur Nagle, of the British Royal Navy, was reported missing after the dire battle at Singapore, in the dark days of 1942.

When more auspicious circumstances smile again, it is hoped to offer a detailed and up-to-date account of the truly great accomplishments that redound to the glory of Mother Nagle's Sisters in India.

CHAPTER 28

FROM THE THRONE OF THE FISHERMAN SOME OF SAINT PETER'S SUCCESSORS BLESS AND PRAISE THE WORK OF MOTHER NAGLE

"FOR ALL her ways are gentleness and all her paths are peace." These words may well be applied to Mother Nagle and to the everlasting message of her work. They are culled from a poem written by a celebrated relative of hers in our own day — the late Sir Cecil Spring-Rice, who was British Ambassador to the United States during the years of the first World War, and who came of an old Irish family.

By holy gentility and education the Presentation Sisters continue to promote the Peace of Christ in the Kingdom of Christ. It is only natural that they, as well as the whole Irish Race, should wish to see raised to the Altars of Holy Church the noble lady who gave inception to a great work by her heroic charity.

In 1939, ere our present wreckage of a world eventuated, two Sisters of the Presentation devotedly journeyed from the United States to Rome, and were received in private audience by the present Pontiff, His Holiness Pope Pius the Twelfth, to whom they humbly presented a special message on their beloved Foundress. The following is a summary of what Mother Carthagh, Superior General of the Presentation Sisters in San Francisco, said to His Holiness on the occasion mentioned:

"Most Holy Father: Prostrate at the feet of Your Holiness, we beg the favour of Your Blessings on the Cause of the Beatification of our holy Foundress, Mother Nano Nagle, for the introduction of which we hope the preliminary steps will very soon be taken.

Nano Nagle was born in County Cork, Ireland, on April 9th, 1728. She died on April 26th, 1784. During a time of great religious persecution, in the year 1776, she founded the Congregation of the Sisters of the Presentation in the city of Cork, Ireland.

The purpose of the Institute was the charitable instruction in the principles of Religion and Christian piety of the children of the poor, deprived of Christian education through the persecution.

The Rules of the Congregation were approved by Pope Pius VI; confirmed by Pope Pius VII, and under Pope Pius XI were brought into accordance with the Code of Canon Law. The Institute spread throughout the English-speaking countries and it now numbers about four thousand members.

As in the case of many founders of Religious Institutes who died in times of persecution, the Cause of their Beatification was not introduced until recent years, so was it with Mother Nagle.

Constant prayers are being offered at the present time in all our Communities and Schools for the success of the Cause of her Beatification and Canonization.

May I ask Your Holiness to give me a word of encouragement for them as an incentive to continue the work of prayer and effort for the success of this Cause so dear to our hearts?

During the audience, Mother Carthagh asked the Blessing of His Holiness on the introduction of the Cause of the holy Foundress, Mother Nano Nagle. He asked if it were yet introduced in Rome. "Not yet, Your Holiness, but we hope it will soon be introduced," replied Mother Carthagh.

His Holiness then asked if it will be introduced in America. The Sisters replied that it will be introduced from Cork, Ireland, where the Parent House is situated.

Sister Mary Patrick Rupert, who accompanied Mother Carthagh, told the Holy Father that a special Crusade of Prayer was going on for the past years. "Prayer is very necessary," he repeated.

Pope Pius XII then asked questions about the Schools

of the Presentation Sisters, and in reply to a request for a farewell Blessing on the Cause, he said: "By all means, a Blessing! A most cordial and fatherly Blessing! Prayer is necessary, the Cause will go on; the Cause is necessary."

Mother Carthagh presented the Holy Father with a beautifully bound book of the recently revised Constitutions of the Presentation Sisters, and reminded him that their Constitutions were approved by Pope Pius VI, and confirmed by Pope Pius VII, that Pope Pius IX gave them their ring, and Pope Pius XI revised their Constitutions in accordance with the Code of Canon Law. Then she added: "And it now remains for Your Holiness, another Pius, to complete the work by beatifying our holy Foundress." The Pope smiled a most gracious smile, nodded approval, and said: "Yes, it must be."

On June 7, 1939, His Eminence Cardinal Maglione wrote the following letter, from the Vatican, to Reverend Mother Carthagh, through the Office of His Excellency, The Most Reverend John J. Mitty, Archbishop of San Francisco:

Reverend Mother Superior General,

I have been charged by the Holy Father to acknowledge receipt of the devoted letter which you addressed to Him under date of May eighteenth, and to thank you for the gifts which accompanied it, . . .

It is the fervent prayer of His Holiness that Our Divine Lord may recompense you and your religious with the treasure of His grace for your goodness to His Vicar upon earth, and He desires that you be assured that your generous gift will enable Him to widen considerably the scope of His fatherly charity. As a mark of particular benevolence and in pledge of abundant favour from on high, He imparts to you and to the Sisters of the Presentation, as also to the children of your schools, His paternal Apostolic Benediction.

At the gracious command of His Holiness, your petition for the Beatification of your Foundress, Mother Nano

Nagle, has been referred for consideration to the Sacred Congregation of Rites.

With the assurance of my religious devotion, I am,
Faithfully yours in Christ,
L. Card. Maglione.

While in Ireland, in 1939, Mother Carthagh visited Bishop Cohalan, of Cork, who has been asked to introduce the Cause of Mother Nagle, and told his Lordship of the Holy Father's gracious interest in the proposed honouring of the worthy Foundress.

It is hoped that, when an arch of Peace beams again over this broken world, the Cause of Mother Nagle will move forward unto happy completion and fondly anticipated outcome. Praying for this devout consummation in the meantime are the countless benefactors of the venerated Foundress, whose abiding work manifests its merit from East to West, and from North to South.

In the United States there are now over one hundred Schools conducted by the Sisters of the Presentation, and there are about thirteen hundred Sisters engaged in the work of teaching in these Schools. This is a fruitful growth from the day that a little group of the Congregation first began their blessed labours on the Pacific Coast, some ninety years ago.

We should add that when Pope Pius the Sixth, in the Eighteenth Century, gave his paternal approval and Apostolic Benediction to the new Institute of Mother Nagle he offered thanks to the Divine Mercy for the fact that Honora Nagle had begun the founding in Ireland of Houses of Conventual Education, at a time when such institutions were being uprooted elsewhere in Europe. As the Pope himself expressed it: "More grateful, indeed, or more seasonable intelligence we could not receive, especially at the present time, when the designs and schemes of wicked men tend to nothing less than ruin and destruction, were such a thing possible, of the Church of Christ, founded and formed by His Precious Blood; we feel and acknowledge it an effect of the boundless Providence of Almighty God, that while elsewhere the institutions and convents of the religious of both sexes are sacrilegiously plundered and destroyed, houses are by the increase of piety in your diocese, (Bishop Moylan's Diocese of Cork), erected and endowed for the reception of pious virgins, whereby the Christian education of young girls is happily assured."

Commending the work of Mother Nagle, and recommending its rules to Rome, at the close of the eighteenth century were Dr. Richard O'Reilly, Archbishop of Armagh; Dr. John Thomas Troy, Archbishop of Dublin; Dr. Thomas Bray, Archbishop of Cashel; Dr. Edward Dillon, Archbishop of Tuam; Dr. James Caulfield, Bishop of Ferns; Dr. James Lanigan, Bishop of Ossory; Dr. Charles Sughrue, Bishop of Kerry.

Referring to the Institute of Mother Nagle, whom he described as "Honora Nagle, an opulent and noble lady of the kingdom of Ireland," Pope Pius, the Seventh, in 1805, declared: "Wonderful, indeed, does the rapid and successful increase of that Institute appear after receiving the apostolical approbation, and not less so the multiplied and abundant fruits it has produced wherever established."

The second century of the Presentation Congregation has been winning for it the same bright crown of immortality that characterized its first. Well may the Sisters rejoice in the Charity of Christ which has always urged them forward, and which has helped them to prosper, proceed and reign. In the words of the Crusaders' cry: "God wills it."

PERSONAL MESSAGES ON MOTHER NAGLE FROM MEMBERS OF THE AMERICAN HIERARCHY TO THE AUTHOR

From His Grace The Most Reverend Francis J.
Spellman, D.D., Archbishop of New York:—

> Permit me to associate myself with you in the publication of the biography of Mother Nagle. Thank you very much for sending me some of the page proofs of your biography. Thank you too for your thoughtfulness and graciousness in dedicating this volume to me. It is an honor which I deeply appreciate.
>
> With prayerful good wishes and kindest regards, I am, Very truly yours in Christ,
> + FRANCIS J. SPELLMAN,
> *Archbishop of New York.*

From His Grace The Most Reverend John J. Cantwell, D.D., Archbishop of Los Angeles:—

> It was most gratifying news to hear of the work you are concluding in the Biography of Mother Nagle. In the providence of Almighty God it may be that you will be instrumental in popularizing this noble woman whom we shall certainly know more of, and who is a glory to our race.
>
> Praying upon you every blessing, I am,
> Very sincerely yours,
> + JOHN J. CANTWELL,
> *Archbishop of Los Angeles.*

From His Excellency The Most Reverend Thomas E.
Molloy, D.D., Bishop of Brooklyn, New York:—

> Permit to assure you that it is a source of pleasure to learn that you propose to provide a biography of Mother Nagle. She richly merits indeed this recognition of her extraordinary sanctity of soul and of her

zealous devotion to the cause of Christian Education, particularly in Ireland, Australia, India, and the United States.

The recollection of her holiness of life which will be stimulated by your publication and the realization of her unselfish service for the moral, intellectual and spiritual welfare of others will be a blessedly useful source of inspiration and guidance to Christian teachers throughout the world.

Please accept the assurance of my commendations of your very timely and useful endeavors in this matter.

+ Thomas E. Molloy,
Bishop of Brooklyn.

From His Excellency The Most Reverend Richard J. Cushing, Auxiliary Bishop of Boston and Diocesan Director of the Society for the Propagation of the Faith:—

It was grand hearing from you on the Biography of Mother Nagle. I extend to you my affectionate greetings and prayerful good wishes.

Your devoted and grateful friend,
+ Richard J. Cushing.

From His Excellency The Most Reverend Joseph T. McGucken, D.D., Auxiliary Bishop of Los Angeles:—

I was delighted to learn that you are engaged in the work of writing the life of Mother Nano Nagle, the Foundress of the Presentation Sisters.

Her life marks a milestone in the history of Catholic Education, and was the beginning of new accomplishments for which we, here in the United States, are indebted more than we know to Mother Nagle. Her biography should have been written long since, but I think it is providential that it has at last fallen into such capable hands.

I pray upon you the blessing and the assistance of the Spirit of God, to enable you to interpret not only

the historical setting but the true interior spirit of
Mother Nagle's work.

Very sincerely in Christ,
+ JOSEPH T. McGUCKEN,
Auxiliary Bishop of Los Angeles, Chancellor.

From His Excellency The Most Reverend Henry Althoff,
D.D., Bishop of Belleville, Illinois:—

You have undertaken the laudable task of completing
the life story of Mother Nagle. This biography will
be received with general enthusiasm and will afford
inspiration to countless souls. It will be truly an
admirable life as your summary so well indicates.

Mother Nagle was indeed favored with a high and
singular vocation. She has left a precious inheritance
to her daughters. Imbued with her saintly spirit they
will appreciate your work.

You are rendering a valuable service to our time.
May you receive every encouragement. I pray God
to bless all your endeavors.

Sincerely yours in Christ,
+ HENRY ALTHOFF,
Bishop of Belleville.

From His Excellency The Most Reverend George L. Leech,
D.D., Bishop of Harrisburg, Pennsylvania:—

I am pleased to acknowledge your esteemed letter in
which you inform me that you are reaching the completion of your Life of Mother Nano Nagle, Foundress of the Sisters of the Presentation of the Blessed
Virgin Mary.

It is good to know that the great Mother Nano
Nagle has found in you so worthy a biographer, and
I am delighted to subscribe to your work beforehand.

With kindest wishes, I remain, dear Mr. Leahy,

Very sincerely yours,
+ G. L. LEECH,
Bishop of Harrisburg.

From His Excellency The Most Reverend Jules B.
Jeanmard, D.D., Bishop of Lafayette, Louisiana:—

> I am more than glad to give you a favorable word in
> your efforts to make better known the life of the
> Saintly Mother Nagle.
>
> In my humble opinion, Ireland is destined to play
> a great and noble part in the re-Christianization of
> Europe after the war.
>
> The publication, at this time, of the life of one of
> her children, who has done so much by her holy
> example in her work of Christian Education, which is
> continued by her spiritual daughters, the Presenta-
> tion Sisters, will serve to call attention to Ireland's
> priceless contribution to the Christian Order we must
> all strive to restore.
>
> Very sincerely yours in Christ,
+ JULES B. JEANMARD,
Bishop of Lafayette.

From His Excellency The Most Reverend Gerald P.
O'Hara, D.D., Bishop of Savannah-Atlanta:—

> I have met the Presentation Sisters, of whom you
> speak, in many parts of the world, especially in the
> East, and this fact adds to my interest in your under-
> taking.
>
> With the assurance of my interest in your cherished
> plans,
>
> I am, my dear Mr. Leahy,
Faithfully yours in Christ,
+ GERALD P. O'HARA,
Bishop of Savannah-Atlanta.

From His Excellency The Most Reverend Eugene J.
McGuinness, D.D., Bishop of Raleigh, North Carolina:—

> It is indeed a joy to know that you are about to
> issue the Biography of Mother Nano Nagle, the great
> pioneer in education in the days when the ordinary
> folk were supposed to be left in ignorance. It took

great courage and a generous dash of the Grace of God to accomplish the things she did, not only for Ireland, but for the Catholic World.

Assuring you that I look forward with delight to the issuance of this book, I beg to remain,

Sincerely in Christ,

+ EUGENE J. McGUINNESS,
Bishop of Raleigh.

From His Excellency The Most Reverend Gerald Shaughnessy, S.M., D.D., Bishop of Seattle:—

I am very pleased to know of your forthcoming biography of Mother Nano Nagle.

I am sure that the story of Mother Nagle will, when better known, inspire our faithful to a greater appreciation of Catholic Education and the contribution which Mother Nagle and her Sisters have made to that cause.

Extending to you and to your work my blessing and best wishes, I remain,

Sincerely yours,

+ GERALD SHAUGHNESSY,
Bishop of Seattle.

From His Excellency The Most Reverend William A. Griffin, D.D., Bishop of Trenton, New Jersey:—

I am very happy that you are about to send to the press the Biography of Mother Nagle. Today, more than ever, the world needs the inspiration of such lives as that of Mother Nagle, noble women indeed who, unhonored and unsung, never fail to leave the world a little better for their lives.

Asking the Lord to bless your noble effort, I remain,

Sincerely yours,

+ WILLIAM A. GRIFFIN,
Bishop of Trenton.

From His Excellency The Most Reverend John L. Swint, D.D., Bishop of Wheeling, West Virginia:—

> His Excellency states that he has only the most pleasant recollections of the fine courtesy shown him by the Presentation Sisters wherever he met them during his stay in Ireland for the Eucharistic Congress. He bespeaks God's blessing on your noble endeavor in making known the holy work of a great Foundress.
>
> Very sincerely yours,
>
> F. J. Schwertz,
> *Chancellor.*

From His Grace The Most Reverend John T. McNicholas, O.P., S.T.M., Archbishop of Cincinnati, a most encouraging and helpful letter has been received, at the time of completion, in which His Grace expresses his very deep interest in this biography of Mother Nagle.

From His Grace The Most Reverend John J. Glennon, D.D., Archbishop of Saint Louis, a number of warm and generous letters have been received expressing his constant interest in this work on Mother Nagle. His Grace's beautiful thoughts are crystallised and enshrined in the delightful Foreword which he contributed to the biography.

Messages From The Presentation Sisters on the Biography of Mother Nagle.

From Reverend Mother M. Carthagh, Mother General of The Presentation Sisters, San Francisco:—

> I can scarcely express in words the joy and enthusiasm I feel that at last the Presentation Congregation has found a worthy exponent of the life and work of Nano Nagle and of her daughters the world over.
>
> Your letters to Monsignor Richard Collins (Archdiocesan Director of the Presentation Sisters) and to me leave no doubt that your deep-seated convictions regarding the nature and the greatness of the task

before you will impart color and spirit to the pages of your book that, perhaps, only a gifted Irishman of deep faith and piety can impart. You are the man, par excellence, to carry this much needed work through.

Your determination combined with help from on High is bound to result in a story of Nano Nagle and her daughters that shall be not only informative but inspirational.

As for obstacles — they should simply be ignored. Go ahead in God's Name. We shall get on our knees, call upon the Most High and help shall be forthcoming. That God has been pleased and glorified by the work of Nano Nagle is more than amply proved by the fruits that have appeared in the wake of her precious life. It was He that raised her up; it was He that inspired her; and now He will glorify His faithful servant by proclaiming her name and her labors throughout the Christian world through the pages of your book.

Go ahead with the work. God will see to the rest. Relying on his largesse you may count on your book's meeting with success. God wills it! He will therefore furnish the means.

You may call me an optimist, and I prefer to be regarded as one in view of such a book as you are capable of writing.

With renewed assurance of our support in your work — God bless it and you.

Very sincerely yours in Christ,

MOTHER M. CARTHAGE.

From Mother M. Raphael McCarthy, Mother Superior, Presentation Motherhouse, Aberdeen, South Dakota:—

It was indeed glorious news to hear that you are about to complete the Biography of our beloved Foundress, Mother Nagle. Accept our sincere thanks for your lively interest in a work that is dear to all our hearts.

May the spirit of Nano Nagle be with you to inspire the telling of a story, which I believe will do much good for the glory of God and the Salvation of Souls. It will be an inspiration to us, Presentation Sisters, in particular; it will enable us to live through the beginnings of our beloved community, to be edified by the example of our holy Foundress, and spurred on to the imitation of her virtues.

Your reputation as a writer and lecturer gives us high hopes of a work well done. We are fortunate in having you to further this contribution to the history of Catholic Education and Catholic Charities. It is something we have long desired, and for which we have earnestly prayed. May God bless you through the successful completion of this life story of Mother Nagle and the history of the origin of the Presentation Sisters. Our continued prayers will be with you.

Sincerely yours in Christ,

PRESENTATION SISTERS.

From Reverend Mother Mary Perpetua, Mother General, Presentation Sisters, Dubuque, Iowa:—

Like Mother M. Carthagh, I am filled with joy and enthusiastic anticipation to know that a story of Mother Nagle and her daughters is in the making.

The prayers of our community shall be offered daily for the success of the undertaking. The Presentation Sisters are highly honored in having such a distinguished scholar take an active interest in our Foundress.

Again assuring you of our support, I am,

Sincerely yours in Christ,

MOTHER MARY PERPETUA.

From the Right Reverend Monsignor Richard Collins,
Archdiocesan Director of the Presentation Sisters,
San Francisco:—

> I am elated at your prospects of completing the life
> story of Mother Nagle. I foresee a needed and attrac-
> tive addition to the just claim of her children in this
> much desired work.
>
> I should not be surprised that the enthusiasm
> created by, and born of your work, will enthuse her
> children throughout the world with the desire for even
> a second edition. I say this because I feel that all
> those having contact with the Presentation Sisters will
> eagerly demand the work. I think there is a place
> awaiting it — and just now. You have my sincerest
> wishes and fondest hopes and blessings for your
> success.
>
> Very sincerely yours,
>
> RICHARD COLLINS.

From the Presentation Sisters, Cathedral Square, St. John's,
Newfoundland:—

> We are glad you are getting so many interested in
> the noble work. You may be assured of the prayers
> of the Sisters and our pupils that you may get every
> help you need to make "The Flower of Her Kindred"
> a success.

PATRONS, AMONG THE HIERARCHY, OF THE WORK ON MOTHER NAGLE.

His Grace The Most Reverend Francis J. Spellman, D.D., Archbishop of New York.

His Grace The Most Reverend John J. Glennon, D.D., Archbishop of Saint Louis.

His Grace The Most Reverend John J. Cantwell, D.D., Archbishop of Los Angeles.

His Grace The Most Reverend John T. McNicholas, O.P., S.T.M., Archbishop of Cincinnati.

His Excellency The Most Reverend Henry Althoff, D.D., Bishop of Belleville.

His Excellency The Most Reverend Richard J. Cushing, D.D., Auxiliary Bishop of Boston.

His Excellency The Most Reverend William A. Griffin, D.D., Bishop of Trenton.

His Excellency The Most Reverend Jules B. Jeanmard, D.D., Bishop of Lafayette.

His Excellency The Most Reverend George L. Leech, D.D., Bishop of Harrisburg.

His Excellency The Most Reverend Joseph T. McGucken, D.D., Auxiliary Bishop of Los Angeles.

His Excellency The Most Reverend Eugene J. McGuinness, D.D., Bishop of Raleigh.

His Excellency The Most Reverend Thomas E. Molloy, D.D., Bishop of Brooklyn.

His Excellency The Most Reverend Gerald P. O'Hara, D.D., Bishop of Savannah-Atlanta.

His Excellency The Most Reverend Gerald Shaughnessy, S.M., D.D., Bishop of Seattle.

His Excellency The Most Reverend John J. Swint, D.D., Bishop of Wheeling.

ADVANCE SUBSCRIBERS TO THE BIOGRAPHY OF MOTHER NAGLE

The Author has not only had the pleasure of writing this Biography but he has also assumed the entire responsibility for its printing and publication. His task of production has been lightened by helpful friends among the Clergy, Sisters and Laity, who encouraged his hopes, during long months of preparation, by being advance subscribers to the book. His everlasting gratitude is extended to all.

Atkinson, Miss Helen E., California
Brosnan, Very Rev. Fr. John, New York
Beardsley, Miss Louise J., San Francisco
Brennan, Very Rev. Fr. Thomas J., Berkeley, California
Barry, Rev. Fr. Denis B., California
Bottomley, Mrs. John T., Boston, Massachusetts
Byrne, The Right Rev. Monsignor John M., San Francisco
Casey, The Very Rev. Fr. Michael J., St. Paul, Minn.
Cantillon, Very Rev. Fr. John R., San Francisco
Cahill, Patrick J., Chicago
Campion, The Very Rev. Fr. Raymond J., Brooklyn
Connor, Rev. Doctor Maurice, Sacramento, California
Cashman, Miss Helena, Los Angeles
Cantwell, The Rt. Rev. Monsignor James P., San Francisco
Cantwell, The Very Rev. Fr. Arthur, San Francisco
Collins, The Right Rev. Monsignor Richard, San Francisco
Coyne, The Rev. Father Thomas F., Maine
Costello, The Very Rev. Fr. John J., Iowa
Cullen, The Right Rev. Monsignor John J., San Francisco
Cusack, The Rev. Fr. John F., Brooklyn
Deenihan, The Very Rev. Fr. James, Los Angeles
Drury, The Rev. Fr. John F., Rhode Island
Durkin, The Very Rev. Fr. John F., Monterey, California
Durkin, The Very Rev. Thomas, Minnesota

Devlin, The Very Rev. Fr. John J., Hollywood, California

Doerbecker, Miss Katherine L., New York

Donovan, The Very Rev. Fr. Joseph P., Kenrick Seminary, St. Louis

Dunn, The Rev. Fr. Joseph E., Dubuque

Friel, The Right Rev. Monsignor Thomas F., Chicago

Farraher, James, San Francisco

Flanagan, The Right Rev. Monsignor William J., San Francisco

Feeley, The Very Rev. Fr. Patrick F. (Requiescat in Pace) New York

Finnegan, The Very Rev. Fr. Denis, New York

Finn, Professor John F. X., New York

Gately, The Rev. Fr. William J., Brooklyn

Guilfoyle, The Rev. Fr. Merlin, San Francisco

Galvin, The Rev. Fr. Timothy, Oakland, California

Galvin, The Rev. Fr. Michael, California

Gilmartin, The Rt. Rev. Monsignor Charles, Illinois

Grealy, The Rt. Rev. Monsignor Patrick, Sacramento, California

Harrington, The Very Rev. Fr. Peter, S.M.A., East St. Louis, Illinois

Hanley, The Very Rev. Fr. Peter A., Rhode Island

Holy Ghost Sisters (The White Sisters), Putnam, Conn.

Hildegard, Mother Hildegard Goff, Ursuline Academy, New York

Harrison, Hon. Maurice, San Francisco

Holy Ghost Fathers, The Very Rev. Fr. George Collins, Washington, D. C.

Hogan, The Rev. Fr. Stephen J., Washington, D. C.

Hayes, The Rev. Fr. John J., California

Healy, Hon. Garth, Irish Consul, Chicago

Hunt, The Very Rev. Fr. Bernard, Iowa

Kane, The Very Rev. Fr. Daniel P., Brooklyn

Keating, The Rt. Rev. Monsignor Martin C., Los Angeles

Kelly, The Rev. Fr. Edward J., California

Kelly, The Rev. Fr. Leo A., Brooklyn

Kelliher, The Very Rev. Fr. M. G., Iowa

Kinkead, Major Eugene F., New York

Leen, The Rt. Rev. Monsignor William, Iowa

Looney, The Very Rev. Fr. Edward M., California

Lynch, The Rt. Rev. Monsignor P. T., Iowa

Linehan, The Rev. Fr. James C., Sulpician Fathers, Washington

Lynch, The Rev. Fr. William F., Detroit

Millett, The Right Rev. Monsignor Thomas, San Francisco

Moclair, The Very Rev. Fr. John, Los Angeles

Motherway, The Very Rev. Fr. E. J., San Francisco

McCarthy, The Rt. Rev. Monsignor John M., Los Angeles

Mulloy, The Rt. Rev. Monsignor William T., Fargo

Murphy, Hon. Matthew, Irish Consul, San Francisco

Mullay, Miss Rose (Requiescat in Pace), Chicago

Monahan, The Very Rev. Fr. John P., New York

McNulty, Miss Alma, San Francisco

Morrill, Miss Lena, San Francisco

Merillion, Mrs. Margaret, San Francisco

Moran, Mrs. Thomas J., California

Murphy, The Very Rev. Fr. Sylvan, Capuchin Franciscan Fathers, Burlingame, California

Moriarty, The Right Rev. Monsignor Patrick G., San Francisco

McHugh, The Very Rev. Fr. Patrick, Sacramento, Calif.

McCauley, Hon. Leo. T., Consul General of Ireland, New York

Nagle, Daniel P., Chicago

Nolan, The Rev. Fr. Thomas F., St. Paul, Minn.

Neagle, The Right Rev. Monsignor Richard, (Requiescat in Pace), Boston

O'Hara, The Right Rev. Monsignor Francis J., Brooklyn, N. Y.

O'Connell, The Very Rev. M. D., California

O'Riordan, The Very Rev. Fr. Daniel B., California

O'Reilly, The Very Rev. Fr. John J. Holy Ghost Fathers, Rhode Island

O'Connell, Miss Emma, New York

O'Connor, Jerry C., San Francisco

O'Neill, The Rev. Fr. Alexander, Alabama

O'Connell, The Rev. Fr. Richard, San Francisco

Parks, The Rev. Fr. Joseph K., Brooklyn

Presentation Sisters, Reverend Mother Carthagh, San Francisco

Presentation Sisters, Sister Moninna, St. Anne's Convent, San Francisco

Presentation Sisters, Cathedral School, San Francisco

Presentation Sisters, St. Francis Convent, San Francisco

Presentation Sisters, Berkeley, California

Presentation Sisters, San Jose, California

Presentation Sisters, St. Agnes Convent, San Francisco

Presentation Sisters, Central Falls, Rhode Island

Presentation Sisters, Gilroy, California

Presentation Sisters, Holy Rosary Hospital, Miles City, Montana

Presentation Sisters, St. John's, Newfoundland

Presentation Sisters, St. Teresa's Convent, San Francisco

Presentation Sisters, Reverend Mother Beatrice, Mount St. Joseph, Newburgh, New York

Presentation Sisters, Reverend Mother Raphael, Aberdeen, South Dakota

Presentation Sisters, Mount Carmel School, Lawler, Iowa

Presentation Sisters, Reverend Mother Vincent, Mount St. Michael, Staten Island, New York

Presentation Sisters, Queen of Peace Convent, New Dorp, New York

Presentation Sisters, Reverend Mother Perpetua, Mount Loretto, Dubuque, Iowa

Presentation Sisters, Reverend Mother Helena, Fitchburg, Massachusetts

Presentation Sisters, Epiphany Convent, San Francisco

Presentation Sisters, Our Lady of Loretto Convent, Los
    Angeles
Presentation Sisters, Langdon, North Dakota
Presentation Sisters, Saint Christopher Parish, Grant City,
    Staten Island, New York
Prindiville, The Rev. Fr. Raymond, Paulist Fathers, San
    Francisco
Reeves, James, New York
Ryan, The Very Rev. Fr. John M., San Francisco

Schley-Behr, Mrs. J., New York
Scott, Hon. Joseph, K.S.G., Los Angeles
Slattery, The Very Rev. Fr. Patrick, East St. Louis, Illinois
Shea, The Rev. Fr. Daniel P., San Francisco
Smith, The Rev. Fr. Matthew A., California
Stapleton, The Rev. Fr. John P., California

Tobin, The Very Rev. Fr. William A., South Carolina
Tobin, The Rt. Rev. Monsignor Walter J., Birmingham,
    Alabama
Walsh, The Rev. Fr. Michael, San Francisco

The following letter was received from His Grace Archbishop Mitty at the completion of this work:—

I am very happy indeed to learn that you have prepared
a biography of Mother Nano Nagle, Foundress of the
Sisters of the Presentation.

Her life and work and what she and her Community
have accomplished in so many parts of the world, mark
another chapter in the religious life of the Church and in
the history of Education.

The publication of this story comes indeed at a most opportune moment, when it has become so necessary to stress
the value of education based upon religion.

Praying every blessing upon your work and with every
best wish, I beg to remain

Faithfully yours

†John J. Mitty

Archbishop of San Francisco.